ISBN 978-0-266-85533-0
PIBN 10532950

MEMORIAL EDITION OF THE WRITINGS OF HENRY GEORGE

VOL I.

Make for thyself a definition or description of the thing which is presented to thee, so as to see distinctly what kind of a thing it is, in its substance, in its nudity, in its complete entirety, and tell thyself its proper name, and the names of the things of which it has been compounded, and into which it will be resolved.   For nothing is so productive of elevation of mind as to be able to examine methodically and truly every object which is presented to thee in life, and always to look at things so as to see at the same time what kind of universe this is, and what kind of use everything performs in it, and what value everything has with reference to the whole, and what with reference to man, who is a citizen of the highest city, of which all other cities are like families; what each thing is, and of what it is composed, and how long it is the nature of this thing to endure.
—*Marcus Aurelius Antoninus.*

Henry George
when writing "Progress and Poverty"
San Francisco, 1879

THE WRITINGS OF HENRY GEORGE

PROGRESS AND POVERTY

AN INQUIRY INTO THE CAUSE OF INDUS-
TRIAL DEPRESSIONS AND OF INCREASE
OF WANT WITH INCREASE OF WEALTH

THE REMEDY

I

NEW YORK: DOUBLEDAY
AND McCLURE COMPANY
1898

THE DE VINNE PRESS.

TO THOSE WHO,
SEEING THE VICE AND MISERY THAT SPRING FROM
THE UNEQUAL DISTRIBUTION
OF WEALTH AND PRIVILEGE,
FEEL THE POSSIBILITY OF A HIGHER SOCIAL STATE
AND WOULD STRIVE FOR ITS ATTAINMENT

SAN FRANCISCO, March, 1879.

There must be refuge!   Men
Perished in winter winds till one smote fire
From flint stones coldly hiding what they held,
The red spark treasured from the kindling sun ;
They gorged on flesh like wolves, till one sowed corn,
Which grew a weed, yet makes the life of man ;
They mowed and babbled till some tongue struck speech,
And patient fingers framed the lettered sound.
What good gift have my brothers, but it came
From search and strife and loving sacrifice?

Edwin Arnold.

Never yet
Share of Truth was vainly set
   In the world's wide fallow ;
After hands shall sow the seed,
   After hands, from hill and mead,
Reap the harvests yellow.

Whittier.

PREFACE TO FOURTH EDITION.

THE views herein set forth were in the main briefly stated in a pamphlet entitled "Our Land and Land Policy," published in San Francisco in 1871. I then intended, as soon as I could, to present them more fully, but the opportunity did not for a long time occur. In the meanwhile I became even more firmly convinced of their truth, and saw more completely and clearly their relations; and I also saw how many false ideas and erroneous habits of thought stood in the way of their recognition, and how necessary it was to go over the whole ground.

This I have here tried to do, as thoroughly as space would permit. It has been necessary for me to clear away before I could build up, and to write at once for those who have made no previous study of such subjects, and for those who are familiar with economic reasonings; and, so great is the scope of the argument that it has been impossible to treat with the fullness they deserve many of the questions raised. What I have most endeavored to do is to establish general principles, trusting to my readers to carry further their applications where this is needed.

In certain respects this book will be best appreciated by those who have some knowledge of economic literature; but no previous reading is necessary to the understanding of the argument or the passing of judgment upon its conclusions. The facts upon which I have relied are not facts which can be verified only by a search through libraries. They are facts of common observation and common knowledge, which every reader can verify for himself, just as he can decide whether the reasoning from them is or is not valid.

Beginning with a brief statement of facts which suggest this inquiry, I proceed to examine the explanation currently given in the name of political economy of the reason why, in spite of the increase of productive power, wages tend to the minimum of a bare living. This examination shows that the current doctrine of wages is founded upon a misconception; that, in truth, wages are produced by the labor for which they are paid, and should, other things being equal, increase with the number of laborers. Here the inquiry meets a doctrine which is the foundation and center of most important economic theories, and which has powerfully influenced thought in all directions—the Malthusian doctrine, that population tends to increase faster than subsistence. Examination, however, shows that this doctrine has no real support either in fact or in analogy, and that when brought to a decisive test it is utterly disproved.

Thus far the results of the inquiry, though extremely important, are mainly negative. They show that current theories do not satisfactorily explain the connection of poverty with material progress, but throw no light upon the problem itself, beyond showing that its solution must be sought in the laws which govern the distribution of wealth. It therefore becomes necessary to carry the inquiry into this field. A preliminary review shows that the three laws of distribution must necessarily correlate with each other, which as laid down by the current political economy they fail to do, and an examination of the terminology in use reveals the confusion of thought by which this discrepancy has been slurred over. Proceeding then to work out the laws of distribution, I first take up the law of rent. This, it is readily seen, is correctly apprehended by the current political economy. But it is also seen that the full scope of this law has not been appreciated, and that it involves as corollaries the laws of wages and interest—the cause which determines what part of the produce shall go to the land owner necessarily determining what part shall be left for labor and capital. Without resting here, I proceed to an independent deduction of the laws of interest and wages. I have stopped to determine the real cause and justification of interest, and to point out a source of much misconception—the confounding of what are really the profits of monopoly with the legitimate earnings of capital. Then returning to the main inquiry, investigation shows that interest must rise and fall with wages, and depends ultimately upon the same thing as rent—the margin of cultivation or point in production where rent begins. A similar but independent investigation of the law of wages yields similar harmonious results. Thus the three laws of distribution are brought into mutual support and harmony, and the fact that with material progress rent everywhere advances is seen to explain the fact that wages and interest do not advance.

What causes this advance of rent is the next question that arises, and it necessitates an examination of the effect of material progress upon the distribution of wealth. Separating the factors of material progress into increase of population and improvements in the arts, it is first seen that increase in population tends constantly, not merely

by reducing the margin of cultivation, but by localizing the economies and powers which come with increased population, to increase
the proportion of the aggregate produce which is taken in rent, and
to reduce that which goes as wages and interest. Then eliminating
increase of population, it is seen that improvement in the methods
and powers of production tends in the same direction, and, land being
held as private property, would produce in a stationary population
all the effects attributed by the Malthusian doctrine to pressure of
population. And then a consideration of the effects of the continuous
increase in land values which thus spring from material progress
reveals in the speculative advance inevitably begotten when land is
private property a derivative but most powerful cause of the increase
of rent and the crowding down of wages. Deduction shows that
this cause must necessarily produce periodical industrial depressions,
and induction proves the conclusion; while from the analysis which
has thus been made it is seen that the necessary result of material
progress, land being private property, is, no matter what the increase in population, to force laborers to wages which give but a
bare living.

This identification of the cause that associates poverty with progress points to the remedy, but it is to so radical a remedy that I have
next deemed it necessary to inquire whether there is any other
remedy. Beginning the investigation again from another starting
point, I have passed in examination the measures and tendencies
currently advocated or trusted in for the improvement of the condition of the laboring masses. The result of this investigation is to
prove the preceding one, as it shows that nothing short of making
land common property can permanently relieve poverty and check
the tendency of wages to the starvation point.

The question of justice now naturally arises, and the inquiry
passes into the field of ethics. An investigation of the nature and
basis of property shows that there is a fundamental and irreconcil-
able difference between property in things which are the product of
labor and property in land; that the one has a natural basis and
sanction while the other has none, and that the recognition of exclusive property in land is necessarily a denial of the right of property in the products of labor. Further investigation shows that
private property in land always has, and always must, as development proceeds, lead to the enslavement of the laboring class; that
land owners can make no just claim to compensation if society choose
to resume its right; that so far from private property in land being
in accordance with the natural perceptions of men, the very reverse

is true, and that in the United States we are already beginning to feel the effects of having admitted this erroneous and destructive principle.

The inquiry then passes to the field of practical statesmanship. It is seen that private property in land, instead of being necessary to its improvement and use, stands in the way of improvement and use, and entails an enormous waste of productive forces; that the recognition of the common right to land involves no shock or dispossession, but is to be reached by the simple and easy method of abolishing all taxation save that upon land values. And this an inquiry into the principles of taxation shows to be, in all respects, the best subject of taxation.

A consideration of the effects of the change proposed then shows that it would enormously increase production; would secure justice in distribution; would benefit all classes; and would make possible an advance to a higher and nobler civilization.

The inquiry now rises to a wider field, and recommences from another starting point. For not only do the hopes which have been raised come into collision with the widespread idea that social progress is possible only by slow race improvement, but the conclusions we have arrived at assert certain laws which, if they are really natural laws, must be manifest in universal history. As a final test, it therefore becomes necessary to work out the law of human progress, for certain great facts which force themselves on our attention, as soon as we begin to consider this subject, seem utterly inconsistent with what is now the current theory. This inquiry shows that differences in civilization are not due to differences in individuals, but rather to differences in social organization; that progress, always kindled by association, always passes into retrogression as inequality is developed; and that even now, in modern civilization, the causes which have destroyed all previous civilizations are beginning to manifest themselves, and that mere political democracy is running its course toward anarchy and despotism. But it also identifies the law of social life with the great moral law of justice, and, proving previous conclusions, shows how retrogression may be prevented and a grander advance begun. This ends the inquiry. The final chapter will explain itself.

The great importance of this inquiry will be obvious. If it has been carefully and logically pursued, its conclusions completely change the character of political economy, give it the coherence and certitude of a true science, and bring it into full sympathy with the aspirations of the masses of men, from which it has long been estranged. What I have done in this book, if I have correctly solved the great problem I have sought to investigate, is, to unite the truth perceived by the school of Smith and Ricardo to the truth perceived by the schools of Proudhon and Lasalle; to show that *laissez faire* (in its full true meaning) opens the way to a realization of the noble dreams of socialism; to identify social law with moral law, and to disprove ideas which in the minds of many cloud grand and elevating perceptions.

This work was written between August, 1877, and March, 1879, and the plates finished by September of that year. Since that time new illustrations have been given of the correctness of the views herein advanced, and the march of events—and especially that great movement which has begun in Great Britain in the Irish land agitation—shows still more clearly the pressing nature of the problem I have endeavored to solve. But there has been nothing in the criticisms they have received to induce the change or modification of these views—in fact, I have yet to see an objection not answered in advance in the book itself. And except that some verbal errors have been corrected and a preface added, this edition is the same as previous ones.

HENRY GEORGE.

NEW YORK, *November*, 1880.

CONTENTS.

CONTENTS.

INTRODUCTORY.

THE PROBLEM.

Ye build! ye build! but ye enter not in,
Like the tribes whom the desert devoured in their sin;
From the land of promise ye fade and die,
Ere its verdure gleams forth on your wearied eye.

—Mrs. Sigourney.

INTRODUCTORY.

THE PROBLEM.

The present century has been marked by a prodigious increase in wealth-producing power. The utilization of steam and electricity, the introduction of improved processes and labor-saving machinery, the greater subdivision and grander scale of production, the wonderful facilitation of exchanges, have multiplied enormously the effectiveness of labor.

At the beginning of this marvelous era it was natural to expect, and it was expected, that labor-saving inventions would lighten the toil and improve the condition of the laborer; that the enormous increase in the power of producing wealth would make real poverty a thing of the past. Could a man of the last century—a Franklin or a Priestley—have seen, in a vision of the future, the steamship taking the place of the sailing vessel, the railroad train of the wagon, the reaping machine of the scythe, the threshing machine of the flail; could he have heard the throb of the engines that in obedience to human will, and for the satisfaction of human desire, exert a power greater than that of all the men and all the beasts of burden of the earth combined; could he have seen the forest tree transformed into finished lumber—into doors, sashes, blinds, boxes or barrels, with hardly the touch of a human hand; the great workshops where boots and shoes are turned out by the case with less labor than the old-fashioned cobbler could have put on a sole; the factories where, under the eye of a girl, cotton becomes cloth faster than hundreds of stalwart weavers could have turned it out with their hand-looms; could he have seen steam hammers shaping mammoth shafts and mighty anchors, and delicate machinery making tiny watches; the diamond drill cutting through the heart of the rocks, and coal oil sparing the whale; could he have realized the enormous saving of labor resulting from improved facilities of exchange and communication—sheep killed in Australia eaten fresh in England, and the order given by the London banker in the afternoon executed in San Francisco in the morning of the same day; could he have conceived of the hundred thousand improvements which these only suggest, what would he have inferred as to the social condition of mankind?

It would not have seemed like an inference; further than the vision went it would have seemed as though he saw; and his heart would have leaped and his nerves would have thrilled, as one who from a height beholds just ahead of the thirst-stricken caravan the living gleam of rustling woods and the glint of laughing waters. Plainly, in the sight of the imagination, he would have beheld these new forces elevating society from its very foundations, lifting the very poorest above the possibility of want, exempting the very lowest from anxiety for the material needs of life; he would have seen these slaves of the lamp of knowledge taking on themselves the traditional curse, these muscles of iron and sinews of steel making the poorest laborer's life a holiday, in which every high quality and noble impulse could have scope to grow.

And out of these bounteous material conditions he would have seen arising, as necessary sequences, moral conditions realizing the golden age of which mankind have always dreamed. Youth no longer stunted and starved; age no longer harried by avarice; the child at play with the tiger; the man with the muck-rake drinking in the glory of the stars! Foul things fled, fierce things tame; discord turned to harmony! For how could there be greed where all had enough? How could the vice, the crime, the ignorance, the brutality, that spring from poverty and the fear of poverty, exist where poverty had vanished? Who should crouch where all were freemen; who oppress where all were peers?

More or less vague or clear, these have been the hopes, these the dreams born of the improvements which give this wonderful century its preëminence. They have sunk so deeply into the popular mind as radically to change the currents of thought, to recast creeds and displace the most fundamental conceptions. The haunting visions of higher possibilities have not merely gathered splendor and vividness, but their direction has changed—instead of seeing behind the faint tinges of an expiring sunset, all the glory of the daybreak has decked the skies before.

It is true that disappointment has followed disappointment, and that discovery upon discovery, and invention after invention, have neither lessened the toil of those who most need respite, nor brought plenty to the poor. But there have been so many things to which it seemed this failure could be laid, that up to our time the new faith has hardly weakened. We have better appreciated the difficulties to be overcome; but not the less trusted that the tendency of the times was to overcome them.

Now, however, we are coming into collision with facts which there can be no mistaking. From all parts of the civilized world come complaints of industrial depression; of labor condemned to involuntary idleness; of capital massed and wasting; of pecuniary distress among business men; of want and suffering and anxiety among the working classes. All the dull, deadening pain, all the keen, maddening anguish, that to great masses of men are involved in the words "hard times," afflict the world to-day. This state of things, common to communities differing so widely in situation, in political institutions, in fiscal and financial systems, in density of population and in social organization, can hardly be accounted for by local causes. There is distress where large standing armies are maintained, but there is also distress where the standing armies are nominal; there is distress where protective tariffs stupidly and wastefully hamper trade, but there is also distress where trade is nearly free; there is distress where autocratic government yet prevails, but there is also distress where political power is wholly in the hands of the people; in countries where paper is money, and in countries where gold and silver are the only currency. Evidently, beneath all such things as these, we must infer a common cause.

That there is a common cause, and that it is either what we call material progress or something closely connected with material progress, becomes more than an inference when it is noted that the phenomena we class together and speak of as industrial depression are but intensifications of phenomena which always accompany material progress, and which show themselves more clearly and strongly as material progress goes on. Where the conditions to which material progress everywhere tends are most fully realized—that is to say, where population is densest, wealth greatest, and the machinery of production and exchange most highly developed—we find the deepest poverty, the sharpest struggle for existence, and the most of enforced idleness.

It is to the newer countries—that is, to the countries where material progress is yet in its earlier stages—that laborers emigrate in search of higher wages, and capital flows in search of higher interest. It is in the older countries—that is to say, the countries where material progress has reached later stages—that widespread destitution is found in the midst of the greatest abundance. Go into one of the new communities where Anglo-Saxon vigor is just beginning the race of progress; where the machinery of production and exchange is yet rude and inefficient; where the increment of wealth is not yet great enough to enable any class to live in ease and luxury; where the best house is but a cabin of logs or a cloth and paper shanty, and the richest man is forced to daily work—and though you will find an absence of wealth and all its concomitants, you will find no beggars. There is no luxury, but there is no destitution. No one makes an easy living, nor a very good living; but every one *can* make a living, and no one able and willing to work is oppressed by the fear of want.

But just as such a community realizes the conditions which all civilized communities are striving for, and advances in the scale of material progress—just as closer settlement and a more intimate connection with the rest of the world, and greater utilization of labor-saving machinery, make possible greater economies in production and exchange, and wealth in consequence increases, not merely in the aggregate, but in proportion to population —so does poverty take a darker aspect. Some get an infinitely better and easier living, but others find it hard to get a living at all. The "tramp" comes with the locomotive, and almshouses and prisons are as surely the marks of "material progress" as are costly dwellings, rich warehouses, and magnificent churches. Upon streets lighted with gas and patrolled by uniformed policemen, beggars wait for the passer-by, and in the shadow of college, and library, and museum, are gathering the more hideous Huns and fiercer Vandals of whom Macaulay prophesied.

This fact—the great fact that poverty and all its concomitants show themselves in communities just as they develop into the conditions toward which material progress tends—proves that the social difficulties existing wherever a certain stage of progress has been reached, do not arise from local circumstances, but are, in some way or another, engendered by progress itself.

And, unpleasant as it may be to admit it, it is at last becoming evident that the enormous increase in productive power which has marked the present century and is still going on with accelerating ratio, has no tendency to extirpate poverty or to lighten the burdens of those compelled to toil. It simply widens the gulf between Dives and Lazarus, and makes the struggle for existence more intense. The march of invention has clothed mankind with powers of which a century ago the boldest imagination could not have dreamed. But in factories where labor-saving machinery has reached its most wonderful development, little children are at work; wherever the new forces are anything like fully utilized, large classes are maintained by charity or live on the verge of recourse to it; amid the greatest accumulations of wealth, men die of starvation, and puny infants suckle dry breasts; while everywhere the greed of gain, the worship of wealth, shows the force of the fear of want. The promised land flies before us like the mirage. The fruits of the tree of knowledge turn as we grasp them to apples of Sodom that crumble at the touch.

It is true that wealth has been greatly increased, and that the average of comfort, leisure, and refinement has been raised; but these gains are not general. In them the lowest class do not share.* I do not mean that the

---

* It is true that the poorest may now in certain ways enjoy what the richest a century ago could not have commanded, but this does not show improvement of condition so long as the ability to obtain the necessaries of life is not increased. The beggar in a great city may enjoy many things from which the backwoods farmer is debarred, but that does not prove the condition of the city beggar better than that of the independent farmer.

condition of the lowest class has nowhere nor in anything been improved; but that there is nowhere any improvement which can be credited to increased productive power. I mean that the tendency of what we call material progress is in nowise to improve the condition of the lowest class in the essentials of healthy, happy human life. Nay, more, that it is still further to depress the condition of the lowest class. The new forces, elevating in their nature though they be, do not act upon the social fabric from underneath, as was for a long time hoped and believed, but strike it at a point intermediate between top and bottom. It is as though an immense wedge were being forced, not underneath society, but through society. Those who are above the point of separation are elevated, but those who are below are crushed down.

This depressing effect is not generally realized, for it is not apparent where there has long existed a class just able to live. Where the lowest class barely lives, as has been the case for a long time in many parts of Europe, it is impossible for it to get any lower, for the next lowest step is out of existence, and no tendency to further depression can readily show itself. But in the progress of new settlements to the conditions of older communities it may clearly be seen that material progress does not merely fail to relieve poverty—it actually produces it. In the United States it is clear that squalor and misery, and the vices and crimes that spring from them, everywhere increase as the village grows to the city, and the march of development brings the advantages of the improved methods of production and exchange. It is in the older and richer sections of the Union that pauperism and distress among the working classes are becoming most painfully apparent. If there is less deep poverty in San Francisco than in New York, is it not because San Francisco is yet behind New York in all that both cities are striving for? When San Francisco reaches the point where New York now is, who can doubt that there will also be ragged and barefooted children on her streets?

This association of poverty with progress is the great enigma of our times. It is the central fact from which spring industrial, social, and political difficulties that perplex the world, and with which statesmanship and philanthropy and education grapple in vain. From it come the clouds that overhang the future of the most progressive and self-reliant nations. It is the riddle which the Sphinx of Fate puts to our civilization, and which not to answer is to be destroyed. So long as all the increased wealth which modern progress brings goes but to build up great fortunes, to increase luxury and make sharper the contrast between the House of Have and the House of Want, progress is not real and cannot be permanent. The reaction must come. The tower leans from its foundations, and every new story but hastens the final catastrophe. To educate men who must be condemned to poverty, is but to make them restive; to base on a state of most glaring social in-equality political institutions under which men are theoretically equal, is to stand a pyramid on its apex.

All-important as this question is, pressing itself from every quarter painfully upon attention, it has not yet re-ceived a solution which accounts for all the facts and points to any clear and simple remedy. This is shown by the widely varying attempts to account for the pre-vailing depression. They exhibit not merely a diver-gence between vulgar notions and scientific theories, but also show that the concurrence which should exist be-tween those who avow the same general theories breaks up upon practical questions into an anarchy of opinion. Upon high economic authority we have been told that the prevailing depression is due to over-consumption; upon equally high authority, that it is due to over-pro-duction; while the wastes of war, the extension of railroads, the attempts of workmen to keep up wages, the demonetization of silver, the issues of paper money, the increase of labor-saving machinery, the opening of shorter avenues to trade, etc., are separately pointed out as the cause, by writers of reputation.

And while professors thus disagree, the ideas that there is a necessary conflict between capital and labor, that machinery is an evil, that competition must be restrained and interest abolished, that wealth may be created by the issue of money, that it is the duty of government to furnish capital or to furnish work, are rapidly making way among the great body of the people, who keenly feel a hurt and are sharply conscious of a wrong. Such ideas, which bring great masses of men, the repositories of ultimate political power, under the leadership of charlatans and demagogues, are fraught with danger; but they cannot be successfully combated until political economy shall give some answer to the great question which shall be consistent with all her teachings, and which shall commend itself to the perceptions of the great masses of men.

It must be within the province of political economy to give such an answer. For political economy is not a set of dogmas. It is the explanation of a certain set of facts. It is the science which, in the sequence of certain phenomena, seeks to trace mutual relations and to identify cause and effect, just as the physical sciences seek to do in other sets of phenomena. It lays its foundations upon firm ground. The premises from which it makes its deductions are truths which have the highest sanction; axioms which we all recognize; upon which we safely base the reasoning and actions of every-day life, and which may be reduced to the metaphysical expression of the physical law that motion seeks the line of least resistance—viz., that men seek to gratify their desires with the least exertion. Proceeding from a basis

thus assured, its processes, which consist simply in
identification and separation, have the same certainty.
In this sense it is as exact a science as geometry, which,
from similar truths relative to space, obtains its conclusions by similar means, and its conclusions when valid
should be as self-apparent. And although in the domain
of political economy we cannot test our theories by arti-
ficially produced combinations or conditions, as may be
done in some of the other sciences, yet we can apply
tests no less conclusive, by comparing societies in which
different conditions exist, or by, in imagination, separating, combining, adding or eliminating forces or factors
of known direction.

I propose in the following pages to attempt to solve by
the methods of political economy the great problem I
have outlined. I propose to seek the law which associates poverty with progress, and increases want with
advancing wealth; and I believe that in the explanation
of this paradox we shall find the explanation of those
recurring seasons of industrial and commercial paralysis
which, viewed independently of their relations to more
general phenomena, seem so inexplicable. Properly
commenced and carefully pursued, such an investigation
must yield a conclusion that will stand every test, and as
truth, will correlate with all other truth. For in the
sequence cf phenomena there is no accident. Every
effect has a cause, and every fact implies a preceding
fact.

That political economy, as at present taught, does not
explain the persistence of poverty amid advancing wealth
in a manner which accords with the deep-seated perceptions of men; that the unquestionable truths which it
does teach are unrelated and disjointed; that it has failed
to make the progress in popular thought that truth,
even when unpleasant, must make; that, on the contrary, after a century of cultivation, during which it has

engrossed the attention of some of the most subtle and powerful intellects, it should be spurned by the statsman, scouted by the masses, and relegated in the opinion of many educated and thinking men to the rank of a pseudo-science in which nothing is fixed or can be fixed— must, it seems to me, be due not to any inability of the science when properly pursued, but to some false step in its premises, or overlooked factor in its estimates. And as such mistakes are generally concealed by the respect paid to authority, I propose in this inquiry to take nothing for granted, but to bring even accepted theories to the test of first principles, and should they not stand the test, freshly to interrogate facts in the endeavor to discover their law.

I propose to beg no question, to shrink from no conclusion, but to follow truth wherever it may lead. Upon us is the responsibility of seeking the law, for in the very heart of our civilization to-day women faint and little children moan. But what that law may prove to be is not our affair. If the conclusions that we reach run counter to our prejudices, let us not flinch; if they challenge institutions that have long been deemed wise and natural, let us not turn back.

BOOK I.

WAGES AND CAPITAL.

He that is to follow philosophy must be a freeman in mind.
—*Ptolemy.*

CHAPTER I.

Reducing to its most compact form the problem we have set out to investigate, let us examine, step by step, the explanation which political economy, as now accepted by the best authority, gives of it.

The cause which produces poverty in the midst of advancing wealth is evidently the cause which exhibits itself in the tendency, everywhere recognized, of wages to a minimum. Let us, therefore, put our inquiry into this compact form:

Why, in spite of increase in productive power, do wages tend to a minimum which will give but a bare living?

The answer of the current political economy is, that wages are fixed by the ratio between the number of laborers and the amount of capital devoted to the employment of labor, and constantly tend to the lowest amount on which laborers will consent to live and reproduce, because the increase in the number of laborers tends naturally to follow and overtake any increase in capital. The increase of the divisor being thus held in check only by the possibilities of the quotient, the dividend may be increased to infinity without greater result.

In current thought this doctrine holds all but undisputed sway. It bears the indorsement of the very highest names among the cultivators of political economy, and though there have been attacks upon it, they are

generally more formal than real.* It is assumed by
Buckle as the basis of his generalizations of universal
history. It is taught in all, or nearly all, the great English and American universities, and is laid down in text-
books which aim at leading the masses to reason correctly
upon practical affairs, while it seems to harmonize with
the new philosophy, which, having in a few years all but
conquered the scientific world, is now rapidly permeating
the general mind.

Thus entrenched in the upper regions of thought, it is
in cruder form even more firmly rooted in what may be
styled the lower. What gives to the fallacies of protection such a tenacious hold, in spite of their evident in-
consistencies and absurdities, is the idea that the sum to
be distributed in wages is in each community a fixed one,
which the competition of "foreign labor" must still
further subdivide. The same idea underlies most of the
theories which aim at the abolition of interest and the
restriction of competition, as the means whereby the
share of the laborer in the general wealth can be increased; and it crops out in every direction among those
who are not thoughtful enough to have any theories, as
may be seen in the columns of newspapers and the
debates of legislative bodies.

---

* This seems to me true of Mr. Thornton's objections, for while
he denies the existence of a predetermined wage fund, consisting of
a portion of capital set apart for the purchase of labor, he yet holds
(which is the essential thing) that wages are drawn from capital,
and that increase or decrease of capital is increase or decrease of the
fund available for the payment of wages. The most vital attack
upon the wage fund doctrine of which I know is that of Professor
Francis A. Walker (The Wages Question: New York, 1876), yet he
admits that wages are in large part advanced from capital—which,
so far as it goes, is all that the stanchest supporter of the wage
fund theory could claim—while he fully accepts the Malthusian
theory. Thus his practical conclusions in nowise differ from those
reached by expounders of the current theory.

And yet, widely accepted and deeply rooted as it is, it seems to me that this theory does not tally with obvious facts. For, if wages depend upon the ratio between the amount of labor seeking employment and the amount of capital devoted to its employment, the relative scarcity or abundance of one factor must mean the relative abundance or scarcity of the other. Thus, capital must be relatively abundant where wages are high, and relatively scarce where wages are low. Now, as the capital used in paying wages must largely consist of the capital constantly seeking investment, the current rate of interest must be the measure of its relative abundance or scarcity. So, if it be true that wages depend upon the ratio between the amount of labor seeking employment and the capital devoted to its employment, then high wages, the mark of the relative scarcity of labor, must be accompanied by low interest, the mark of the relative abundance of capital, and reversely, low wages must be accompanied by high interest.

This is not the fact, but the contrary. Eliminating from interest the element of insurance, and regarding only interest proper, or the return for the use of capital, is it not a general truth that interest is high where and when wages are high, and low where and when wages are low? Both wages and interest have been higher in the United States than in England, in the Pacific than in the Atlantic States. Is it not a notorious fact that where labor flows for higher wages, capital also flows for higher interest? Is it not true that wherever there has been a general rise or fall in wages there has been at the same time a similar rise or fall in interest? In California, for instance, when wages were higher than anywhere else in the world, so also was interest higher. Wages and interest have in California gone down together. When common wages were $5 a day, the ordinary bank rate of interest was twenty-four per cent. per annum. Now that common wages are $2 or $2.50 a day, the ordinary bank rate is from ten to twelve per cent.

Now, this broad, general fact, that wages are higher in new countries, where capital is relatively scarce, than in old countries, where capital is relatively abundant, is too glaring to be ignored. And although very lightly touched upon, it is noticed by the expounders of the current political economy. The manner in which it is noticed proves what I say, that it is utterly inconsistent with the accepted theory of wages. For in explaining it such writers as Mill, Fawcett, and Price virtually give up the theory of wages upon which, in the same treatises, they formally insist. Though they declare that wages are fixed by the ratio between capital and laborers, they explain the higher wages and interest of new countries by the greater relative production of wealth. I shall hereafter show that this is not the fact, but that, on the contrary, the production of wealth is relatively larger in old and densely populated countries than in new and sparsely populated countries. But at present I merely wish to point out the inconsistency. For to say that the higher wages of new countries are due to greater proportionate production, is clearly to make the ratio with production, and not the ratio with capital, the determinator of wages.

Though this inconsistency does not seem to have been perceived by the class of writers to whom I refer, it has been noticed by one of the most logical of the expounders of the current political economy. Professor Cairnes* endeavors in a very ingenious way to reconcile the fact with the theory, by assuming that in new countries, where industry is generally directed to the production of food and what in manufactures is called raw material, a

---

* Some Leading Principles of Political Economy Newly Expounded, Chapter 1, Part 2.

much larger proportion of the capital used in production is devoted to the payment of wages than in older countries where a greater part must be expended in machinery and material, and thus, in the new country, though capital is scarcer, and interest is higher, the amount determined to the payment of wages is really larger, and wages are also higher. For instance, of $100,000 devoted in an old country to manufactures, $80,000 would probably be expended for buildings, machinery and the purchase of materials, leaving but $20,000 to be paid out in wages; whereas in a new country, of $30,000 devoted to agriculture, etc., not more than $5,000 would be required for tools, etc., leaving $25,000 to be distributed in wages. In this way it is explained that the wage fund may be comparatively large where capital is comparatively scarce, and high wages and high interest accompany each other.

In what follows I think I shall be able to show that this explanation is based upon a total misapprehension of the relations of labor to capital—a fundamental error as to the fund from which wages are drawn; but at present it is necessary only to point out that the connection in the fluctuation of wages and interest in the same countries and in the same branches of industry cannot thus be explained. In those alternations known as "good times" and "hard times" a brisk demand for labor and good wages is always accompanied by a brisk demand for capital and stiff rates of interest. While, when laborers cannot find employment and wages droop, there is always an accumulation of capital seeking investment at low rates.* The present depression has been no less marked by want of employment and distress among the working classes than by the accumulation of unemployed capital in all the great centers, and by nominal rates of interest

---

* Times of commercial panic are marked by high rates of discount, but this is evidently not a high rate of interest, properly socalled, but a high rate of insurance against risk.

on undoubted security. Thus, under conditions which admit of no explanation consistent with the current theory, do we find high interest coinciding with high wages, and low interest with low wages—capital seemingly scarce when labor is scarce, and abundant when labor is abundant.

All these well known facts, which coincide with each other, point to a relation between wages and interest, but it is to a relation of conjunction, not of opposition. Evidently they are utterly inconsistent with the theory that wages are determined by the ratio between labor and capital, or any part of capital.

How, then, it will be asked, could such a theory arise? How is it that it has been accepted by a succession of economists, from the time of Adam Smith to the present day?

If we examine the reasoning by which in current treatises this theory of wages is supported, we see at once that it is not an induction from observed facts, but a deduction from a previously assumed theory—viz., that wages are drawn from capital. It being assumed that capital is the source of wages, it necessarily follows that the gross amount of wages must be limited by the amount of capital devoted to the employment of labor, and hence that the amount individual laborers can receive must be determined by the ratio between their number and the amount of capital existing for their recompense.* This reasoning is valid, but the conclusion,

* For instance McCulloch (Note VI to Wealth of Nations) says: "That portion of the capital or wealth of a country which the employers of labor intend to or are willing to pay out in the purchase of labor, may be much larger at one time than another. But whatever may be its absolute magnitude, it obviously forms the only source from which any portion of the wages of labor can be derived. No other fund is in existence from which the laborer, as such, can draw a single shilling. And hence *it follows* that the average rate

as we have seen, does not correspond with the facts. The fault, therefore, must be in the premises. Let us see.

I am aware that the theorem that wages are drawn from capital is one of the most fundamental and apparently best settled of current political economy, and that it has been accepted as axiomatic by all the great thinkers who have devoted their powers to the elucidation of the science. Nevertheless, I think it can be demonstrated to be a fundamental error—the fruitful parent of a long series of errors, which vitiate most important practical conclusions. This demonstration I am about to attempt. It is necessary that it should be clear and conclusive, for a doctrine upon which so much important reasoning is based, which is supported by such a weight of authority, which is so plausible in itself, and is so liable to recur in different forms, cannot be safely brushed aside in a paragraph.

The proposition I shall endeavor to prove, is:

That wages, instead of being drawn from capital, are in reality drawn from the product of the labor for which they are paid. *

Now, inasmuch as the current theory that wages are drawn from capital also holds that capital is reimbursed from production, this at first glance may seem a distinction without a difference—a mere change in terminology,

---

of wages, or the share of the national capital appropriated to the employment of labor falling, at an average, to each laborer, must entirely depend on its amount as compared with the number of those amongst whom it has to be divided." Similar citations might be made from all the standard economists.

* We are speaking of labor expended in production, to which it is best for the sake of simplicity to confine the inquiry. Any question which may arise in the reader's mind as to wages for unproductive services had best therefore be deferred.

to discuss which would be but to add to those unprofitable disputes that render so much that has been written upon politico-economic subjects as barren and worthless as the controversies of the various learned societies about the true reading of the inscription on the stone that Mr. Pickwick found. But that it is much more than a formal distinction will be apparent when it is considered that upon the difference between the two propositions are built up all the current theories as to the relations of capital and labor; that from it are deduced doctrines that, themselves regarded as axiomatic, bound, direct, and govern the ablest minds in the discussion of the most momentous questions. For, upon the assumption that wages are drawn directly from capital, and not from the product of the labor, is based, not only the doctrine that wages depend upon the ratio between capital and labor, but the doctrine that industry is limited by capital—that capital must be accumulated before labor is employed, and labor cannot be employed except as capital is accumulated; the doctrine that every increase of capital gives or is capable of giving additional employment to industry; the doctrine that the conversion of circulating capital into fixed capital lessens the fund applicable to the maintenance of labor; the doctrine that more laborers can be employed at low than at high wages; the doctrine that capital applied to agriculture will maintain more laborers than if applied to manufactures ; the doctrine that profits are high or low as wages are low or high, or that they depend upon the cost of the subsistence of laborers; together with such paradoxes as that a demand for commodities is not a demand for labor, or that certain commodities may be increased in cost by a reduction in wages or diminished in cost by an increase in wages.

In short, all the teachings of the current political economy, in the widest and most important part of its domain, are based more or less directly upon the assumption that labor is maintained and paid out of existing capital before the product which constitutes the ultimate object is secured. If it be shown that this is an error, and that on the contrary the maintenance and payment of labor do not even temporarily trench on capital, but are directly drawn from the product of the labor, then all this vast superstructure is left without support and must fall. And so likewise must fall the vulgar theories which also have their base in the belief that the sum to be distributed in wages is a fixed one, the individual shares in which must necessarily be decreased by an increase in the number of laborers.

The difference between the current theory and the one I advance is, in fact, similar to that between the mercantile theory of international exchanges and that with which Adam Smith supplanted it. Between the theory that commerce is the exchange of commodities for money, and the theory that it is the exchange of commodities for commodities, there may seem no real difference when it is remembered that the adherents of the mercantile theory did not assume that money had any other use than as it could be exchanged for commodities. Yet, in the practical application of these two theories, there arises all the difference between rigid governmental protection and free trade.

If I have said enough to show the reader the ultimate importance of the reasoning through which I am about to ask him to follow me, it will not be necessary to apologize in advance either for simplicity or prolixity. In arraigning a doctrine of such importance—a doctrine supported by such a weight of authority, it is necessary to be both clear and thorough.

Were it not for this I should be tempted to dismiss with a sentence the assumption that wages are drawn from capital. For all the vast superstructure which the current political economy builds upon this doctrine is in truth based upon a foundation which has been merely taken for granted, without the slightest attempt to distinguish the apparent from the real. Because wages are generally paid in money, and in many of the operations of production are paid before the product is fully completed, or can be utilized, it is inferred that wages are drawn from pre-existing capital, and, therefore, that industry is limited by capital—that is to say that labor cannot be employed until capital has been accumulated, and can only be employed to the extent that capital has been accumulated.

Yet in the very treatises in which the limitation of industry by capital is laid down without reservation and made the basis for the most important reasonings and elaborate theories, we are told that capital is stored-up or accumulated labor—"that part of wealth which is saved to assist future production." If we substitute for the word "capital" this definition of the word, the propositiou carries its own refutation, for that labor cannot be employed until the results of labor are saved becomes too absurd for discussion.

Should we, however, with this *reductio ad absurdum*, attempt to close the argument, we should probably be met with the explanation, not that the first laborers were supplied by Providence with the capital necessary to set them to work, but that the proposition merely refers to a state of society in which production has become a complex operation.

But the fundamental truth, that in all economic reasoning must be firmly grasped, and never let go, is that society in its most highly developed form is but an elaboration of society in its rudest beginnings, and that principles obvious in the simpler relations of men are merely disguised and not abrogated or reversed by the more intricate relations that result from the division of labor and the use of complex tools and methods. The steam grist mill, with its complicated machinery exhibiting every diversity of motion, is simply what the rude stone mortar dug up from an ancient river bed was in its day —an instrument for grinding corn. And every man engaged in it, whether tossing wood into the furnace, running the engine, dressing stones, printing sacks or keeping books, is really devoting his labor to the same purpose that the pre-historic savage did when he used his mortar—the preparation of grain for human food.

And so, if we reduce to their lowest terms all the complex operations of modern production, we see that each individual who takes part in this infinitely subdivided and intricate network of production and exchange is really doing what the primeval man did when he climbed the trees for fruit or followed the receding tide for shell-fish—endeavoring to obtain from nature by the exertion of his powers the satisfaction of his desires. If we keep this firmly in mind, if we look upon production as a whole—as the co-operation of all embraced in any of its great groups to satisfy the various desires of each, we plainly see that the reward each obtains for his exertions comes as truly and as directly from nature as the result of that exertion, as did that of the first man.

To illustrate: In the simplest state of which we can conceive, each man digs his own bait and catches his own fish. The advantages of the division of labor soon become apparent, and one digs bait while the others fish. Yet evidently the one who digs bait is in reality doing as much toward the catching of fish as any of those who actually take the fish. So when the advantages of canoes are discovered, and instead of all going a-fishing, one stays behind and makes and repairs canoes, the canoe-maker is in reality devoting his labor to the taking of fish as much as the actual fishermen, and the fish which he eats at night when the fishermen come home are as truly the product of his labor as of theirs. And thus when the division of labor is fairly inaugurated, and instead of each attempting to satisfy all of his wants by direct resort to nature, one fishes, another hunts, a third picks berries, a fourth gathers fruit, a fifth makes tools, a sixth builds huts, and a seventh prepares clothing—each one is to the extent he exchanges the direct product of his own labor for the direct product of the labor of others really applying his own labor to the production of the things he uses—is in effect satisfying his particular desires by the exertion of his particular powers; that is to say, what he receives he in reality produces. If he digs roots and exchanges them for venison, he is in effect as truly the procurer of the venison as though he had gone in chase of the deer and left the huntsman to dig his own roots. The common expression, "I made so and so," signifying "I earned so and so," or "I earned money with which I purchased so and so," is, economically speaking, not metaphorically but literally true. Earning is making.

Now, if we follow these principles, obvious enough in a simpler state of society, through the complexities of the state we call civilized, we shall see clearly that in every case in which labor is exchanged for commodities, production really precedes enjoyment; that wages are the earnings—that is to say, the makings of labor—not the advances of capital, and that the laborer who receives his wages in money (coined or printed, it may be, before his labor commenced) really receives in return for the addition his labor has made to the general stock of wealth, a draft upon that general stock, which he may utilize in any particular form of wealth that will best satisfy his desires; and that neither the money, which is but the draft, nor the particular form of wealth which he uses it to call for, represents advances of capital for his maintenance, but on the contrary represents the wealth, or a portion of the wealth, his labor has already added to the general stock.

Keeping these principles in view we see that the draughtsman, who, shut up in some dingy office on the banks of the Thames, is drawing the plans for a great marine engine, is in reality devoting his labor to the production of bread and meat as truly as though he were garnering the grain in California or swinging a lariat on a La Plata pampa; that he is as truly making his own clothing as though he were shearing sheep in Australia or weaving cloth in Paisley, and just as effectually producing the claret he drinks at dinner as though he gathered the grapes on the banks of the Garonne. The miner who, two thousand feet under ground in the heart of the Comstock, is digging out silver ore, is, in effect, by virtue of a thousand exchanges, harvesting crops in valleys five thousand feet nearer the earth's center; chasing the whale through Arctic icefields; plucking tobacco leaves in Virginia; picking coffee berries in Honduras; cutting sugar cane on the Hawaiian Islands; gathering cotton in Georgia or weaving it in Manchester or Lowell; making quaint wooden toys for his children in the Hartz Mountains; or plucking amid the green and gold of Los Angeles orchards the oranges which, when his shift is relieved, he will take home to his sick wife. The wages which he receives on Saturday night at the mouth of the shaft, what are they but the certificate to all the world that he has done these things—the primary exchange in the long series which transmutes his labor into the things he has really been laboring for?

All this is clear when looked at in this way; but to meet this fallacy in all its strongholds and lurking places we must change our investigation from the deductive to the inductive form. Let us now see, if, beginning with facts and tracing their relations, we arrive at the same conclusions as are thus obvious when, beginning with first principles, we trace their exemplification in complex facts.

CHAPTER II.

Before proceeding further in our inquiry, let us make sure of the meaning of our terms, for indistinctness in their use must inevitably produce ambiguity and indeterminateness in reasoning. Not only is it requisite in economic reasoning to give to such words as "wealth," "capital," "rent," "wages," and the like, a much more definite sense than they bear in common discourse, but, unfortunately, even in political economy there is, as to some of these terms, no certain meaning assigned by common consent, different writers giving to the same term different meanings, and the same writers often using a term in different senses. Nothing can add to the force of what has been said by so many eminent authors as to the importance of clear and precise definitions, save the example, not an infrequent one, of the same authors falling into grave errors from the very cause they warned against. And nothing so shows the importance of language in thought as the spectacle of even acute thinkers basing important conclusions upon the use of the same word in varying senses. I shall endeavor to avoid these dangers. It will be my effort throughout, as any term becomes of importance, to state clearly what I mean by it, and to use it in that sense and in no other. Let me ask the reader to note and to bear in mind the definitions thus given, as otherwise I cannot hope to make myself properly understood. I shall not attempt to attach arbitrary meanings to words, or to coin terms, even when it would be convenient to do so, but shall conform to usage as closely as is possible, only endeavoring so to fix the meaning of words that they may clearly express thought.

What we have now on hand is to discover whether, as a matter of fact, wages are drawn from capital. As a preliminary, let us settle what we mean by wages and what we mean by capital. To the former word a sufficiently definite meaning has been given by economic writers, but the ambiguities which have attached to the use of the latter in political economy will require a detailed examination.

As used in common discourse "wages" means a compensation paid to a hired person for his services; and we speak of one man "working for wages," in contradistinction to another who is "working for himself." The use of the term is still further narrowed by the habit of applying it solely to compensation paid for manual labor. We do not speak of the wages of professional men, managers or clerks, but of their fees, commissions, or salaries. Thus the common meaning of the word wages is the compensation paid to a hired person for manual labor. But in political economy the word wages has a much wider meaning, and includes all returns for exertion. For, as political economists explain, the three agents or factors in production are land, labor, and capital, and that part of the produce which goes to the second of these factors is by them styled wages.

Thus the term labor includes all human exertion in the production of wealth, and wages, being that part of the produce which goes to labor, includes all reward for such exertion. There is, therefore, in the politico-economic sense of the term wages no distinction as to the kind of labor, or as to whether its reward is received through an employer or not, but wages means the return received for the exertion of labor, as distinguished from the return received for the use of capital, and the return received by the landholder for the use of land. The man who cultivates the soil for himself receives his wages in its produce, just as, if he uses his own capital and owns his own land, he may also receive interest and rent; the hunter's wages are the game he kills; the fisherman's wages are the fish he takes. The gold washed out by the self-employing gold-digger is as much his wages as the money paid to the hired coal miner by the purchaser of his labor,* and, as Adam Smith shows, the high profits of retail storekeepers are in large part wages, being the recompense of their labor and not of their capital. In short, whatever is received as the result or reward of exertion is "wages."

This is all it is now necessary to note as to "wages," but it is important to keep this in mind. For in the standard economic works this sense of the term wages is recognized with greater or less clearness only to be subsequently ignored.

But it is more difficult to clear away from the idea of capital the ambiguities that beset it, and to fix the scientific use of the term. In general discourse, all sorts of things that have a value or will yield a return are vaguely spoken of as capital, while economic writers vary so widely that the term can hardly be said to have a fixed meaning. Let us compare with each other the definitions of a few representative writers:

"That part of a man's stock," says Adam Smith (Book II, Chap. I), "which he expects to afford him a revenue, is called his capital," and the capital of a country or society, he goes on to say, consists of (1) machines and instruments of trade which facilitate and abridge labor;

---

* This was recognized in common speech in California, where the placer miners styled their earnings their "wages," and spoke of making high wages or low wages according to the amount of gold taken out.

(2) buildings, not mere dwellings, but which may be considered instruments of trade—such as shops, farmhouses, etc.; (3) improvements of land which better fit it for tillage or culture; (4) the acquired and useful abilities of all the inhabitants; (5) money; (6) provisions in the hands of producers and dealers, from the sale of which they expect to derive a profit; (7) the material of, or partially completed, manufactured articles still in the hands of producers or dealers; (8) completed articles still in the hands of producers or dealers. The first four of these he styles fixed capital, and the last four circulating capital, a distinction of which it is not necessary to our purpose to take any note.

Ricardo's definition is:

"Capital is that part of the wealth of a country which is employed in production, and consists of food, clothing, tools, raw materials, machinery, etc., necessary to give effect to labor."— *Principles of Political Economy, Chapter V.*

This definition, it will be seen, is very different from that of Adam Smith, as it excludes many of the things which he includes—as acquired talents, articles of mere taste or luxury in the possession of producers or dealers; and includes some things he excludes—such as food, clothing, etc., in the possession of the consumer.

McCulloch's definition is:

" The capital of a nation really comprises all those portions of the produce of industry existing in it that *may be* directly employed either to support human existence or to facilitate production."— *Notes on Wealth of Nations, Book II, Chap. I.*

This definition follows the line of Ricardo's, but is wider. While it excludes everything that is not capable of aiding production, it includes everything that is so capable, without reference to actual use or necessity for use—the horse drawing a pleasure carriage being, according to McCulloch's view, as he expressly states, as much capital as the horse drawing a plow, because he may, if need arises, be used to draw a plow.

John Stuart Mill, following the same general line as Ricardo and McCulloch, makes neither the use nor the capability of use, but the determination to use, the test of capital. He says:

"Whatever things are destined to supply productive labor with the shelter, protection, tools and materials which the work requires, and to feed and otherwise maintain the laborer during the process, are capital."—*Principles of Political Economy, Book I, Chap. IV.*

These quotations sufficiently illustrate the divergence of the masters. Among minor authors the variance is still greater, as a few examples will suffice to show.

Professor Wayland, whose "Elements of Political Economy" has long been a favorite text-book in American educational institutions, where there has been any pretense of teaching political economy, gives this lucid definition:

"The word capital is used in two senses. In relation to product it means any substance on which industry is to be exerted. In relation to industry, the material on which industry is about to confer value, that on which it has conferred value; the instruments which are used for the conferring of value, as well as the means of sustenance by which the being is supported while he is engaged in performing the operation."—*Elements of Political Economy, Book I, Chap. I.*

Henry C. Carey, the American apostle of protectionism, defines capital as "the instrument by which man obtains mastery over nature, including in it the physical and mental powers of man himself." Professor Perry, a Massachusetts free trader, very properly objects to this that it hopelessly confuses the boundaries between capital and labor, and then himself hopelessly confuses the boundaries between capital and land by defining capital as "any valuable thing outside of man himself from whose use springs a pecuniary increase or profit." An

English economic writer of high standing, Mr. Wm. Thornton, begins an elaborate examination of the relations of labor and capital ("On Labor") by stating that he will include land with capital, which is very much as if one who proposed to teach algebra should begin with the declaration that he would consider the signs plus and minus as meaning the same thing and having the same value. An American writer, also of high standing, Professor Francis A. Walker, makes the same declaration in his elaborate book on "The Wages Question." Another English writer, N. A. Nicholson ("The Science of Exchanges," London, 1873), seems to cap the climax of absurdity by declaring in one paragraph (p. 26) that "capital must of course be accumulated by saving," and in the very next paragraph stating that "the land which produces a crop, the plow which turns the soil, the labor which secures the produce, and the produce itself, if a material profit is to be derived from its employment, are all alike capital." But how land and labor are to be accumulated by saving them he nowhere condescends to explain. In the same way a standard American writer, Professor Amasa Walker (p. 66, "Science of Wealth"), first declares that capital arises from the net savings of labor and then immediately afterward declares that land is capital.

I might go on for pages, citing contradictory and self-contradictory definitions. But it would only weary the reader. It is unnecessary to multiply quotations. Those already given are sufficient to show how wide a difference exists as to the comprehension of the term capital. Any one who wants further illustration of the "confusion worse confounded" which exists on this subject among the professors of political economy may find it in any library where the works of these professors are ranged side by side.

Now, it makes little difference what name we give to

things, if when we use the name we always keep in view the same things and no others. But the difficulty arising in economic reasoning from these vague and varying definitions of capital is that it is only in the premises of reasoning that the term is used in the peculiar sense assigned by the definition, while in the practical conclusions that are reached it is always used, or at least it is always understood, in one general and definite sense. When, for instance, it is said that wages are drawn from capital, the word capital is understood in the same sense as when we speak of the scarcity or abundance, the increase or decrease, the destruction or increment, of capital—a commonly understood and definite sense which separates capital from the other factors of production, land and labor, and also separates it from like things used merely for gratification. In fact, most people understand well enough what capital is until they begin to define it, and I think their works will show that the economic writers who differ so widely in their definitions use the term in this commonly understood sense in all cases except in their definitions and the reasoning based on them.

This common sense of the term is that of wealth devoted to procuring more wealth. Dr. Adam Smith correctly expresses this common idea when he says: "That part of a man's stock which he expects to afford him revenue is called his capital." And the capital of a community is evidently the sum of such individual stocks, or that part of the aggregate stock which is expected to procure more wealth. This also is the derivative sense of the term. The word capital, as philologists trace it, comes down to us from a time when wealth was estimated in cattle, and a man's income depended upon the number of head he could keep for their increase.

The difficulties which beset the use of the word capital, as an exact term, and which are even more strikingly exemplified in current political and social discussions than in the definitions of economic writers, arise from two facts—first, that certain classes of things, the possession of which to the individual is precisely equivalent to the possession of capital, are not part of the capital of the community; and, second, that things of the same kind may or may not be capital, according to the purpose to which they are devoted.

With a little care as to these points, there should be no difficulty in obtaining a sufficiently clear and fixed idea of what the term capital as generally used properly includes; such an idea as will enable us to say what things are capital and what are not, and to use the word without ambiguity or slip.

Land, labor, and capital are the three factors of production. If we remember that capital is thus a term used in contradistinction to land and labor, we at once see that nothing properly included under either one of these terms can be properly classed as capital. The term land necessarily includes, not merely the surface of the earth as distinguished from the water and the air, but the whole material universe outside of man himself, for it is only by having access to land, from which his very body is drawn, that man can come in contact with or use nature. The term land embraces, in short, all natural materials, forces, and opportunities, and, therefore, nothing that is freely supplied by nature can be properly classed as capital. A fertile field, a rich vein of ore, a falling stream which supplies power, may give to the possessor advantages equivalent to the possession of capital, but to class such things as capital would be to put an end to the distinction between land and capital, and, so far as they relate to each other, to make the two terms meaningless. The term labor, in like manner, includes all human exertion, and hence human powers whether natural or acquired can never properly be classed as capital. In common parlance we often speak of a man's knowledge, skill, or industry as constituting his capital; but this is evidently a metaphorical use of language that must be eschewed in reasoning that aims at exactness. Superiority in such qualities may augment the income of an individual just as capital would, and an increase in the knowledge, skill, or industry of a community may have the same effect in increasing its production as would an increase of capital; but this effect is due to the increased power of labor and not to capital. Increased velocity may give to the impact of a cannon ball the same effect as increased weight, yet, nevertheless, weight is one thing and velocity another.

Thus we must exclude from the category of capital everything that may be included either as land or labor. Doing so, there remain only things which are neither land nor labor, but which have resulted from the union of these two original factors of production. Nothing can be properly capital that does not consist of these—that is to say, nothing can be capital that is not wealth.

But it is from ambiguities in the use of this inclusive term wealth that many of the ambiguities which beset the term capital are derived.

As commonly used the word "wealth" is applied to anything having an exchange value. But when used as a term of political economy it must be limited to a much more definite meaning, because many things are commonly spoken of as wealth which in taking account of collective or general wealth cannot be considered as wealth at all. Such things have an exchange value, and are commonly spoken of as wealth, insomuch as they represent as between individuals, or between sets of individuals, the power of obtaining wealth; but they are not truly wealth, inasmuch as their increase or decrease does not affect the sum of wealth. Such are bonds, mortgages, promissory notes, bank bills, or other stipulations for the transfer of wealth. Such are slaves, whose value represents merely the power of one class to appropriate the earnings of another class. Such are lands, or other natural opportunities, the value of which is but the result of the acknowledgment in favor of certain persons of an exclusive right to their use, and which represents merely the power thus given to the owners to demand a share of the wealth produced by those who use them. Increase in the amount of bonds, mortgages, notes, or bank bills cannot increase the wealth of the community that includes as well those who promise to pay as those who are entitled to receive. The enslavement of a part of their number could not increase the wealth of a people, for what the enslavers gained the enslaved would lose. Increase in land values does not represent increase in the common wealth, for what land owners gain by higher prices, the tenants or purchasers who must pay them will lose. And all this relative wealth, which, in common thought and speech, in legislation and law, is undistinguished from actual wealth, could, without the destruction or consumption of anything more than a few drops of ink and a piece of paper, be utterly annihilated. By enactment of the sovereign political power debts might be canceled, slaves emancipated, and land resumed as the common property of the whole people, without the aggregate wealth being diminished by the value of a pinch of snuff, for what some would lose others would gain. There would be no more destruction of wealth than there was creation of wealth when Elizabeth Tudor enriched her favorite courtiers by the grant of monopolies, or when Boris Godoonof made Russian peasants merchantable property.

All things which have an exchange value are, therefore, not wealth, in the only sense in which the term can be used in political economy. Only such things can be wealth the production of which increases and the destruction of which decreases the aggregate of wealth. If we consider what these things are, and what their nature is, we shall have no difficulty in defining wealth.

When we speak of a community increasing in wealth —as when we say that England has increased in wealth since the accession of Victoria, or that California is a wealthier country than when it was a Mexican territory —we do not mean to say that there is more land, or that the natural powers of the land are greater, or that there are more people, for when we wish to express that idea we speak of increase of population; or that the debts or dues owing by some of these people to others of their number have increased; but we mean that there is an increase of certain tangible things, having an actual and not merely a relative value—such as buildings, cattle, tools, machinery, agricultural and mineral products, manufactured goods, ships, wagons, furniture, and the like. The increase of such things constitutes an increase of wealth; their decrease is a lessening of wealth; and the community that, in proportion to its numbers, has most of such things is the wealthiest community. The common character of these things is that they consist of natural substances or products which have been adapted by human labor to human use or gratification, their value depending on the amount of labor which upon the average would be required to produce things of like kind.

Thus wealth, as alone the term can be used in political economy, consists of natural products that have been secured, moved, combined, separated, or in other ways modified by human exertion, so as to fit them for the gratification of human desires. It is, in other words, labor impressed upon matter in such a way as to store up, as the heat of the sun is stored up in coal, the power of human labor to minister to human desires. Wealth is not the sole object of labor, for labor is also expended in ministering directly to desire; but it is the object and result of what we call productive labor—that is, labor which gives value to material things. Nothing which nature supplies to man without his labor is wealth, nor yet does the expenditure of labor result in wealth unless there is a tangible product which has and retains the power of ministering to desire.

Now, as capital is wealth devoted to a certain purpose, nothing can be capital which does not fall within this definition of wealth. By recognizing and keeping this in mind, we get rid of misconceptions which vitiate all reasoning in which they are permitted, which befog popular thought, and have led into mazes of contradiction even acute thinkers.

But though all capital is wealth, all wealth is not capital. Capital is only a part of wealth—that part, namely, which is devoted to the aid of production. It is in drawing this line between the wealth that is and the wealth that is not capital that a second class of misconceptions are likely to occur.

The errors which I have been pointing out, and which consist in confounding with wealth and capital things essentially distinct, or which have but a relative existence, are now merely vulgar errors. They are widespread, it is true, and have a deep root, being held, not merely by the less educated classes, but seemingly by a large majority of those who in such advanced countries as England and the United States mold and guide public opinion, make the laws in Parliaments, Congresses and Legislatures, and administer them in the courts. They crop out, moreover, in the disquisitions of many of those flabby writers who have burdened the press and darkened counsel by numerous volumes which are dubbed political economy, and which pass as text-books with the ignorant and as authority with those who do not think for themselves. Neverthless, they are only vulgar errors, inasmuch as they receive no countenance from the best writers on political economy. By one of those lapses

which flaw his great work and strikingly evince the im-
perfections of the highest talent, Adam Smith counts as
capital certain personal qualities, an inclusion which is
not consistent with his original definition of capital as
stock from which revenue is expected. But this error
has been avoided by his most eminent successors, and in
the definitions, previously given, of Ricardo, McCulloch,
and Mill, it is not involved. Neither in their definitions nor in that of Smith is involved the vulgar error
which confounds as real capital things which are only relatively capital, such as evidences of debt, land values, etc.
But as to things which are really wealth, their definitions
differ from each other, and widely from that of Smith,
as to what is and what is not to be considered as capital.
The stock of a jeweler would, for instance, be included
as ˉcapital by the definition of Smith, and the food or
clothing in possession of a laborer would be excluded.
But the definitions of Ricardo and McCulloch would exclude the stock of the jeweler, as would also that of Mill,
if understood as most persons would understand the
words I have quoted. But as explained by him, it is
neither the nature nor the destination of the things
themselves which determines whether they are or are not
capital, but the intention of the owner to devote either
the things or the value received from their sale to the
supply of productive labor with tools, materials, and
maintenance. All these definitions, however, agree in
including as capital the provisions and clothing of the
laborer, which Smith excludes.

Let us consider these three definitions, which represent the best teachings of current political economy:

To McCulloch's definition of capital as "all those portions of the produce of industry that may be directly
employed either to support human existence or to facilitate production," there are obvious objections. One
may pass along any principal street in a thriving town

or city and see stores filled with all sorts of valuable things, which, though they cannot be employed either to support human existence or to facilitate production, undoubtedly constitute part of the capital of the store-keepers and part of the capital of the community. And he can also see products of industry capable of supporting human existence or facilitating production being consumed in ostentation or useless luxury. Surely these, though they might, *do not* constitute part of capital.

Ricardo's definition avoids including as capital things which might be but are not employed in production, by covering only such as are employed. But it is open to the first objection made to McCulloch's. If only wealth that may be, or that is, or that is destined to be, used in supporting producers, or assisting production, is capital, then the stocks of jewelers, toy dealers, tobacconists, confectioners, picture dealers, etc.—in fact, all stocks that consist of, and all stocks in so far as they consist of articles of luxury, are not capital.

If Mill, by remitting the distinction to the mind of the capitalist, avoids this difficulty (which does not seem to me clear), it is by making the distinction so vague that no power short of omnisicence could tell in any given country at any given time what was and what was not capital.

But the great defect which these definitions have in common is that they include what clearly cannot be accounted capital, if any distinction is to be made between laborer and capitalist. For they bring into the category of capital the food, clothing, etc., in the possession of the day laborer, which he will consume whether he works or not, as well as the stock in the hands of the capitalist, with which he proposes to pay the laborer for his work.

Yet, manifestly, this is not the sense in which the term capital is used by these writers when they speak of labor and capital as taking separate parts in the work of production and separate shares in the distribution of its proceeds; when they speak of wages as drawn from capital, or as depending upon the ratio between labor and capital, or in any of the ways in which the term is generally used by them. In all these cases the term capital is used in its commonly understood sense, as that portion of wealth which its owners do not propose to use directly for their own gratification, but for the purpose of obtaining more wealth. In short, by political economists, in everything except their definitions and first principles, as well as by the world at large, "that part of a man's stock," to use the words of Adam Smith, "which he expects to afford him revenue is called his capital." This is the only sense in which the term capital expresses any fixed idea—the only sense in which we can with any clearness separate it from wealth and contrast it with labor. For, if we must consider as capital everything which supplies the laborer with food, clothing, shelter, etc., then to find a laborer who is not a capitalist we shall be forced to hunt up an absolutely naked man, destitute even of a sharpened stick, or of a burrow in the ground —a situation in which, save as the result of exceptional circumstances, human beings have never yet been found.

It seems to me that the variance and inexactitude in these definitions arise from the fact that the idea of what capital is has been deduced from a preconceived idea of how capital assists production. Instead of determining what capital is, and then observing what capital does, the functions of capital have first been assumed, and then a definition of capital made which includes all things which do or may perform those functions. Let us reverse this process, and, adopting the natural order, ascertain what the thing is before settling what it does. All we are trying to do, all that it is necessary to do, is to fix, as it were, the metes and bounds of a term that in the main is well apprehended—to make definite, that is, sharp and clear on its verges, a common idea.

If the articles of actual wealth existing at a given time in a given community were presented *in situ* to a dozen intelligent men who had never read a line of political economy, it is doubtful if they would differ in respect to a single item, as to whether it should be accounted capital or not. Money which its owner holds for use in his business or in speculation would be accounted capital; money set aside for household or personal expenses would not. That part of a farmer's crop held for sale or for seed, or to feed his help in part payment of wages, would be accounted capital; that held for the use of his own family would not be. The horses and carriage of a hackman would be classed as capital, but an equipage kept for the pleasure of its owner would not. So no one would think of counting as capital the false hair on the head of a woman, the cigar in the mouth of a smoker, or the toy with which a child is playing; but the stock of a hair dealer, of a tobacconist, or of the keeper of a toy store, would be unhesitatingly set down as capital. A coat which a tailor had made for sale would be accounted capital, but not the coat he had made for himself. Food in the possession of a hotel-keeper or a restaurateur would be accounted capital, but not the food in the pantry of a housewife, or in the lunch basket of a workman. Pig iron in the hands of the smelter, or founder, or dealer, would be accounted capital, but not the pig iron used as ballast in the hold of a yacht. The bellows of a blacksmith, the looms of a factory, would be capital, but not the sewing machine of a woman who does only her own work; a building let for hire, or used for business or productive purposes, but not a homestead. In short, I think we should find that now, as when Dr. Adam Smith wrote, "that part of a man's stock which he expects to yield him a revenue is called his capital."

And, omitting his unfortunate slip as to personal qualities, and qualifying somewhat his enumeration of money,
it is doubtful if we could better list the different articles
of capital than did Adam Smith in the passage which in
the previous part of this chapter I have condensed.

Now, if, after having thus separated the wealth that is
capital from the wealth that is not capital, we look for
the distinction between the two classes, we shall not find
it to be as to the character, capabilities, or final destination of the things themselves, as has been vainly attempted to draw it; but it seems to me that we shall find
it to be as to whether they are or are not in the possession of the consumer.* Such articles of wealth as in
themselves, in their uses, or in their products, are yet to
be exchanged are capital; such articles of wealth as are in
the hands of the consumer are not capital.   Hence, if we
define capital as *wealth in course of exchange,* understanding exchange to include not merely the passing from hand
to hand, but also such transmutations as occur when the
reproductive or transforming forces of nature are utilized
for the increase of wealth, we shall, I think, comprehend
all the things that the general idea of capital properly
includes, and shut out all it does not.   Under this definition, it seems to me, for instance, will fall all such tools
as are really capital.   For it is as to whether its services
or uses are to be exchanged or not which makes a tool
an article of capital or merely an article of wealth.

---

* Money may be said to be in the hands of the consumer when
devoted to the procurement of gratification, as, though not in itself
devoted to consumption, it represents wealth which is; and thus
what in the previous paragraph I have given as the common classifi-
cation would be covered by this distinction, and would be substantially correct.   In speaking of money in this connection, I am of
course speaking of coin, for although paper money may perform all
the functions of coin, it is not wealth, and cannot therefore be
capital.

Thus, the lathe of a manufacturer used in making things which are to be exchanged is capital, while the lathe kept by a gentleman for his own amusement is not. Thus, wealth used in the construction of a railroad, a public telegraph line, a stage coach, a theater, a hotel, etc., may be said to be placed in the course of exchange. The exchange is not effected all at once, but little by little, with an indefinite number of people. Yet there is an exchange, and the "consumers" of the railroad, the telegraph line, the stage coach, theater or hotel, are not the owners, but the persons who from time to time use them.

Nor is this definition inconsistent with the idea that capital is that part of wealth devoted to production. It is too narrow an understanding of production which confines it merely to the making of things. Production includes not merely the making of things, but the bringing of them to the consumer. The merchant or storekeeper is thus as truly a producer as is the manufacturer, or farmer, and his stock or capital is as much devoted to production as is theirs. But it is not worth while now to dwell upon the functions of capital, which we shall be better able to determine hereafter. Nor is the definition of capital I have suggested of any importance. I am not writing a text-book, but only attempting to discover the laws which control a great social problem, and if the reader has been led to form a clear idea of what things are meant when we speak of capital my purpose is served.

But before closing this digression let me call attention to what is often forgotten—namely, that the terms "wealth," "capital," "wages," and the like, as used in political economy are abstract terms, and that nothing can be generally affirmed or denied of them that cannot be affirmed or denied of the whole class of things they represent. The failure to bear this in mind has led to much confusion of thought, and permits fallacies, otherwise transparent, to pass for obvious truths. Wealth

being an abstract term, the idea of wealth, it must be
remembered, involves the idea of exchange ability.   The
possession of wealth to a certain amount is potentially
the possession of any or all species of wealth to that
equivalent in exchange.   And, consequently, so of
capital.

CHAPTER III

WAGES NOT DRAWN FROM CAPITAL, BUT PRODUCED BY THE LABOR.

The importance of this digression will, I think, become more and more apparent as we proceed in our inquiry, but its pertinency to the branch we are now engaged in may at once be seen.

It is at first glance evident that the economic meaning of the term wages is lost sight of, and attention is concentrated upon the common and narrow meaning of the word, when it is affirmed that wages are drawn from capital. For, in all those cases in which the laborer is his own employer and takes directly the produce of his labor as its reward, it is plain enough that wages are not drawn from capital, but result directly as the product of the labor. If, for instance, I devote my labor to gathering birds' eggs or picking wild berries, the eggs or berries I thus get are my wages. Surely no one will contend that in such a case wages are drawn from capital. There is no capital in the case. An absolutely naked man, thrown on an island where no human being has before trod, may gather birds' eggs or pick berries.

Or if I take a piece of leather and work it up into a pair of shoes, the shoes are my wages—the reward of my exertion. Surely they are not drawn from capital—either my capital or any one else's capital—but are brought into existence by the labor of which they become the wages; and in obtaining this pair of shoes as the wages of my labor, capital is not even momentarily lessened one iota. For, if we call in the idea of capital, my capital at the beginning consists of the piece of leather, the thread, etc. As my labor goes on, value is steadily added, until, when my labor results in the finished shoes, I have my capital plus the difference in value between the material and the shoes. In obtaining this additional value—my wages—how is capital at any time drawn upon?

Adam Smith, who gave the direction to economic thought that has resulted in the current elaborate theories of the relation between wages and capital, recognized the fact that in such simple cases as I have instanced, wages are the produce of labor, and thus begins his chapter upon the wages of labor (Chapter VIII):

> "*The produce of labor constitutes the natural recompense or wages of labor.* In that original state of things which precedes both the appropriation of land and the accumulation of stock, the whole produce of labor belongs to the laborer. He has neither landlord nor master to share with him."

Had the great Scotchman taken this as the initial point of his reasoning, and continued to regard the produce of labor as the natural wages of labor, and the landlord and master but as sharers, his conclusions would have been very different, and political economy to-day would not embrace such a mass of contradictions and absurdities; but instead of following the truth obvious in the simple modes of production as a clew through the perplexities of the more complicated forms, he momentarily recognizes it, only immediately to abandon it, and stating that "in every part of Europe twenty workmen serve under a master for one that is independent," he recommences the inquiry from a point of view in which the master is considered as providing from his capital the wages of his workmen.

It is evident that in thus placing the proportion of

self-employing workmen as but one in twenty, Adam Smith had in mind but the mechanic arts, and that, including all laborers, the proportion who take their earnings directly, without the intervention of an employer, must, even in Europe a hundred years ago, have been much greater than this. For, besides the independent laborers who in every community exist in considerable numbers, the agriculture of large districts of Europe has, since the time of the Roman Empire, been carried on by the metayer system, under which the capitalist receives his return from the laborer instead of the laborer from the capitalist. At any rate, in the United States, where any general law of wages must apply as fully as in Europe, and where in spite of the advance of manufactures a very large part of the people are yet self-employing farmers, the proportion of laborers who get their wages through an employer must be comparatively small.

But it is not necessary to discuss the ratio in which self-employing laborers anywhere stand to hired laborers, nor is it necessary to multiply illustrations of the truism that where the laborer takes directly his wages they are the product of his labor, for as soon as it is realized that the term wages includes all the earnings of labor, as well when taken directly by the laborer in the results of his labor as when received from an employer, it is evident that the assumption that wages are drawn from capital, on which as a universal truth such a vast superstructure is in standard politico-economic treatises so unhesitatingly built, is at least in large part untrue, and the utmost that can with any plausibility be affirmed, is that some wages, *i.e.* wages received by the laborer from an employer, are drawn from capital. This restriction of the major premise at once invalidates all the deductions that are made from it; but without resting here, let us see whether even in this restricted sense it accords with the facts. Let us pick up the clew where Adam Smith dropped it, and advancing step by step, see whether the relation of facts which is obvious in the simplest forms of production does not run through the most complex.

Next in simplicity to "that original state of things," of which many examples may yet be found, where the whole produce of labor belongs to the laborer, is the arrangement in which the laborer, though working for another person, or with the capital of another person, receives his wages in kind—that is to say, in the things his labor produces. In this case it is as clear as in the case of the self-employing laborer that the wages are really drawn from the product of the labor, and not at all from capital. If I hire a man to gather eggs, to pick berries, or to make shoes, paying him from the eggs, the berries, or the shoes that his labor secures, there can be no question that the source of the wages is the labor for which they are paid. Of this form of hiring is the saer-and-daer stock tenancy, treated of with such perspicuity by Sir Henry Maine in his "Early History of Institutions," and which so clearly involved the relation of employer and employed as to render the acceptor of cattle the man or vassal of the capitalist who thus employed him. It was on such terms as these that Jacob worked for Laban, and to this day, even in civilized countries, it is not an infrequent mode of employing labor. The farming of land on shares, which prevails to a considerable extent in the Southern States of the Union and in California, the metayer system of Europe, as well as the many cases in which superintendents, salesmen, etc., are paid by a percentage of profits, what are they but the employment of labor for wages which consist of part of its produce?

The next step in the advance from simplicity to complexity is where the wages, though estimated in kind, are paid in an equivalent of something else. For instance, on American whaling ships the custom is not to pay fixed wages, but a "lay," or proportion of the catch, which varies from a sixteenth to a twelfth to the captain down to a three-hundredth to the cabin-boy. Thus, when a whaleship comes into New Bedford or San Francisco after a successful cruise, she carries in her hold the wages of her crew, as well as the profits of her owners, and an equivalent which will reimburse them for all the stores used up during the voyage. Can anything be clearer than that these wages—this oil and bone which the crew of the whaler have taken—have not been drawn from capital, but are really a part of the produce of their labor? Nor is this fact changed or obscured in the slightest degree where, as a matter of convenience, instead of dividing up between the crew their proportion of the oil and bone, the value of each man's share is estimated at the market price, and he is paid for it in money. The money is but the equivalent of the real wages, the oil and bone. In no way is there any advance of capital in this payment. The obligation to pay wages does not accrue until the value from which they are to be paid is brought into port. At the moment when the owner takes from his capital money to pay the crew he adds to his capital oil and bone.

So far there can be no dispute. Let us now take another step, which will bring us to the usual method of employing labor and paying wages.

The Farallone Islands, off the Bay of San Francisco, are a hatching ground of sea-fowl, and a company who claim these islands employ men in the proper season to collect the eggs. They might employ these men for a proportion of the eggs they gather, as is done in the whale fishery and probably would do so if there were much uncertainty attending the business; but as the fowl are plentiful and tame, and about so many eggs can be gathered by so much labor, they find it more convenient to pay their men fixed wages. The men go out and remain on the islands, gathering the eggs and bringing them to a landing, whence, at intervals of a few days, they are taken in a small vessel to San Francisco and sold. When the season is over the men return and are paid their stipulated wages in coin. Does not this transaction amount to the same thing as if, instead of being paid in coin, the stipulated wages were paid in an equivalent of the eggs gathered? Does not the coin represent the eggs, by the sale of which it was obtained, and are not these wages as much the product of the labor for which they are paid as the eggs would be in the possession of a man who gathered them for himself without the intervention of any employer?

To take another example, which shows by reversion the identity of wages in money with wages in kind. In San Buenaventura lives a man who makes an excellent living by shooting for their oil and skins the common hair seals which frequent the islands forming the Santa Barbara Channel. When on these sealing expeditions he takes two or three Chinamen along to help him, whom at first he paid wholly in coin. But it seems that the Chinese highly value some of the organs of the seal, which they dry and pulverize for medicine, as well as the long hairs in the whiskers of the male seal, which, when over a certain length, they greatly esteem for some purpose that to outside barbarians is not very clear. And this man soon found that the Chinamen were very willing to take instead of money these parts of the seals killed, so that now, in large part, he thus pays them their wages.

Now, is not what may be seen in all these cases—the identity of wages in money with wages in kind—true of all cases in which wages are paid for productive labor? Is not the fund created by the labor really the fund from which the wages are paid?

It may, perhaps, be said: "There is this difference—

where a man works for himself, or where, when working
for an employer, he takes his wages in kind, his wages
depend upon the result of his labor. Should that, from
any misadventure, prove futile, he gets nothing. When
he works for an employer, however, he gets his wages
anyhow—they depend upon the performance of the labor,
not upon the result of the labor." But this is evidently
not a real distinction. For on the average, the labor
that is rendered for fixed wages not only yields the
amount of the wages, but more; else employers could
make no profit. When wages are fixed, the employer
takes the whole risk and is compensated for this assurance, for wages when fixed are always somewhat less than
wages contingent. But though when fixed wages are
stipulated the laborer who has performed his part of the
contract has usually a legal claim upon the employer, it
is frequently, if not generally, the case that the disaster
which prevents the employer from reaping benefit from
the labor prevents him from paying the wages. And in
one important department of industry the employer is
legally exempt in case of disaster, although the contract
be for wages certain and not contingent. For the maxim
of admiralty law is, that "freight is the mother of
wages," and though the seaman may have performed his
part, the disaster which prevents the ship from earning
freight deprives him of claim for his wages.

In this legal maxim is embodied the truth for which I
am contending. Production is always the mother of
wages. Without production, wages would not and could
not be. It is from the produce of labor, not from the
advances of capital that wages come.

Wherever we analyze the facts this will be found to be
true. For labor always precedes wages. This is as uni-
versally true of wages received by the laborer from an
employer as it is of wages taken directly by the laborer
who is his own employer. In the one class of cases as

in the other, reward is conditioned upon exertion. Paid sometimes by the day, oftener by the week or month, occasionally by the year, and in many branches of production by the piece, the payment of wages by an employer to an employee always implies the previous rendering of labor by the employee for the benefit of the employer, for the few cases in which advance payments are made for personal services are evidently referable either to charity or to guarantee and purchase. The name "retainer," given to advance payments to lawyers, shows the true character of the transaction, as does the name "blood money" given in 'longshore vernacular to a payment which is nominally wages advanced to sailors, but which in reality is purchase money—both English and American law considering a sailor as much a chattel as a pig.

I dwell on this obvious fact that labor always precedes wages, because it is all-important to an understanding of the more complicated phenomena of wages that it should be kept in mind. And obvious as it is, as I have put it, the plausibility of the proposition that wages are drawn from capital—a proposition that is made the basis for such important and far-reaching deductions—comes in the first instance from a statement that ignores and leads the attention away from this truth. That statement is, that labor cannot exert its productive power unless supplied by capital with maintenance.* The unwary reader

---

* Industry is limited by capital. . . There can be no more industry than is supplied with materials to work up and food to eat. Self-evident as the thing is, it is often forgotten that the people of a country are maintained and have their wants supplied not by the produce of present labor, but of past. They consume what has been produced, not what is about to be produced. Now, of what has been produced a part only is allotted to the support of productive labor, and there will not and cannot be more of that labor

at once recognizes the fact that the laborer must have food, clothing, etc., in order to enable him to perform the work, and having been told that the food, clothing, etc., used by productive laborers are capital, he assents to the conclusion that the consumption of capital is necessary to the application of labor, and from this it is but an obvious deduction that industry is limited by capital —that the demand for labor depends upon the supply of capital, and hence that wages depend upon the ratio between the number of laborers looking for employment and the amount of capital devoted to hiring them.

But I think the discussion in the previous chapter will enable any one to see wherein lies the fallacy of this reasoning—a fallacy which has entangled some of the most acute minds in a web of their own spinning. It is in the use of the term capital in two senses. In the primary proposition that capital is necessary to the exertion of productive labor, the term "capital" is understood as including all food, clothing, shelter, etc.; whereas, in the deductions finally drawn from it, the term is used in its common and legitimate meaning of wealth devoted, not to the immediate gratification of desire, but to the procurement of more wealth—of wealth in the hands of employers as distinguished from laborers. The conclusion is no more valid than it would be from the acceptance of the proposition that a laborer cannot go to work without his breakfast and some clothes, to infer that no more laborers can go to work than employers first furnish with breakfasts and clothes. Now, the fact is that laborers generally furnish their own breakfasts and the clothes in which they go to work; and the further fact is that

---

than the portion so allotted (which is the capital of the country) can feed and provide with the materials and instruments of production. —*John Stuart Mill, Principles of Political Economy, Book I, Chap. V, Sec. I.*

capital (in the sense in which the word is used in distinction to labor) in exceptional cases sometimes may, but is
never compelled to make advances to labor before the
work begins. Of all the vast number of unemployed
laborers in the civilized world to-day, there is probably
not a single one willing to work who could not be employed without any advance of wages. A great proportion would doubtless gladly go to work on terms which
did not require the payment of wages before the end of
a month; it is doubtful if there are enough to be called
a class who would not go to work and wait for their
wages until the end of the week, as most laborers habitually do; while there are certainly none who would not
wait for their wages until the end of the day, or if you
please, until the next meal hour. The precise time of
the payment of wages is immaterial; the essential point
—the point I lay stress on—is that it is *after* the performance of work.

The payment of wages, therefore, always implies the
previous rendering of labor. Now, what does the rendering of labor in production imply? Evidently the production of wealth, which, if it is to be exchanged or used in
production, is capital. Therefore, the payment of capital in wages pre-supposes a production of capital by the
labor for which the wages are paid. And as the employer generally makes a profit, the payment of wages is,
so far as he is concerned, but the return to the laborer
of a portion of the capital he has received from the labor.
So far as the employee is concerned, it is but the receipt
of a portion of the capital his labor has previously produced. As the value paid in the wages is thus exchanged
for a value brought into being by the labor, how can it
be said that wages are drawn from capital or advanced by
capital? As in the exchange of labor for wages the employer always gets the capital created by the labor before

he pays out capital in the wages, at what point is his capital lessened even temporarily? *

Bring the question to the test of facts. Take, for instance, an employing manufacturer who is engaged in turning raw material into finished products—cotton into cloth, iron into hardware, leather into boots, or so on, as may be, and who pays his hands, as is generally the case, once a week. Make an exact inventory of his capital on Monday morning before the beginning of work, and it will consist of his buildings, machinery, raw materials, money on hand, and finished products in stock. Suppose, for the sake of simplicity, that he neither buys nor sells during the week, and after work has stopped and he has paid his hands on Saturday night, take a new inventory of his capital. The item of money will be less, for it has been paid out in wages; there will be less raw material, less coal, etc., and a proper deduction must be made from the value of the buildings and machinery for the week's wear and tear. But if he is doing a remunerative business, which must on the average be the case, the item of finished products will be so much greater as to compensate for all these deficiencies and show in the summing up an increase of capital. Manifestly, then, the value he paid his hands in wages was not drawn from

---

* I speak of labor producing capital for the sake of greater clearness. What labor always procures is either wealth, which may or may not be capital, or services, the cases in which nothing is obtained being merely exceptional cases of misadventure. Where the object of the labor is simply the gratification of the employer, as where I hire a man to black my boots, I do not pay the wages from capital, but from wealth which I have devoted, not to reproductive uses, but to consumption for my own satisfaction. Even if wages thus paid be considered as drawn from capital, then by that act they pass from the category of capital to that of wealth devoted to the gratification of the possessor, as when a cigar dealer takes a dozen cigars from the stock he has for sale and puts them in his pocket for his own use.

his capital, or from any one else's capital. It came, not from capital, but from the value created by the labor itself. There was no more advance of capital than if he had hired his hands to dig clams, and paid them with a part of the clams they dug. Their wages were as truly the produce of their labor as were the wages of the primitive man, when, long "before the appropriation of land and the accumulation of stock," he obtained an oyster by knocking it with a stone from the rocks.

As the laborer who works for an employer does not get his wages until he has performed the work, his case is similar to that of the depositor in a bank who cannot draw money out until he has put money in. And as by drawing out what he has previously put in, the bank depositor does not lessen the capital of the bank, neither can laborers by receiving wages lessen even temporarily either the capital of the employer or the aggregate capital of the community. Their wages no more come from capital than the checks of depositors are drawn against bank capital. It is true that laborers in receiving wages do not generally receive back wealth in the same form in which they have rendered it, any more than bank depositors receive back the identical coins or bank notes they have deposited, but they receive it in equivalent form, and as we are justified in saying that the depositor receives from the bank the money he paid in, so are we justified in saying that the laborer receives in wages the wealth he has rendered in labor.

That this universal truth is so often obscured, is largely due to that fruitful source of economic obscurities, the confounding of wealth with money; and it is remarkable to see so many of those who, since Dr. Adam Smith made the egg stand on its head, have copiously demonstrated the fallacies of the mercantile system, fall into delusions of the very same kind in treating of the relations of capital and labor. Money being the general medium of exchanges, the common flux through which all transmutations of wealth from one form to another take place, whatever difficulties may exist to an exchange will generally show themselves on the side of reduction to money, and thus it is sometimes easier to exchange money for any other form of wealth than it is to exchange wealth in a particular form into money, for the reason that there are more holders of wealth who desire to make some exchange than there are who desire to make any particular exchange. And so a producing employer who has paid out his money in wages may sometimes find it difficult to turn quickly back into money the increased value for which his money has really been exchanged, and is spoken of as having exhausted or advanced his capital in the payment of wages. Yet, unless the new value created by the labor is less than the wages paid, which can be only an exceptional case, the capital which he had before in money he now has in goods—it has been changed in form, but not lessened.

There is one branch of production in regard to which the confusions of thought which arise from the habit of estimating capital in money are least likely to occur, inasmuch as its product is the general material and standard of money. And it so happens that this business furnishes us, almost side by side, with illustrations of production passing from the simplest to most complex forms.

In the early days of California, as afterward in Australia, the placer miner, who found in river bed or surface deposit the glittering particles which the slow processes of nature had for ages been accumulating, picked up or washed out his "wages" (so, too, he called them) in actual money, for coin being scarce, gold dust passed as currency by weight, and at the end of the day had his wages in money in a buckskin bag in his pocket. There can be no dispute as to whether these wages came from capital or not.   They were manifestly the produce of his labor.   Nor could there be any dispute when the holder of a specially rich claim hired men to work for him and paid them off in the identical money which their labor had taken from gulch or bar.   As coin became more abundant, its greater convenience in saving the trouble and loss of weighing assigned gold dust to the place of a commodity, and with coin obtained by the sale of the dust their labor had procured, the employing miner paid off his hands.   Where he had coin enough to do so, instead of selling his gold dust at the nearest store and paying a dealer's profit, he retained it until he got enough to take a trip, or send by express to San Francisco, where at the mint he could have it turned into coin without charge.   While thus accumulating gold dust he was lessening his stock of coin; just as the manufacturer, while accumulating a stock of goods, lessens his stock of money.   Yet no one would be obtuse enough to imagine that in thus taking in gold dust and paying out coin the miner was lessening his capital.

But the deposits that could be worked without preliminary labor were soon exhausted, and gold mining rapidly took a more elaborate character.   Before claims could be opened so as to yield any return deep shafts had to be sunk, great dams constructed, long tunnels cut through the hardest rock, water brought for miles over mountain ridges and across deep valleys, and expensive machinery put up.   These works could not be constructed without capital.   Sometimes their construction required years, during which no return could be hoped for, while the men employed had to be paid their wages every week, or every month.   Surely, it will be said, in such cases, even if in no others, that wages do actually come from capital; are actually advanced by capital; and must necessarily lessen capital in their payment!   Surely here, at least, industry is limited by capital, for without capital such works could not be carried on! Let us see:

It is cases of this class that are always instanced as showing that wages are advanced from capital. For where wages are paid before the object of the labor is obtained, or is finished—as in agriculture, where plowing and sowing must precede by several months the harvesting of the crop; as in the erection of buildings, the construction of ships, railroads, canals, etc.—it is clear that the owners of the capital paid in wages cannot expect an immediate return, but, as the phrase is, must "outlay it," or "lie out of it" for a time, which sometimes amounts to many years. And hence, if first principles are not kept in mind, it is easy to jump to the conclusion that wages are advanced by capital.

But such cases will not embarrass the reader to whom in what has preceded I have made myself clearly understood. An easy analysis will show that these instances where wages are paid before the product is finished, or even produced, do not afford any exception to the rule apparent where the product is finished before wages are paid.

If I go to a broker to exchange silver for gold, I lay down my silver, which he counts and puts away, and then hands me the equivalent in gold, minus his commission. Does the broker advance me any capital? Manifestly not. What he had before in gold he now has in silver, plus his profit. And as he got the silver before he paid out the gold, there is on his part not even momentarily an advance of capital.

Now, this operation of the broker is precisely analogous to what the capitalist does, when, in such cases as we are now considering, he pays out capital in wages. As the rendering of labor precedes the payment of wages, and as the rendering of labor in production implies the creation of value, the employer receives value before he pays out value—he but exchanges capital of one form for capital of another form. For the creation of value does not depend upon the finishing of the product; it takes place at every stage of the process of production, as the immediate result of the application of labor, and hence, no matter how long the process in which it is engaged, labor always adds to capital by its exertion before it takes from capital in its wages.

Here is a blacksmith at his forge making picks. Clearly he is making capital—adding picks to his employer's capital before he draws money from it in wages. Here is a machinist or boilermaker working on the keel-plates of a Great Eastern. Is not he also just as clearly creating value—making capital? The giant steamship, as the pick, is an article of wealth, an instrument of production, and though the one may not be completed for years, while the other is completed in a few minutes, each day's work, in the one case as in the other, is as clearly a production of wealth—an addition to capital. In the case of the steamship, as in the case of the pick, it is not the last blow, any more than the first blow, that creates the value of the finished product—the creation of value is continuous, it immediately results from the exertion of labor.

We see this very clearly wherever the division of labor has made it customary for different parts of the full process of production to be carried on by different sets of producers—that is to say, wherever we are in the habit of estimating the amount of value which the labor expended in any preparatory stage of production has created. And a moment's reflection will show that this is the case as to the vast majority of products. Take a ship, a building, a jack-knife, a book, a lady's thimble or a loaf of bread. They are finished products. But they were not produced at one operation or by one set of producers. And this being the case, we readily distinguish different points or stages in the creation of the value which as completed articles they represent. When we do not distinguish different parts in the final process of production we do distinguish the value of the materials. The value of these materials may often be again decomposed many times, exhibiting as many clearly defined steps in the creation of the final value. At each of these steps we habitually estimate a creation of value, an addition to capital. The batch of bread which the baker is taking from the oven has a certain value. But this is composed in part of the value of the flour from which the dough was made. And this again is composed of the value of the wheat, the value given by milling, etc. Iron in the form of pigs is very far from being a completed product. It must yet pass through several, or, perhaps, through many, stages of production before it results in the finished articles that were the ultimate objects for which the iron ore was extracted from the mine. Yet, is not pig iron capital? And so the process of production is not really completed when a crop of cotton is gathered, nor yet when it is ginned and pressed; nor yet when it arrives at Lowell or Manchester; nor yet when it is converted into yarn; nor yet when it becomes cloth; but only when it is finally placed in the hands of the consumer. Yet at each step in this progress there is clearly enough a creation of value—an addition to capital. Why, therefore, although we do not so habitually distinguish and estimate it, is there not a creation of value —an addition to capital—when the ground is plowed for the crop? Is it because it may possibly be a bad season and the crop may fail? Evidently not; for a like possibility of misadventure attends every one of the many steps in the production of the finished article. On the average a crop is sure to come up, and so much plowing and sowing will on the average result in so much cotton in the boll, as surely as so much spinning of cotton yarn will result in so much cloth.

In short, as the payment of wages is always conditioned upon the rendering of labor, the payment of wages in production, no matter how long the process, never involves any advance of capital, or even temporarily lessens capital. It may take a year, or even years, to build a ship, but the creation of value of which the finished ship will be the sum goes on day by day, and hour by hour, from the time the keel is laid or even the ground is cleared. Nor by the payment of wages before the ship is completed, does the master builder lessen either his capital or the capital of the community, for the value of the partially completed ship stands in place of the value paid out in wages. There is no advance of capital in this payment of wages, for the labor of the workmen during the week or month creates and renders to the builder more capital than is paid back to them at the end of the week or month, as is shown by the fact that if the builder were at any stage of the construction asked to sell a partially completed ship he would expect a profit.

And so, when a Sutro or St. Gothard tunnel or a Suez canal is cut, there is no advance of capital. The tunnel or canal, as it is cut, becomes capital as much as the money spent in cutting it—or, if you please, the powder, drills, etc., used in the work, and the food, clothes, etc., used by the workmen—as is shown by the fact that the value of the capital stock of the company is not lessened as capital in these forms is gradually changed into capital in the form of tunnel or canal. On the contrary, it probably, and on the average, increases as the work progresses, just as the capital invested in a speedier mode of production would on the average increase.

And this is obvious in agriculture also. That the

creation of value does not take place all at once when the crop is gathered, but step by step during the whole process which the gathering of the crop concludes, and that no payment of wages in the interim lessens the farmer's capital, is tangible enough when land is sold or rented during the process of production, as a plowed field will bring more than an unplowed field, or a field that has been sown more than one merely plowed. It is tangible enough when growing crops are sold, as is sometimes done, or where the farmer does not harvest himself, but lets a contract to the owner of harvesting machinery. It is tangible in the case of orchards and vineyards which, though not yet in bearing, bring prices proportionate to their age. It is tangible in the case of horses, cattle and sheep, which increase in value as they grow toward maturity. And if not always tangible between what may be called the usual exchange points in production, this increase of value as surely takes place with every exertion of labor. Hence, where labor is rendered before wages are paid, the advance of capital is really made by labor, and is from the employed to the employer, not from the employer to the employed.

"Yet," it may be said, "in such cases as we have been considering capital is required!" Certainly; I do not dispute that. But it is not required in order to make advances to labor. It is required for quite another purpose. What that purpose is we may readily see.

When wages are paid in kind—that is to say, in wealth of the same species as the labor produces; as, for instance, if I hire men to cut wood, agreeing to give them as wages a portion of the wood they cut, a method sometimes adopted by the owners or lessees of woodland, it is evident that no capital is required for the payment of wages. Nor yet when, for the sake of mutual convenience, arising from the fact that a large quantity of wood can be more readily and more advantageously exchanged than a number of small quantities, I agree to pay wages in money, instead of wood, shall I need any capital, provided I can make the exchange of the wood for money before the wages are due. It is only when I cannot make such an exchange, or such an advantageous exchange as I desire, until I accumulate a large quantity of wood that I shall need capital. Nor even then shall I need capital if I can make a partial or tentative exchange by borrowing on my wood. If I cannot, or do not choose, either to sell the wood or to borrow upon it, and yet wish to go ahead accumulating a large stock of wood, I shall need capital. But manifestly, I need this capital, not for the payment of wages, but for the accumulation of a stock of wood. Likewise in cutting a tunnel. If the workmen were paid in tunnel (which, if convenient, might easily be done by paying them in stock of the company), no capital for the payment of wages would be required. It is only when the undertakers wish to accumulate capital in the shape of a tunnel that they will need capital. To recur to our first illustration: The broker to whom I sell my silver cannot carry on his business without capital. But he does not need this capital because he makes any advance of capital to me when he receives my silver and hands me gold. He needs it because the nature of the business requires the keeping of a certain amount of capital on hand, in order that when a customer comes he may be prepared to make the exchange the customer desires.

And so we shall find it in every branch of production. Capital has never to be set aside for the payment of wages when the produce of the labor for which the wages are paid is exchanged as soon as produced; it is only required when this produce is stored up, or what is to the individual the same thing, placed in the general current of exchanges without being at once drawn against— that is, sold on credit. But the capital thus required is not required for the payment of wages, nor for advances to labor, as it is always represented in the produce of the labor. It is never as an employer of labor that any producer needs capital; when he does need capital, it is because he is not only an employer of labor, but a merchant or speculator in, or an accumulator of, the products of labor. This is generally the case with employers.

To recapitulate: The man who works for himself gets his wages in the things he produces, as he produces them, and exchanges this value into another form whenever he sells the produce. The man who works for another for stipulated wages in money works under a contract of exchange. He also creates his wages as he renders his labor, but he does not get them except at stated times, in stated amounts, and in a different form. In performing the labor he is advancing in exchange; when he gets his wages the exchange is completed. During the time he is earning the wages he is advancing capital to his employer, but at no time, unless wages are paid before work is done, is the employer advancing capital to him. Whether the employer who receives this produce in exchange for the wages immediately re-exchanges it, or keeps it for awhile, no more alters the character of the transaction than does the final disposition of the product made by the ultimate receiver, who may, perhaps, be in another quarter of the globe and at the end of a series of exchanges numbering hundreds.

CHAPTER IV.

THE MAINTENANCE OF LABORERS NOT DRAWN FROM CAPITAL.

But a stumbling block may yet remain, or may recur, in the mind of the reader.

As the plowman cannot eat the furrow, nor a partially completed steam engine aid in any way in producing the clothes the machinist wears, have I not, in the words of John Stuart Mill, "forgotten that the people of a country are maintained and have their wants supplied, not by the produce of present labor, but of past?" Or, to use the language of a popular elementary work—that of Mrs. Fawcett — have I not "forgotten that many months must elapse between the sowing of the seed and the time when the produce of that seed is converted into a loaf of bread," and that "it is, therefore, evident that laborers cannot live upon that which their labor is assisting to produce, but are maintained by that wealth which their labor, or the labor of others, has previously produced, which wealth is capital?" *

The assumption made in these passages—the assumption that it is so self-evident that labor must be subsisted from capital that the proposition has but to be stated to compel recognition—runs through the whole fabric of current political economy. And so confidently is it held that the maintenance of labor is drawn from capital that

* Political Economy for Beginners, by Millicent Garrett Fawcett, Chap. III, p. 25.

the proposition that "population regulates itself by the funds which are to employ it, and, therefore, always increases or diminishes with the increase or diminution of capital,"* is regarded as equally axiomatic, and in its turn made the basis of important reasoning.

Yet being resolved, these propositions are seen to be, not self-evident, but absurd; for they involve the idea that labor cannot be exerted until the products of labor are saved—thus putting the product before the producer.

And being examined, they will be seen to derive their apparent plausibility from a confusion of thought.

I have already pointed out the fallacy, concealed by an erroneous definition, which underlies the proposition that because food, raiment and shelter are necessary to productive labor, therefore industry is limited by capital. To say that a man must have his breakfast before going to work is not to say that he cannot go to work unless a capitalist furnishes him with a breakfast, for his breakfast may, and in point of fact in any country where there is not actual famine will, come not from wealth set apart for the assistance of production, but from wealth set apart for subsistence. And, as has been previously shown, food, clothing, etc.—in short, all articles of wealth—are only capital so long as they remain in the possession of those who propose, not to consume, but to exchange them for other commodities or for productive services, and cease to be capital when they pass into the possession of those who will consume them; for in that transaction they pass from the stock of wealth held for the purpose of procuring other wealth, and pass into the stock of wealth held for purposes of gratification, irrespective of whether their consumption will aid in the production of wealth or not. Unless this distinction is preserved it is impossible to draw the line between the

* The words quoted are Ricardo's (Chap. II); but the idea is common in standard works.

wealth that is capital and the wealth that is not capital, even by remitting the distinction to the "mind of the possessor," as does John Stuart Mill.   For men do not eat or abstain, wear clothes or go naked, as they propose to engage in productive labor or not.   They eat because they are hungry, and wear clothes because they would be uncomfortable without them.   Take the food on the breakfast table of a laborer who will work or not that day as he gets the opportunity.   If the distinction between capital and non-capital be the support of productive labor, is this food capital or not?   It is as impossible for the laborer himself as for any philosopher of the Ricardo-Mill school to tell.   Nor yet can it be told when it gets into his stomach; nor, supposing that he does not get work at first, but continues the search, can it be told until it has passed into the blood and tissues.   Yet the man will eat his breakfast all the same.

But, though it would be logically sufficient, it is hardly safe to rest here and leave the argument to turn on the distinction between wealth and capital.   Nor is it necessary.   It seems to me that the proposition that present labor must be maintained by the produce of past labor will upon analysis prove to be true only in the sense that the afternoon's labor must be performed by the aid of the noonday meal, or that before you eat the hare he must be caught and cooked.   And this, manifestly, is not the sense in which the proposition is used to support the important reasoning that is made to hinge upon it. That sense is, that before a work which will not immediately result in wealth available for subsistence can be carried on, there must exist such a stock of subsistence as will support the laborers during the process.   Let us see if this be true:

The canoe which Robinson Crusoe made with such infinite toil and pains was a production in which his labor could not yield an immediate return.   But was it necessary that, before he commenced, he should accumulate a stock of food sufficient to maintain him while he felled the tree, hewed out the canoe, and finally launched her into the sea? Not at all. It was necessary only that he should devote part of his time to the procurement of food while he was devoting part of his time to the building and launching of the canoe. Or supposing a hundred men to be landed, without any stock of provisions, in a new country. Will it be necessary for them to accumulate a season's stock of provisions before they can begin to cultivate the soil? Not at all. It will be necessary only that fish, game, berries, etc., shall be so abundant that the labor of a part of the hundred may suffice to furnish daily enough of these for the maintenance of all, and that there shall be such a sense of mutual interest, or such a correlation of desires, as shall lead those who in the present get the food to divide (exchange) with those whose efforts are directed to future recompense.

What is true in these cases is true in all cases. It is not necessary to the production of things that cannot be used as subsistence, or cannot be immediately utilized, that there should have been a previous production of the wealth required for the maintenance of the laborers while the production is going on. It is only necessary that there should be, somewhere within the circle of exchange, a contemporaneous production of sufficient subsistence for the laborers, and a willingness to exchange this subsistence for the thing on which the labor is being bestowed.

And as a matter of fact, is it not true, in any normal condition of things, that consumption is supported by contemporaneous production?

Here is a luxurious idler, who does no productive work either with head or hand, but lives, we say, upon wealth which his father left him securely invested in government bonds. Does his subsistence, as a matter of fact, come from wealth accumulated in the past or from the productive labor that is going on around him? On his table are new-laid eggs, butter churned but a few days before, milk which the cow gave this morning, fish which twenty-four hours ago were swimming in the sea, meat which the butcher boy has just brought in time to be cooked, vegetables fresh from the garden, and fruit from the orchard—in short, hardly anything that has not recently left the hand of the productive laborer (for in this category must be included transporters and distributors as well as those who are engaged in the first stages of production), and nothing that has been produced for any considerable length of time, unless it may be some bottles of old wine. What this man inherited from his father, and on which we say he lives, is not actually wealth at all, but only the power of commanding wealth as others produce it. And it is from this contemporaneous production that his subsistence is drawn.

The fifty square miles of London undoubtedly contain more wealth than within the same space anywhere else exists. Yet were productive labor in London absolutely to cease, within a few hours people would begin to die like rotten sheep, and within a few weeks, or at most a few months, hardly one would be left alive. For an entire suspension of productive labor would be a disaster more dreadful than ever yet befell a beleaguered city. It would not be a mere external wall of circumvallation, such as Titus drew around Jerusalem, which would prevent the constant incoming of the supplies on which a great city lives, but it would be the drawing of a similar wall around each household. Imagine such a suspension of labor in any community, and you will see how true it is that mankind really live from hand to mouth; that it is the daily labor of the community that supplies the community with its daily bread.

Just as the subsistence of the laborers who built the Pyramids was drawn not from a previously hoarded stock, but from the constantly recurring crops of the Nile Valley; just as a modern government when it undertakes a great work of years does not appropriate to it wealth already produced, but wealth yet to be produced, which is taken from producers in taxes as the work progresses; so it is that the subsistence of the laborers engaged in production which does not directly yield subsistence comes from the production of subsistence in which others are simultaneously engaged.

If we trace the circle of exchange by which work done in the production of a great steam engine secures to the worker bread, meat, clothes and shelter, we shall find that though between the laborer on the engine and the producers of the bread, meat, etc., there may be a thousand intermediate exchanges, the transaction, when reduced to its lowest terms, really amounts to an exchange of labor between him and them. Now the cause which induces the expenditure of the labor on the engine is evidently that some one who has power to give what is desired by the laborer on the engine wants in exchange an engine—that is to say, there exists a demand for an engine on the part of those producing bread, meat, etc., or on the part of those who are producing what the producers of the bread, meat, etc., desire. It is this demand which directs the labor of the machinist to the production of the engine, and hence, reversely, the demand of the machinist for bread, meat, etc., really directs an equivalent amount of labor to the production of these things, and thus his labor, actually exerted in the production of the engine, virtually produces the things in which he expends his wages.

Or, to formularize this principle:

The demand for consumption determines the direction in which labor will be expended in production.

This principle is so simple and obvious that it needs no further illustration, yet in its light all the complexities of our subject disappear, and we thus reach the same view of the real objects and rewards of labor in the intricacies of modern production that we gained by observing in the first beginnings of society the simpler forms of production and exchange. We see that now, as then, each laborer is endeavoring to obtain by his exertions the satisfaction of his own desires; we see that although the minute division of labor assigns to each producer the production of but a small part, or perhaps nothing at all, of the particular things he labors to get, yet, in aiding in the production of what other producers want, he is directing other labor to the production of the things he wants—in effect, producing them himself. And thus, if he make jack-knives and eat wheat, the wheat is really as much the produce of his labor as if he had grown it for himself and left wheat-growers to make their own jack-knives.

We thus see how thoroughly and completely true it is, that in whatever is taken or consumed by laborers in return for labor rendered, there is no advance of capital to the laborers. If I have made jack-knives, and with the wages received have bought wheat, I have simply exchanged jack-knives for wheat—added jack-knives to the existing stock of wealth and taken wheat from it. And as the demand for consumption determines the direction in which labor will be expended in production, it cannot even be said, so long as the limit of wheat production has not been reached, that I have lessened the stock of wheat, for, by placing jack-knives in the exchangeable stock of wealth and taking wheat out, I have determined labor at the other end of a series of exchanges to the production of wheat, just as the wheat grower, by putting in wheat and demanding jack-knives, determined labor to the production of jack-knives, as the easiest way by which wheat could be obtained.

And so the man who is following the plow—though the crop for which he is opening the ground is not yet sown, and after being sown will take months to arrive at maturity—he is yet, by the exertion of his labor in plowing, virtually producing the food he eats and the wages he receives. For, though plowing is but a part of the operation of producing a crop, it *is* a part, and as necessary a part as harvesting. The doing of it is a step toward procuring a crop, which, by the assurance which it gives of the future crop, sets free from the stock constantly held the subsistence and wages of the plowman. This is not merely theoretically true, it is practically and literally true. At the proper time for plowing, let plowing cease. Would not the symptoms of scarcity at once manifest themselves without waiting for the time of the harvest? Let plowing cease, and would not the effect at once be felt in counting-room, and machine shop, and factory? Would not loom and spindle soon stand as idle as the plow? That this would be so, we see in the effect which immediately follows a bad season. And if this would be so, is not the man who plows really producing his subsistence and wages as much as though during the day or week his labor actually resulted in the things for which his labor is exchanged?

As a matter of fact, where there is labor looking for employment, the want of capital does not prevent the owner of land which promises a crop for which there is a demand from hiring it. Either he makes an agreement to cultivate on shares, a common method in some parts of the United States, in which case the laborers, if they are without means of subsistence, will, on the strength of the work they are doing, obtain credit at the nearest store; or, if he prefers to pay wages, the farmer will himself obtain credit, and thus the work done in cultivation is immediately utilized or exchanged as it is done. If anything more will be used up than would be used up if the laborers were forced to beg instead of to work (for in any civilized country during a normal condition of things the laborers must be supported anyhow), it will be the reserve capital drawn out by the prospect of replacement, and which is in fact replaced by the work as it is done. For instance, in the purely agricultural districts of Southern California there was in 1877 a total failure of the crop, and of millions of sheep nothing remained but their bones. In the great San Joaquin Valley were many farmers without food enough to support their families until the next harvest time, let alone to support any laborers. But the rains came again in proper season, and these very farmers proceeded to hire hands to plow and to sow. For every here and there was a farmer who had been holding back part of his crop. As soon as the rains came he was anxious to sell before the next harvest brought lower prices, and the grain thus held in reserve, through the machinery of exchanges and advances, passed to the use of the cultivators—set free, in effect produced, by the work done for the next crop.

The series of exchanges which unite production and consumption may be likened to a curved pipe filled with water. If a quantity of water is poured in at one end, a like quantity is released at the other. It is not identically the same water, but is its equivalenc. And so they who do the work of production put in as they take out—they receive in subsistence and wages but the produce of their labor.

CHAPTER V.

It may now be asked, If capital is not required for the payment of wages or the support of labor during production, what, then, are its functions?

The previous examination has made the answer clear. Capital, as we have seen, consists of wealth used for the procurement of more wealth, as distinguished from wealth used for the direct satisfaction of desire; or, as I think it may be defined, of wealth in the course of exchange.

Capital, therefore, increases the power of labor to produce wealth: (1) By enabling labor to apply itself in more effective ways, as by digging up clams with a spade instead of the hand, or moving a vessel by shoveling coal into a furnace, instead of tugging at an oar. (2) By enabling labor to avail itself of the reproductive forces of nature, as to obtain corn by sowing it, or animals by breeding them. (3) By permitting the division of labor, and thus, on the one hand, increasing the efficiency of the human factor of wealth, by the utilization of special capabilities, the acquisition of skill, and the reduction of waste; and, on the other, calling in the powers of the natural factor at their highest, by taking advantage of the diversities of soil, climate and situation, so as to obtain each particular species of wealth where nature is most favorable to its production.

Capital does not supply the materials which labor works up into wealth, as is erroneously taught; the materials of wealth are supplied by nature. But such materials partially worked up and in the course of exchange are capital.

Capital does not supply or advance wages, as is erroneously taught. Wages are that part of the produce of his labor obtained by the laborer.

Capital does not maintain laborers during the progress of their work, as is erroneously taught. Laborers are maintained by their labor, the man who produces, in whole or in part, anything that will exchange for articles of maintenance, virtually producing that maintenance.

Capital, therefore, does not limit industry, as is erroneouly taught, the only limit to industry being the access to natural material. But capital may limit the form of industry and the productiveness of industry, by limiting the use of tools and the division of labor.

That capital may limit the form of industry is clear. Without the factory, there could be no factory operatives; without the sewing machine, no machine sewing; without the plow, no plowman; and without a great capital engaged in exchange, industry could not take the many special forms which are concerned with exchanges. It is also as clear that the want of tools must greatly limit the productiveness of industry. If the farmer must use the spade because he has not capital enough for a plow, the sickle instead of the reaping machine, the flail instead of the thresher; if the machinist must rely upon the chisel for cutting iron; the weaver on the hand loom, and so on, the productiveness of industry cannot be a tithe of what it is when aided by capital in the shape of the best tools now in use. Nor could the division of labor go further than the very rudest and almost imperceptible beginnings, nor the exchanges which make it possible extend beyond the nearest neighbors, unless a portion of the things produced were constantly kept in stock or in transit. Even the pursuits of hunting, fishing, gathering nuts, and making weapons could not be specialized so that an individual could devote himself to any one, unless some part of what was procured by each was reserved from immediate consumption, so that he who devoted himself to the procurement of things of one kind could obtain the others as he wanted them, and could make the good luck of one day supply the short-comings of the next. While to permit the minute sub-division of labor that is characteristic of, and necessary to, high civilization, a great amount of wealth of all descrip-tions must be constantly kept in stock or in transit. To enable the resident of a civilized community to exchange his labor at option with the labor of those around him and with the labor of men in the most remote parts of the globe, there must be stocks of goods in warehouses, in stores, in the holds of ships, and in railway cars, just as to enable the denizen of a great city to draw at will a cupful of water, there must be thousands of millions of gallons stored in reservoirs and moving through miles of pipe.

But to say that capital may limit the form of industry or the productiveness of industry is a very different thing from saying that capital limits industry. For the dictum of the current political economy that "capital limits in-dustry," means not that capital limits the form of labor or the productiveness of labor, but that it limits the ex-ertion of labor. This proposition derives its plausibility from the assumption that capital supplies labor with ma-terials and maintenance—an assumption that we have seen to be unfounded, and which is indeed transparently preposterous the moment it is remembered that capital is produced by labor, and hence that there must be labor before there can be capital. Capital may limit the form of industry and the productiveness of industry; but this is not to say that there could be no industry without capi-tal, any more than it is to say that without the power loom there could be no weaving; without the sewing machine no sewing; no cultivation without the plow; or that in a community of one, like that of Robinson Crusoe, there could be no labor because there could be no exchange.

And to say that capital *may* limit the form and pro- ductiveness of industry is a different thing from saying that capital *does*. For the cases in which it can be truly said that the form of productiveness of the industry of a community is limited by its capital, will, I think, appear upon examination to be more theoretical than real. It is evident that in such a country as Mexico or Tunis the larger and more general use of capital would greatly change the forms of industry and enormously increase its productiveness; and it is often said of such countries that they need capital for the development of their re- sources. But is there not something back of this—a want which includes the want of capital? Is it not the rapacity and abuses of government, the insecurity of property, the ignorance and prejudice of the people, that prevent the accumulation and use of capital? Is not the real limitation in these things, and not in the want of capital, which would not be used even if placed there? We can, of course, imagine a community in which the want of capital would be the only obstacle to an increased productiveness of labor, but it is only by imagining a conjunction of conditions that seldom, if ever, occurs, except by accident or as a passing phase. A community in which capital has been swept away by war, conflagra- tion, or convulsion of nature, and, possibly, a community composed of civilized people just settled in a new land, seem to me to furnish the only examples. Yet how quickly the capital habitually used is reproduced in a community that has been swept by war, has long been noticed, while the rapid production of the capital it can, or is disposed to use, is equally noticeable in the case of a new community.

I am unable to think of any other than such rare and passing conditions in which the productiveness of labor is really limited by the want of capital. For, although there may be in a community individuals who from want of capital cannot apply their labor as efficiently as they would, yet so long as there is a sufficiency of capital in the community at large, the real limitation is not the want of capital, but the want of its proper distribution. If bad government rob the laborer of his capital, if unjust laws take from the producer the wealth with which he would assist production, and hand it over to those who are mere pensioners upon industry, the real limitation to the effectiveness of labor is in misgovernment, and not in want of capital. And so of ignorance, or custom, or other conditions which prevent the use of capital. It is they, not the want of capital, that really constitute the limitation. To give a circular saw to a Terra del Fuegan, a locomotive to a Bedouin Arab, or a sewing machine to a Flathead squaw, would not be to add to the efficiency of their labor. Neither does it seem possible by giving anything else to add to their capital, for any wealth beyond what they had been accustomed to use as capital would be consumed or suffered to waste. It is not the want of seeds and tools that keeps the Apache and the Sioux from cultivating the soil. If provided with seeds and tools they would not use them productively unless at the same time restrained from wandering and taught to cultivate the soil. If all the capital of a London were given them in their present condition, it would simply cease to be capital, for they would only use productively such infinitesimal part as might assist in the chase, and would not even use that until all the edible part of the stock thus showered upon them had been consumed. Yet such capital as they do want they manage to acquire, and in some forms in spite of the greatest difficulties. These wild tribes hunt and fight with the best weapons that American and English factories produce, keeping up with the latest improvements. It is only as they became civilized that they would care for such other capital as the civilized state requires, or that it would be of any use to them.

In the reign of George IV., some returning missionaries took with them to England a New Zealand chief called Hongi. His noble appearance and beautiful tatooing attracted much attention, and when about to return to his people he was presented by the monarch and some of the religious societies with a considerable stock of tools, agricultural instruments, and seeds. The grateful New Zealander did use this capital in the production of food, but it was in a manner of which his English entertainers little dreamed. In Sydney, on his way back, he exchanged it all for arms and ammunition, with which, on getting home, he began war against another tribe with such success that on the first battle field three hundred of his prisoners were cooked and eaten, Hongi having preluded the main repast by scooping out and swallowing the eyes and sucking the warm blood of his mortally wounded adversary, the opposing chief.* But now that their once constant wars have ceased, and the remnant of the Maoris have largely adopted European habits, there are among them many who have and use considerable amounts of capital.

Likewise it would be a mistake to attribute the simple modes of production and exchange which are resorted to in new communities solely to a want of capital. These modes, which require little capital, are in themselves rude and inefficient, but when the conditions of such

* New Zealand and its Inhabitants. Rev. Richard Taylor. London, 1855. Chap. **XXI.**

communities are considered, they will be found in reality the most effective. A great factory with all the latest improvements is the most efficient instrument that has yet been devised for turning wool or cotton into cloth, but only so where large quantities are to be made. The cloth required for a little village could be made with far less labor by the spinning wheel and hand loom. A perfecting press will, for each man required, print many thousand impressions while a man and a boy would be printing a hundred with a Stanhope or Franklin press; yet to work off the small edition of a country newspaper the old-fashioned press is by far the most efficient machine. To carry occasionally two or three passengers, a canoe is a better instrument than a steamboat; a few sacks of flour can be transported with less expenditure of labor by a pack horse than by a railroad train; to put a great stock of goods into a cross-roads store in the backwoods would be but to waste capital. And, generally, it will be found that the rude devices of production and exchange which obtain among the sparse populations of new countries result not so much from the want of capital as from inability profitably to employ it.

As, no matter how much water is poured in, there can never be in a bucket more than a bucketful, so no greater amount of wealth will be used as capital than is required by the machinery of production and exchange that under all the existing conditions—intelligence, habit, security, density of population, etc.—best suit the people. And I am inclined to think that as a general rule this amount will be had—that the social organism secretes, as it were, the necessary amount of capital just as the human organism in a healthy condition secretes the requisite fat.

But whether the amount of capital ever does limit the productiveness of industry, and thus fix a maximum which wages cannot exceed, it is evident that it is not from any scarcity of capital that the poverty of the masses in civilized countries proceeds. For not only do wages nowhere reach the limit fixed by the productiveness of industry, but wages are relatively the lowest where capital is most abundant. The tools and machinery of production are in all the most progressive coun‧tries evidently in excess of the use made of them, and any prospect of remunerative employment brings out more than the capital needed. The bucket is not only full; it is overflowing. So evident is this, that not only among the ignorant, but by men of high economic reputation, is industrial depression attributed to the abundance of machinery and the accumulation of capital; and war, which is the destruction of capital, is looked upon as the cause of brisk trade and high wages—an idea strangely enough, so great is the confusion of thought on such matters, countenanced by many who hold that capital employs labor and pays wages.

Our purpose in this inquiry is to solve the problem to which so many self-contradictory answers are given. In ascertaining clearly what capital really is and what capital really does, we have made the first, and an all-important step. But it is only a first step. Let us recapitulate and proceed.

We have seen that the current theory that wages depend upon the ratio between the number of laborers and the amount of capital devoted to the employment of labor is inconsistent with the general fact that wages and interest do not rise and fall inversely, but conjointly.

This discrepancy having led us to an examination of the grounds of the theory, we have seen, further, that, contrary to the current idea, wages are not drawn from capital at all, but come directly from the produce of the labor for which they are paid. We have seen that capital does not advance wages or subsist laborers, but that its functions are to assist labor in production with tools, seed, etc., and with the wealth required to carry on exchanges.

We are thus irresistibly led to practical conclusions so important as amply to justify the pains taken to make sure of them.

For if wages are drawn, not from capital, but from the produce of labor, the current theories as to the relations of capital and labor are invalid, and all remedies, whether proposed by professors of political economy or workingmen, which look to the alleviation of poverty either by the increase of capital or the restriction of the number of laborers or the efficiency of their work, must be condemned.

If each laborer in performing the labor really creates the fund from which his wages are drawn, then wages cannot be diminished by the increase of laborers, but, on the contrary, as the efficiency of labor manifestly increases with the number of laborers, the more laborers, other things being equal, the higher should wages be.

But this necessary proviso, "other things being equal," brings us to a question which must be considered and disposed of before we can further proceed. That question is, Do the productive powers of nature tend to diminish with the increasing drafts made upon them by increasing population?

BOOK II.

POPULATION AND SUBSISTENCE.

Are God and Nature then at strife,
  That Nature lends such evil dreams?
  So careful of the type she seems,
So careless of the single life.
                    —*Tennyson.*

CHAPTER I.

Behind the theory we have been considering lies a theory we have yet to consider. The current doctrine as to the derivation and law of wages finds its strongest support in a doctrine as generally accepted—the doctrine to which Malthus has given his name—that population naturally tends to increase faster than subsistence. These two doctrines, fitting in with each other, frame the answer which the current political economy gives to the great problem we are endeavoring to solve.

In what has preceded, the current doctrine that wages are determined by the ratio between capital and laborers has, I think, been shown to be so utterly baseless as to excite surprise as to how it could so generally and so long obtain. It is not to be wondered at that such a theory should have arisen in a state of society where the great body of laborers seem to depend for employment and wages upon a separate class of capitalists, nor yet that under these conditions it should have maintained itself among the masses of men, who rarely take the trouble to separate the real from the apparent. But it is surprising that a theory which on examination appears to be so groundless could have been successively accepted by so many acute thinkers as have during the present century devoted their powers to the elucidation and development of the science of political economy.

The explanation of this otherwise unaccountable fact is to be found in the general acceptance of the Malthusian theory. The current theory of wages has never been fairly put upon its trial, because, backed by the

Malthusian theory, it has seemed in the minds of political economists a self-evident truth.　These two theories
mutually blend with, strengthen, and defend each other,
while they both derive additional support from a principle brought prominently forward in the discussions of
the theory of rent—viz., that past a certain point the
application of capital and labor to land yields a diminishing return.　Together they give such an explanation of
the phenomena presented in a highly organized and
advancing society as seems to fit all the facts, and which
has thus prevented closer investigation.

Which of these two theories is entitled to historical
precedence it is hard to say.　The theory of population
was not formulated in such a way as to give it the standing of a scientific dogma until after that had been done
for the theory of wages.　But they naturally spring up
and grow with each other, and were both held in a form
more or less crude long prior to any attempt to construct
a system of political economy.　It is evident, from several
passages, that though he never fully developed it, the
Malthusian theory was in rudimentary form present in
the mind of Adam Smith, and to this, it seems to me,
must be largely due the misdirection which on the subject of wages his speculations took.　But, however this
may be, so closely are the two theories connected, so
completely do they complement each other, that Buckle,
reviewing the history of the development of political
economy in his "Examination of the Scotch Intellect
during the Eighteenth Century," attributes mainly to
Malthus the honor of "decisively proving" the current
theory of wages by advancing the current theory of the
pressure of population upon subsistence.　He says in
his "History of Civilization in England," Vol. 3, Chap. 5:

"Scarcely had the Eighteenth Century passed away when it was
decisively proved that the reward of labor depends solely on two
things; namely, the magnitude of that national fund out of which

all labor is paid, and the number of laborers among whom the fund is to be divided. This vast step in our knowledge is due, mainly, though not entirely, to Malthus, whose work on population, besides marking an epoch in the history of speculative thought, has already produced considerable practical results, and will probably give rise to others more considerable still. It was published in 1798; so that Adam Smith, who died in 1790, missed what to him would have been the intense pleasure of seeing how, in it, his own views were expanded rather than corrected. Indeed, it is certain that without Smith there would have been no Malthus; that is, unless Smith had laid the foundation, Malthus could not have raised the super-structure."

The famous doctrine which ever since its enunciation has so powerfully influenced thought, not alone in the province of political economy, but in regions of even higher speculation, was formulated by Malthus in the proposition that, as shown by the growth of the North American colonies, the natural tendency of population is to double itself at least every twenty-five years, thus increasing in a geometrical ratio, while the subsistence that can be obtained from land "under circumstances the most favorable to human industry could not possibly be made to increase faster than in an arithmetical ratio, or by an addition every twenty-five years of a quantity equal to what it at present produces." "The necessary effects of these two different rates of increase, when brought together," Mr. Malthus naïvely goes on to say, "will be very striking." And thus (Chap. I) he brings them together:

"Let us call the population of this island eleven millions; and suppose the present produce equal to the easy support of such a number. In the first twenty-five years the population would be twenty-two millions, and the food being also doubled, the means of subsistence would be equal to this increase. In the next twenty-five years the population would be forty-four millions, and the means of subsistance only equal to the support of thirty-three millions. In the next period the population would be equal to eighty-eight millions, and the means of subsistence just equal to the support of half that number. And at the conclusion of the first century, the population would be a hundred and seventy-six millions, and the means of subsistence only equal to the support of fifty-five millions; leaving a population of a hundred and twenty-one millions totally unprovided for.

"Taking the whole earth instead of this island, emigration would of course be excluded; and supposing the present population equal to a thousand millions, the human species would increase as the numbers 1, 2, 4, 8, 16, 32, 64, 128, 256, and subsistence as 1, 2, 3, 4, 5, 6, 7, 8, 9. In two centuries the population would be to the means of subsistence as 256 to 9; in three centuries, 4,096 to 13, and in two thousand years the difference would be almost incalculable."

Such a result is of course prevented by the physical fact that no more people can exist than can find subsistence, and hence Malthus' conclusion is, that this tendency of population to indefinite increase must be held back either by moral restraint upon the reproductive faculty, or by the various causes which increase mortality, which he resolves into vice and misery. Such causes as prevent propagation he styles the preventive check; such causes as increase mortality he styles the positive check. This is the famous Malthusian doctrine, as promulgated by Malthus himself in the "Essay on Population."

It is not worth while to dwell upon the fallacy involved in the assumption of geometrical and arithmetical rates of increase, a play upon proportions which hardly rises to the dignity of that in the familiar puzzle of the hare and the tortoise, in which the hare is made to chase the tortoise through all eternity without coming up with him. For this assumption is not necessary to the Malthusian doctrine, or at least is expressly repudiated by some of those who fully accept that doctrine; as, for instance, John Stuart Mill, who speaks of it as "an unlucky attempt to give precision to things which do not admit of it, which every person capable of reasoning must see is wholly superfluous to the argument." * The essence of the Malthusian doctrine is, that population tends to increase faster than the power of providing food, and whether this difference be stated as a geometrical ratio for population and an arithmetical ratio for subsistence, as by Malthus; or as a constant ratio for population and a diminishing ratio for subsistence, as by Mill, is only a matter of statement. The vital point, on which both agree, is, to use the words of Mathus, "that there is a natural tendency and constant effort in population to increase beyond the means of subsistence."

The Malthusian doctrine, as at present held, may be thus stated in its strongest and least objectionable form:

That population, constantly tending to increase, must, when unrestrained, ultimately press against the limits of subsistence, not as against a fixed, but as against an elastic barrier, which makes the procurement of subsistence progressively more and more difficult. And thus, wherever reproduction has had time to assert its power, and is unchecked by prudence, there must exist that degree of want which will keep population within the bounds of subsistence.

Although in reality not more repugnant to the sense of harmonious adaptation by creative beneficence and wisdom than the complacent no-theory which throws the responsibility for poverty and its concomitants upon the inscrutable decrees of Providence, without attempting to trace them, this theory, in avowedly making vice and suffering the necessary results of a natural instinct with

---

*Principles of Political Economy, Book II, Chap. IX., Sec. VI. —Yet notwithstanding what Mill says, it is clear that Malthus himself lays great stress upon his geometrical and arithmetical ratios, and it is also probable that it is to these ratios that Malthus is largely indebted for his fame, as they supplied one of those high-sounding formulas that with many people carry far more weight than the clearest reasoning.

which are linked the purest and sweetest affections, comes rudely in collision with ideas deeply rooted in the human mind, and it was, as soon as formally promulgated, fought with a bitterness in which zeal was often more manifest than logic. But it has triumphantly withstood the ordeal, and in spite of the refutations of the Godwins, the denunciations of the Cobbetts, and all the shafts that argument, sarcasm, ridicule, and sentiment could direct against it, to-day it stands in the world of thought as an accepted truth, which compels the recognition even of those who would fain disbelieve it.

The causes of its triumph, the sources of its strength, are not obscure. Seemingly backed by an indisputable arithmetical truth—that a continuously increasing population must eventually exceed the capacity of the earth to furnish food or even standing room, the Malthusian theory is supported by analogies in the animal and vegetable kingdoms, where life everywhere beats wastefully against the barriers that hold its different species in check—analogies to which the course of modern thought, in leveling distinctions between different forms of life, has given a greater and greater weight; and it is apparently corroborated by many obvious facts, such as the prevalence of poverty, vice, and misery amid dense populations; the general effect of material progress in increasing population without relieving pauperism; the rapid growth of numbers in newly settled countries and the evident retardation of increase in more densely settled countries by the mortality among the class condemned to want.

The Malthusian theory furnishes a general principle which accounts for these and similar facts, and accounts for them in a way which harmonizes with the doctrine that wages are drawn from capital, and with all the principles that are deduced from it. According to the current doctrine of wages, wages fall as increase in the number of laborers necessitates a more minute division of capital; according to the Malthusian theory, poverty appears as increase in population necessitates the more minute division of subsistence. It requires but the identification of capital with subsistence, and number of laborers with population, an identification made in the current treatises on political economy, where the terms are often converted, to make the two propositions as identical formally as they are substantially.* And thus it is, as stated by Buckle in the passage previously quoted, that the theory of population advanced by Malthus has appeared to prove decisively the theory of wages advanced by Smith.

Ricardo, who a few years subsequent to the publication of the "Essay on Population" corrected the mistake into which Smith had fallen as to the nature and cause of rent, furnished the Malthusian theory an additional support by calling attention to the fact that rent would increase as the necessities of increasing population forced cultivation to less and less productive lands, or to less and less productive points on the same lands, thus explaining the rise of rent. In this way was formed a triple combination, by which the Malthusian theory has been buttressed on both sides—the previously received doctrine of wages and the subsequently received doctrine of rent exhibiting in this view but special examples of the operation of the general principle to which the name of Malthus has been attached—the fall in wages and the rise in rents which come with increasing population being but modes in which the pressure of population upon subsistence shows itself.

Thus taking its place in the very framework of polit-

---

* The effect of the Malthusian doctrine upon the definitions of capital may, I think, be seen by comparing (see pp. 32, 33, 34) the definition of Smith, who wrote prior to Malthus, with the definitions of Ricardo, McCulloch and Mill, who wrote subsequently.

ical economy (for the science as currently accepted has undergone no material change or improvement since the time of Ricardo, though in some minor points it has been cleared and illustrated), the Malthusian theory, though repugnant to sentiments before alluded to, is not repugnant to other ideas, which, in older countries at least, generally prevail among the working classes; but, on the contrary, like the theory of wages by which it is supported and in turn supports, it harmonizes with them. To the mechanic or operative the cause of low wages and of the inability to get employment is obviously the competition caused by the pressure of numbers, and in the squalid abodes of poverty what seems clearer than that there are too many people?

But the great cause of the triumph of this theory is, that, instead of menacing any vested right or antagonizing any powerful interest, it is eminently soothing and reassuring to the classes who, wielding the power of wealth, largely dominate thought. At a time when old supports were falling away, it came to the rescue of the special privileges by which a few monopolize so much of the good things of this world, proclaiming a natural cause for the want and misery which, if attributed to political institutions, must condemn every government under which they exist. The "Essay on Population" was avowedly a reply to William Godwin's "Inquiry concerning Political Justice," a work asserting the principle of human equality; and its purpose was to justify existing inequality by shifting the responsibility for it from human institutions to the laws of the Creator. There was nothing new in this, for Wallace, nearly forty years before, had brought forward the danger of excessive multiplication as the answer to the demands of justice for an equal distribution of wealth; but the circumstances of the times were such as to make the same idea, when brought forward by Malthus, peculiarly grateful

to a powerful class, in whom an intense fear of any ques-
tioning of the existing state of things had been generated
by the outburst of the French Revolution.

Now, as then, the Malthusian doctrine parries the demand for reform, and shelters selfishness from question
and from conscience by the interposition of an inevitable
necessity. It furnishes a philosophy by which Dives as he
feasts can shut out the image of Lazarus who faints with
hunger at his door; by which wealth may complacently but-
ton up its pocket when poverty asks an alms, and the rich
Christian bend on Sundays in a nicely upholstered pew
to implore the good gifts of the All Father without any
feeling of responsibility for the squalid misery that is
festering but a square away. For poverty, want, and
starvation are by this theory not chargeable either to individual greed or to social mal-adjustments; they are
the inevitable results of universal laws, with which, if it
were not impious, it were as hopeless to quarrel as with
the law of gravitation. In this view, he who in the
midst of want has accumulated wealth, has but fenced
in a little oasis from the driving sand which else would
have overwhelmed it. He has gained for himself, but
has hurt nobody. And even if the rich were literally to
obey the injunctions of Christ and divide their wealth
among the poor, nothing would be gained. Population
would be increased, only to press again upon the limits
of subsistence or capital, and the equality that would be
produced would be but the equality of common misery.
And thus reforms which would interfere with the interests of any powerful class are discouraged as hopeless.
As the moral law forbids any forestalling of the methods
by which the natural law gets rid of surplus population
and thus holds in check a tendency to increase potent
enough to pack the surface of the globe with human
beings as sardines are packed in a box, nothing can
really be done, either by individual or by combined

effort, to extirpate poverty, save to trust to the efficacy of education and preach the necessity of prudence.

A theory that, falling in with the habits of thought of the poorer classes, thus justifies the greed of the rich and the selfishness of the powerful, will spread quickly and strike its roots deep. This has been the case with the theory advanced by Malthus.

And of late years the Malthusian theory has received new support in the rapid change of ideas as to the origin of man and the genesis of species. That Buckle was right in saying that the promulgation of the Malthusian theory marked an epoch in the history of speculative thought could, it seems to me, be easily shown; yet to trace its influence in the higher domains of philosophy, of which Buckle's own work is an example, would, though extremely interesting, carry us beyond the scope of this investigation. But how much be reflex and how much original, the support which is given to the Malthusian theory by the new philosophy of development, now rapidly spreading in every direction, must be noted in any estimate of the sources from which this theory derives its present strength. As in political economy, the support received from the doctrine of wages and the doctrine of rent combined to raise the Malthusian theory to the rank of a central truth, so the extension of similar ideas to the development of life in all its forms has the effect of giving it a still higher and more impregnable position. Agassiz, who, to the day of his death, was a strenuous opponent of the new philosophy, spoke of Darwinism as "Malthus all over," * and Darwin himself says the struggle for existence "is the doctrine of Malthus applied with manifold force to the whole animal and vegetable kingdoms."†

---

* Address before Massachusetts State Board of Agriculture, 1872. Report U. S. Department of Agriculture, 1873.

† Origin of Species, Chap. III.

It does not, however, seem to me exactly correct to say that the theory of development by natural selection or survival of the fittest is extended Malthusianism, for the doctrine of Malthus did not originally and does not necessarily involve the idea of progression. But this was soon added to it. McCulloch* attributes to the "principle of increase" social improvement and the progress of the arts, and declares that the poverty that it engenders acts as a powerful stimulus to the development of industry, the extension of science and the accumulation of wealth by the upper and middle classes, without which stimulus society would quickly sink into apathy and decay. What is this but the recognition in regard to human society of the developing effects of the "struggle for existence" and "survival of the fittest," which we are now told on the authority of natural science have been the means which Nature has employed to bring forth all the infinitely diversified and wonderfully adapted forms which the teeming life of the globe assumes? What is it but the recognition of the force, which, seemingly cruel and remorseless, has yet in the course of unnumbered ages developed the higher from the lower type, differentiated the man and the monkey, and made the Nineteenth Century succeed the age of stone?

Thus commended and seemingly proved, thus linked and buttressed, the Malthusian theory—the doctrine that poverty is due to the pressure of population against subsistence, or, to put it in its other form, the doctrine that the tendency to increase in the number of laborers must always tend to reduce wages to the minimum on which laborers can reproduce—is now generally accepted as an unquestionable truth, in the light of which social phenomena are to be explained, just as for ages the

---

* Note IV. to Wealth of Nations.

phenomena of the sidereal heavens were explained upon the supposition of the fixity of the earth, or the facts of geology upon that of the literal inspiration of the Mosaic record. If authority were alone to be considered, formally to deny this doctrine would require almost as much audacity as that of the colored preacher who recently started out on a crusade against the opinion that the earth moves around the sun, for in one form or another, the Malthusian doctrine has received in the intellectual world an almost universal indorsement, and in the best as in the most common literature of the day may be seen cropping out in every direction. It is indorsed by economists and by statesmen, by historians and by natural investigators; by social science congresses and by trade unions; by churchmen and by materialists; by conservatives of the strictest sect and by the most radical of radicals. It is held and habitually reasoned from by many who never heard of Malthus and who have not the slightest idea of what his theory is.

Nevertheless, as the grounds of the current theory of wages have vanished when subjected to a candid examination, so, do I believe, will vanish the grounds of this, its twin. In proving that wages are not drawn from capital we have raised this Antæus from the earth.

CHAPTER II.

The general acceptance of the Malthusian theory and the high authority by which it is indorsed have seemed to me to make it expedient to review its grounds and the causes which have conspired to give it such a dominating influence in the discussion of social questions.

But when we subject the theory itself to the test of straightforward analysis, it will, I think, be found as utterly untenable as the current theory of wages.

In the first place, the facts which are marshaled in support of this theory do not prove it, and the analogies do not countenance it.

And in the second place, there are facts which conclusively disprove it.

I go to the heart of the matter in saying that there is no warrant, either in experience or analogy, for the assumption that there is any tendency in population to increase faster than subsistence. The facts cited to show this simply show that where, owing to the sparseness of population, as in new countries, or where, owing to the unequal distribution of wealth, as among the poorer classes in old countries, human life is occupied with the physical necessities of existence, the tendency to reproduce is at a rate which would, were it to go on unchecked, some time exceed subsistence. But it is not a legitimate inference from this that the tendency to reproduce would show itself in the same force where population was sufficiently dense and wealth distributed with sufficient evenness to lift a whole community above the necessity of devoting their energies to a struggle for mere existence. Nor can it be assumed that the tendency to reproduce, by causing poverty, must prevent the existence of such a community; for this, manifestly, would be assuming the very point at issue, and reasoning in a circle. And even if it be admitted that the tendency to multiply must ultimately produce poverty, it cannot from this alone be predicated of existing poverty that it is due to this cause, until it be shown that there are no other causes which can account for it—a thing in the present state of government, laws, and customs, manifestly impossible.

This is abundantly shown in the "Essay on Population" itself. This famous book, which is much oftener spoken of than read, is still well worth perusal, if only as a literary curiosity. The contrast between the merits of the book itself and the effect it has produced, or is at least credited with (for though Sir James Stewart, Mr. Townsend, and others, share with Malthus the glory of discovering "the principle of population," it was the publication of the "Essay on Population" that brought it prominently forward), is, it seems to me, one of the most remarkable things in the history of literature; and it is easy to understand how Godwin, whose "Political Justice" provoked the "Essay on Population," should until his old age have disdained a reply. It begins with the assumption that population tends to increase in a geometrical ratio, while subsistence can at best be made to increase only in an arithmetical ratio—an assumption just as valid, and no more so, than it would be, from the fact that a puppy doubled the length of his tail while he added so many pounds to his weight, to assert a geometric progression of tail and an arithmetical progression of weight. And, the inference from the assumption is

just such as Swift in satire might have credited to the
savans of a previously dogless island, who, by bringing
these two ratios together, might deduce the very "striking consequence" that by the time the dog grew to a
weight of fifty pounds his tail would be over a mile long,
and extremely difficult to wag, and hence recommend
the prudential check of a bandage as the only alternative to the positive check of constant amputations.
Commencing with such an absurdity, the essay includes
a long argument for the imposition of a duty on the im-
portation, and the payment of a bounty for the exportation of corn, an idea that has long since been sent to the
limbo of exploded fallacies. And it is marked throughout the argumentative portions by passages which show
on the part of the reverend gentleman the most ridicu-
lous incapacity for logical thought—as, for instance,
that if wages were to be increased from eighteen pence
or two shillings per day to five shillings, meat would
necessarily increase in price from eight or nine pence to
two or three shillings per pound, and the condition of
the laboring classes would therefore not be improved, a
statement to which I can think of no parallel so close as
a proposition I once heard a certain printer gravely advance—that because an author, whom he had known,
was forty years old when he was twenty, the author must
now be eighty years old because he (the printer) was
forty. This confusion of thought does not merely crop
out here and there; it characterizes the whole work.*

---

* Malthus' other works, though written after he became famous,
made no mark, and are treated with contempt even by those who
find in the Essay a great discovery. The Encyclopædia Britannica,
for instance, though fully accepting the Malthusian theory, says of
Malthus' Political Economy: "It is very ill arranged, and is in no
respect either a practical or a scientific exposition of the subject. It
is in great part occupied with an examination of parts of Mr.
Ricardo's peculiar doctrines, and with an inquiry into the nature and

The main body of the book is taken up with what is in reality a refutation of the theory which the book advances, for Malthus' review of what he calls the positive checks to population is simply the showing that the results which he attributes to over-population actually arise from other causes. Of all the cases cited, and pretty much the whole globe is passed over in the survey, in which vice and misery check increase by limiting marriages or shortening the term of human life, there is not a single case in which the vice and misery can be traced to an actual increase in the number of mouths over the power of the accompanying hands to feed them; but in every case the vice and misery are shown to spring either from unsocial ignorance and rapacity, or from bad government, unjust laws or destructive warfare.

Nor what Malthus failed to show has any one since him shown. The globe may be surveyed and history may be reviewed in vain for any instance of a considerable country* in which poverty and want can be fairly attributed to the pressure of an increasing population. Whatever be the possible dangers involved in the power of human increase, they have never yet appeared. Whatever may some time be, this never yet has been the evil that has afflicted mankind. Population always tending

---

causes of value. Nothing, however, can be more unsatisfactory than these discussions. In truth Mr. Malthus never had any clear or accurate perception of Mr. Ricardo's theories, or of the principles which determine the value in exchange of different articles."

* I say considerable country, because there may be small islands, such as Pitcairn's Island, cut off from communication with the rest of the world and consequently from the exchanges which are necessary to the improved modes of production resorted to as population becomes dense, which may seem to offer examples in point. A moment's reflection, however, will show that these exceptional cases are not in point.

to overpass the limit of subsistence! How is it, then, that this globe of ours, after all the thousands, and it is now thought millions, of years that man has been upon the earth, is yet so thinly populated? How is it, then, that so many of the hives of human life are now deserted —that once cultivated fields are rank with jungle, and the wild beast licks her cubs where once were busy haunts of men?

It is a fact, that, as we count our increasing millions, we are apt to lose sight of—nevertheless it is a fact—that in what we know of the world's history decadence of population is as common as increase. Whether the aggregate population of the earth is now greater than at any previous epoch is a speculation which can deal only with guesses. Since Montesquieu, in the early part of the last century, asserted, what was then probably the prevailing impression, that the population of the earth had, since the Christian era, greatly declined, opinion has run the other way. But the tendency of recent investigation and exploration has been to give greater credit to what have been deemed the exaggerated accounts of ancient historians and travelers, and to reveal indications of denser populations and more advanced civilizations than had before been suspected, as well as of a higher antiquity in the human race. And in basing our estimates of population upon the development of trade, the advance of the arts, and the size of cities, we are apt to underrate the density of population which the intensive cultivations, characteristic of the earlier civilizations, are capable of maintaining—especially where irrigation is resorted to. As we may see from the closely cultivated districts of China and Europe a very great population of simple habits can readily exist with very little commerce and a much lower stage of those arts in which modern progress has been most marked, and without that tendency to concentrate in cities which modern populations show.*

Be this as it may, the only continent which we can be sure now contains a larger population than ever before is Europe. But this is not true of all parts of Europe. Certainly Greece, the Mediterranean Islands, and Turkey in Europe, probably Italy, and possibly Spain, have contained larger populations than now, and this may be likewise true of Northwestern and parts of Central and Eastern Europe.

America also has increased in population during the time we know of it; but this increase is not so great as is popularly supposed, some estimates giving to Peru alone at the time of the discovery a greater population than now exists on the whole continent of South America. And all the indications are that previous to the discovery the population of America had been declining. What great nations have run their course, what empires have arisen and fallen in "that new world which is the old," we can only imagine. But fragments of massive ruins yet attest a grander pre-Incan civilization; amid the tropical forests of Yucatan and Central America are the remains of great cities forgotten ere the Spanish conquest; Mexico, as Cortez found it, showed the superimposition of barbarism upon a higher social development, while through a great

---

* As may be seen from the map in H. H. Bancroft's "Native Races," the State of Vera Cruz is not one of those parts of Mexico noticeable for its antiquities. Yet Hugo Fink, of Cordova, writing to the Smithsonian Institute (Reports 1870), says there is hardly a foot in the whole State in which by excavation either a broken obsidian knife or a broken piece of pottery is not found; that the whole country is intersected with parallel lines of stones intended to keep the earth from washing away in the rainy season, which show that even the very poorest land was put into requisition, and that it is impossible to resist the conclusion that the ancient population was at least as dense as it is at present in the most populous districts of Europe.

part of what is now the United States are scattered mounds which prove a once relatively dense population, and here and there, as in the Lake Superior copper mines, are traces of higher arts than were known to the Indians with whom the whites came in contact.

As to Africa there can be no question. Northern Africa can contain but a fraction of the population that it had in ancient times; the Nile Valley once held an enormously greater population than now, while south of the Sahara there is nothing to show increase within historic times, and widespread depopulation was certainly caused by the slave trade.

As for Asia, which even now contains more than half the human race, though it is not much more than half as densely populated as Europe, there are indications that both India and China once contained larger populations than now, while that great breeding ground of men from which issued swarms that overran both countries and sent great waves of people rolling upon Europe, must have been once far more populous. But the most marked change is in Asia Minor, Syria, Babylonia, Persia, and in short that vast district which yielded to the conquering arms of Alexander. Where were once great cities and teeming populations are now squalid villages and barren wastes.

It is somewhat strange that among all the theories that have been raised, that of a fixed quantity to human life on this earth has not been broached. It would at least better accord with historical facts than that of the constant tendency of population to outrun subsistence. It is clear that population has here ebbed and there flowed; its centers have changed; new nations have arisen and old nations declined; sparsely settled districts have become populous and populous districts have lost their population; but as far back as we can go without abandoning ourselves wholly to inference, there is nothing to show continuous increase, or even clearly to show an aggregate increase from time to time. The advance of the pioneers of peoples has, so far as we can discern, never been into uninhabited lands—their march has always been a battle with some other people previously in possession; behind dim empires vaguer ghosts of empire loom. That the population of the world must have had its small beginnings we confidently infer, for we know that there was a geologic era when human life could not have existed, and we cannot believe that men sprang up all at once, as from the dragon teeth sowed by Cadmus; yet through long vistas, where history, tradition and antiquities shed a light that is lost in faint glimmers, we may discern large populations. And during these long periods the principle of population has not been strong enough fully to settle the world, or even so far as we can clearly see materially to increase its aggregate population. Compared with its capacities to support human life the earth as a whole is yet most sparsely populated.

There is another broad, general fact which cannot fail to strike any one who, thinking of this subject, extends his view beyond modern society. Malthusianism predicates a universal law—that the natural tendency of population is to outrun subsistence. If there be such a law, it must, wherever population has attained a certain density, become as obvious as any of the great natural laws which have been everywhere recognized. How is it, then, that neither in classical creeds and codes, nor in those of the Jews, the Egyptians, the Hindoos, the Chinese, nor any of the peoples who have lived in close association and have built up creeds and codes, do we find any injunctions to the practice of the prudential restraints of Malthus; but that, on the contrary, the wisdom of the centuries, the religions of the world, have always inculcated ideas of civic and religious duty the very reverse of those which the current political economy enjoins, and which Annie Besant is now trying to popularize in England?

And it must be remembered that there have been societies in which the community guaranteed to every member employment and subsistence. John Stuart Mill says (Book II, Chap. XII, Sec. 2), that to do this without state regulation of marriages and births, would be to produce a state of general misery and degradation. "These consequences," he says, "have been so often and so clearly pointed out by authors of reputation that ignorance of them on the part of educated persons is no longer pardonable." Yet in Sparta, in Peru, in Paraguay, as in the industrial communities which appear almost everywhere to have constituted the primitive agricultural organization, there seems to have been an utter ignorance of these dire consequences of a natural tendency.

Besides the broad, general facts I have cited, there are facts of common knowledge which seem utterly inconsistent with such an overpowering tendency to multiplication. If the tendency to reproduce be so strong as Malthusianism supposes, how is it that families so often become extinct—families in which want is unknown? How is it, then, that when every premium is offered by hereditary titles and hereditary possessions, not alone to the principle of increase, but to the preservation of genealogical knowledge and the proving up of descent, that in such an aristocracy as that of England, so many peerages should lapse, and the House of Lords be kept up from century to century only by fresh creations?

For the solitary example of a family that has survived any great lapse of time, even though assured of subsistence and honor, we must go to unchangeable China. The descendants of Confucius still exist there, and enjoy peculiar privileges and consideration, forming, in fact, the only hereditary aristocracy. On the presumption that population tends to double every twenty-five years, they should, in 2,150 years after the death of Confucius, have amounted to 859,559,193,106,709,670,198,710,528 souls. Instead of any such unimaginable number, the descendants of Confucius, 2,150 years after his death, in the reign of Kanghi, numbered 11,000 males, or say 22,000 souls. This is quite a discrepancy, and is the more striking when it is remembered that the esteem in which this family is held on account of their ancestor, "the Most Holy Ancient Teacher," has prevented the operation of the positive check, while the maxims of Confucius inculcate anything but the prudential check.

Yet, it may be said, that even this increase is a great one. Twenty-two thousand persons descended from a single pair in 2,150 years is far short of the Malthusian rate. Nevertheless, it is suggestive of possible overcrowding.

But consider. Increase of descendants does not show increase of population. It could only do this when the breeding was in and in. Smith and his wife have a son and daughter, who marry respectively some one else's daughter and son, and each have two children. Smith and his wife would thus have four grandchildren; but there would be in the one generation no greater number than in the other—each child would have four grandparents. And supposing this process were to go on, the line of descent might constantly spread out into hundreds, thousands and millions; but in each generation of descendants there would be no more individuals than in any previous generation of ancestors. The web of generations is like lattice-work or the diagonal threads in cloth. Commencing at any point at the top, the eye follows lines which at the bottom widely diverge; but beginning at any point at the bottom, the lines diverge in the same way to the top. How many children a man may have is problematical. But that he had two parents is certain, and that these again had two parents each is also certain. Follow this geometrical progression through a few generations and see if it does not lead to quite as "striking consequences" as Mr. Malthus' peopling of the solar systems.

But from such considerations as these let us advance to a more definite inquiry. I assert that the cases commonly cited as instances of over-population will not bear investigation. India, China, and Ireland furnish the strongest of these cases. In each of these countries, large numbers have perished by starvation and large classes are reduced to abject misery or compelled to emigrate. But is this really due to over-population?

Comparing total population with total area, India and China are far from being the most densely populated countries of the world. According to the estimates of MM. Behm and Wagner, the population of India is but 132 to the square mile and that of China 119, whereas Saxony has a population of 442 to the square mile; Belgium 441; England 422; the Netherlands 291; Italy 234 and Japan 233.* There are thus in both countries large areas unused or not fully used, but even in their more densely populated districts there can be no doubt that either could maintain a much greater population in a much higher degree of comfort, for in both countries is labor applied to production in the rudest and most inefficient ways, and in both countries great natural resources are wholly neglected. This arises from no innate

---

* I take these figures from the Smithsonian Report for 1873, leaving out decimals. MM. Behm and Wagner put the population of China at 446,500,000, though there are some who contend that it does not exceed 150,000,000. They put the population of Hither India at 206,225,580, giving 132.29 to the square mile; of Ceylon at 2,405,287 or 97.36 to the square mile; of Further India at 21,018,062, or 27.94 to the square mile. They estimate the population of the world at 1,377,000,000, an average of 26.64 to the square mile.

deficiency in the people, for the Hindoo, as comparative philology has shown, is of our own blood, and China possessed a high degree of civilization and the rudiments of the most important modern inventions when our ancestors were wandering savages. It arises from the form which the social organization has in both countries taken, which has shackled productive power and robbed industry of its reward.

In India from time immemorial, the working classes have been ground down by exactions and oppressions into a condition of helpless and hopeless degradation. For ages and ages the cultivator of the soil has esteemed himself happy if, of his produce, the extortion of the strong hand left him enough to support life and furnish seed; capital could nowhere be safely accumulated or to any considerable extent be used to assist production; all wealth that could be wrung from the people was in the possession of princes who were little better than robber chiefs quartered on the country, or in that of their farmers or favorites, and was wasted in useless or worse than useless luxury, while religion, sunken into an elaborate and terrible superstition, tyrannized over the mind as physical force did over the bodies of men. Under these conditions, the only arts that could advance were those that ministered to the ostentation and luxury of the great. The elephants of the rajah blazed with gold of exquisite workmanship, and the umbrellas that symbolized his regal power glittered with gems; but the plow of the ryot was only a sharpened stick. The ladies of the rajah's harem wrapped themselves in muslins so fine as to take the name of woven wind, but the tools of the artisan were of the poorest and rudest description, and commerce could only be carried on, as it were, by stealth.

Is it not clear that this tyranny and insecurity have produced the want and starvation of India; and not, as according to Buckle, the pressure of population upon subsistence that has produced the want, and the want the tyranny.* Says the Rev. William Tennant, a chaplain in the service of the East India Company, writing in 1796, two years before the publication of the "Essay on Population:"

" When we reflect upon the great fertility of Hindostan, it is amazing to consider the frequency of famine. It is evidently not owing to any sterility of soil or climate; the evil must be traced to some political cause, and it requires but little penetration to discover it in the avarice and extortion of the various governments. The great spur to industry, that of security, is taken away. Hence no man raises more grain than is barely sufficient for himself, and the first unfavorable season produces a famine.

" The Mogul government at no period offered full security to the prince, still less to his vassals; and to peasants the most scanty protection of all. It was a continued tissue of violence and insurrection, treachery and punishment, under which neither commerce nor the arts could prosper, nor agriculture assume the appearance of a system. Its downfall gave rise to a state still more afflictive, since anarchy is worse than misrule. The Mohammedan government, wretched as it was, the European nations have not the merit of overturning. It fell beneath the weight of its own corruption, and had already been succeeded by the multifarious tyranny of petty chiefs, whose right to govern consisted in their treason to the state, and whose exactions on the peasants were as boundless as their avarice. The rents to government were, and, where natives rule, still are, levied twice a year by a merciless banditti, under the semblance of an army, who wantonly destroy or carry off whatever part of the produce may satisfy their caprice or satiate their avidity, after having hunted the ill-fated peasants from the villages to the woods. Any attempt of the peasants to defend their persons or property within the mud walls of their villages only calls for the more signal vengeance on those useful, but ill-fated mortals. They are then sur-

---

* History of Civilization. Vol. I., Chap. 2. In this chapter Buckle has collected a great deal of evidence of the oppression and degradation of the people of India from the most remote times, a condition which, blinded by the Malthusian doctrine, he has accepted and made the cornerstone of his theory of the development of civilization, he attributes to the ease with which food can there be produced.

rounded and attacked with musketry and field pieces till resistance ceases, when the survivors are sold, and their habitations burned and leveled with the ground. Hence you will frequently meet with the ryots gathering up the scattered remnants of what had yesterday been their habitation, if fear has permitted them to return; but oftener the ruins are seen smoking, after a second visitation of this kind, without the appearance of a human being to interrupt the awful silence of desolation. This description does not apply to the Mohammedan chieftains alone; it is equally applicable to the Rajahs in the districts governed by Hindoos." *

To this merciless rapacity, which would have produced want and famine were the population but one to a square mile and the land a Garden of Eden, succeeded, in the first era of British rule in India, as merciless a rapacity, backed by a far more irresistible power. Says Macaulay, in his essay on Lord Clive:

"Enormous fortunes were rapidly accumulated at Calcutta, while millions of human beings were reduced to the extremity of wretchedness. They had been accustomed to live under tyranny, but never under tyranny like this. They found the little finger of the Company thicker than the loins of Surajah Dowlah. * * * It resembled the government of evil genii, rather than the government of human tyrants. Sometimes they submitted in patient misery. Sometimes they fled from the white man as their fathers had been used to fly from the Maharatta, and the palanquin of the English traveler was often carried through silent villages and towns that the report of his approach had made desolate."

Upon horrors that Macaulay thus but touches, the vivid eloquence of Burke throws a stronger light—whole districts surrendered to the unrestrained cupidity of the worst of human kind, poverty-stricken peasants fiendishly tortured to compel them to give up their little hoards, and once populous tracts turned into deserts.

But the lawless license of early English rule has been long restrained. To all that vast population the strong

---

* Indian Recreations. By Rev. Wm. Tennant. London, 1804. Vol. I., Sec. XXXIX.

hand of England has given a more than Roman peace; the just principles of English law have been extended by an elaborate system of codes and law officers designed to secure to the humblest of these abject peoples the rights of Anglo-Saxon freemen; the whole peninsula has been intersected by railways, and great irrigation works have been constructed. Yet, with increasing frequency, famine has succeeded famine, raging with greater intensity over wider areas.

Is not this a demonstration of the Malthusian theory? Does it not show that no matter how much the possibilities of subsistence are increased, population still continues to press upon it? Does it not show, as Malthus contended, that, to shut up the sluices by which superabundant population is carried off, is but to compel nature to open new ones, and that unless the sources of human increase are checked by prudential regulation, the alternative of war is famine? This has been the orthodox explanation. But the truth, as may be seen in the facts brought forth in recent discussions of Indian affairs in the English periodicals, is that these famines, which have been, and are now, sweeping away their millions, are no more due to the pressure of population upon the natural limits of subsistence than was the desolation of the Carnatic when Hyder Ali's horsemen burst upon it in a whirlwind of destruction.

The millions of India have bowed their necks beneath the yokes of many conquerors, but worst of all is the steady, grinding weight of English domination—a weight which is literally crushing millions out of existence, and, as shown by English writers, is inevitably tending to a most frightful and widespread catastrophe. Other conquerors have lived in the land, and, though bad and tyrannous in their rule, have understood and been understood by the people; but India now is like a great estate owned by an absentee and alien landlord. A most expensive military and civil establishment is kept up, managed and officered by Englishmen who regard India as but a place of temporary exile; and an enormous sum, estimated as at least £20,000,000 annually, raised from a population where laborers are in many places glad in good times to work for 1½d. to 4d. a day, is drained away to England in the shape of remittances, pensions, home charges of the government, etc.—a tribute for which there is no return. The immense sums lavished on railroads have, as shown by the returns, been economically unproductive; the great irrigation works are for the most part costly failures. In large parts of India the English, in their desire to create a class of landed proprietors, turned over the soil in absolute possession to hereditary tax-gatherers, who rack-rent the cultivators most mercilessly. In other parts, where the rent is still taken by the State in the shape of a land tax, assessments are so high, and taxes are collected so relentlessly, as to drive the ryots, who get but the most scanty living in good seasons, into the claws of money lenders, who are, if possible, even more rapacious than the zemindars. Upon salt, an article of prime necessity everywhere, and of especial necessity where food is almost exclusively vegetable, a tax of nearly twelve hundred per cent. is imposed, so that its various industrial uses are prohibited, and large bodies of the people cannot get enough to keep either themselves or their cattle in health. Below the English officials are a horde of native employees who oppress and extort. The effect of English law, with its rigid rules, and, to the native, mysterious proceedings, has been but to put a potent instrument of plunder into the hands of the native money lenders, from whom the peasants are compelled to borrow on the most extravagant terms to meet their taxes, and to whom they are easily induced to give obligations of which they know not the meaning. "We do not care for the people of

India," writes Florence Nightingale, with what seems like a sob. "The saddest sight to be seen in the East—nay, probably in the world—is the peasant of our Eastern Empire." And she goes on to show the causes of the terrible famines, in taxation which takes from the cultivators the very means of cultivation, and the actual slavery to which the ryots are reduced as "the consequences of our own laws;" producing in "the most fertile country in the world, a grinding, chronic semi-starvation in many places where what is called famine does not exist." * "The famines which have been devastating India," says H. M. Hyndman,† "are in the main financial famines. Men and women cannot get food, because they cannot save the money to buy it. Yet we are driven, so we say, to tax these people more." And he shows how, even from famine stricken districts, food is exported in payment of taxes, and how the whole of India is subjected to a steady and exhausting drain, which, combined with the enormous expenses of government, is making the population year by year poorer. The exports of India consist almost exclusively of agricultural products. For at least one-third of these, as Mr. Hyndman shows, no return whatever is received;

---

* Miss Nightingale (The People of India, in "Nineteenth Century" for August, 1878) gives instances, which she says represent millions of cases, of the state of peonage to which the cultivators of Southern India have been reduced through the facilities afforded by the Civil Courts to the frauds and oppressions of money lenders and minor native officials. "Our Civil Courts are regarded as institutions for enabling the rich to grind the faces of the poor, and many are fain to seek a refuge from their jurisdiction within native territory," says Sir David Wedderburn, in an article on Protected Princes in India, in a previous (July) number of the same magazine, in which he also gives a native State, where taxation is comparatively light, as an instance of the most prosperous population of India.

† See articles in "Nineteenth Century" for October, 1878, and March, 1879.

they represent tribute—remittances made by Englishmen in India, or expenses of the English branch of the
Indian government.*   And for the rest, the return is for
the most part government stores, or articles of comfort
and luxury used by the English masters of India.   He
shows that the expenses of government have been enormously increased under Imperial rule; that the relentless
taxation of a population so miserably poor that the
masses are not more than half fed, is robbing them of
their scanty means for cultivating the soil; that the
number of bullocks (the Indian draft animal) is decreasing, and the scanty implements of culture being given up
to money lenders, from whom "we, a business people, are
forcing the cultivators to borrow at 12, 24, 60 per cent.†
to build and pay the interest on the cost of vast public
works, which have never paid nearly five per cent."
Says Mr. Hyndman: "The truth is that Indian society
as a whole has been frightfully impoverished under our
rule, and that the process is now going on at an exceed-
ingly rapid rate"—a statement which cannot be doubted,
in view of the facts presented not only by such writers
as I have referred to, but by Indian officials themselves.
The very efforts made by the government to alleviate
famines do, by the increased taxation imposed, but in-
tensify and extend their real cause.   Although in the
recent famine in Southern India six millions of people,
it is estimated, perished of actual starvation, and the
great mass of those who survived were actually stripped,

---

* Prof. Fawcett, in a recent article on the Proposed Loans to India,
calls attentions to such items as £1,200 for outfit and passage of a
member of the Governor General's Council; £2,450 for outfit and
passage of Bishops of Calcutta and Bombay.

† Florence Nightingale says 100 per cent. is common, and even
then the cultivator is robbed in ways which she illustrates. It is
hardly necessary to say that these rates, like those of the pawnbroker,
are not interest in the economic sense of the term.

yet the taxes were not remitted and the salt tax, already prohibitory to the great bulk of these poverty stricken people, was increased forty per cent., just as after the terrible Bengal famine in 1770 the revenue was actually driven up, by raising assessments upon the survivors and rigorously enforcing collection.

In India now, as in India in past times, it is only the most superficial view that can attribute want and starvation to pressure of population upon the ability of the land to produce subsistence. Could the cultivators retain their little capital—could they be released from the drain which, even in non-famine years, reduces great masses of them to a scale of living not merely below what is deemed necessary for the sepoys, but what English humanity gives to the prisoners in the jails—reviving industry, assuming more productive forms, would undoubtedly suffice to keep a much greater population. There are still in India great areas uncultivated, vast mineral resources untouched, and it is certain that the population of India does not reach, as within historical times it never has reached, the real limit of the soil to furnish subsistence, or even the point where this power begins to decline with the increasing drafts made upon it. The real cause of want in India has been, and yet is, the rapacity of man, not the niggardliness of nature.

What is true of India is true of China. Densely populated as China is in many parts, that the extreme poverty of the lower classes is to be attributed to causes similar to those which have operated in India, and not to too great population, is shown by many facts. Insecurity prevails, production goes on under the greatest disadvantages, and exchange is closely fettered. Where the government is a succession of squeezings, and security for capital of any sort must be purchased of a mandarin; where men's shoulders are the great reliance for inland transportation; where the junk is obliged to be constructed so as to unfit it for a sea-boat; where piracy is a regular trade, and robbers often march in regiments, poverty would prevail and the failure of a crop result in famine, no matter how sparse the population.* That China is capable of supporting a much greater population is shown not only by the great extent of uncultivated land to which all travelers testify, but by the immense unworked mineral deposits which are there known to exist. China, for instance, is said to contain the largest and finest deposit of coal yet anywhere discovered. How much the working of these coal beds would add to the ability to support a greater population, may readily be imagined. Coal is not food, it is true; but its production is equivalent to the production of food. For, not only may coal be exchanged for food, as is done in all mining districts, but the force evolved by its consumption may be used in the production of food, or may set labor free for the production of food.

Neither in India nor China, therefore, can poverty and starvation be charged to the pressure of population against subsistence. It is not dense population, but the causes which prevent social organization from taking its natural development and labor from securing its full return, that keep millions just on the verge of starvation, and every now and again force millions beyond it. That the Hindoo laborer thinks himself fortunate to get a handful of rice, that the Chinese eat rats and puppies, is no more due to the pressure of population than it is due to the pressure of population that the Digger Indians live on grasshoppers, or the aboriginal inhabitants of Australia eat the worms found in rotten wood.

Let me be understood. I do not mean merely to say that India or China could, with a more highly developed

* The seat of recent famine in China was not the most thickly settled districts.

civilization, maintain a greater population, for to this any Malthusian would agree. The Malthusian doctrine does not deny that an advance in the productive arts would permit a greater population to find subsistence. But the Malthusian theory affirms—and this is its essence —that, whatever be the capacity for production, the natural tendency of population is to come up with it, and, in the endeavor to press beyond it, to produce, to use the phrase of Malthus, that degree of vice and misery which is necessary to prevent further increase; so that as productive power is increased, population will correspondingly increase, and in a little time produce the same results as before. What I say is this: that nowhere is there any instance which will support this theory; that nowhere can want be properly attributed to the pressure of population against the power to procure subsistence in the then existing degree of human knowledge; that everywhere the vice and misery attributed to over-population can be traced to the warfare, tyranny, and oppression which prevent knowledge from being utilized and deny the security essential to production. The reason why the natural increase of population does not produce want, we shall come to hereafter. The fact that it has not yet anywhere done so, is what we are now concerned with. This fact is obvious with regard to India and China. It will be obvious, too, wherever we trace to their causes the results which on superficial view are often taken to proceed from over-population.

Ireland, of all European countries, furnishes the great stock example of over-population. The extreme poverty of the peasantry and the low rate of wages there prevailing, the Irish famine, and Irish emigration, are constantly referred to as a demonstration of the Malthusian theory worked out under the eyes of the civilized world. I doubt if a more striking instance can be cited of the power of a preaccepted theory to blind men as to the true relations of facts. The truth is, and it lies on the surface, that Ireland has never yet had a population which the natural powers of the country, in the existing state of the productive arts, could not have maintained in ample comfort. At the period of her greatest population (1840–45) Ireland contained something over eight millions of people. But a very large proportion of them managed merely to exist—lodging in miserable cabins, clothed with miserable rags, and with but potatoes for their staple food. When the potato blight came, they died by thousands. But was it the inability of the soil to support so large a population that compelled so many to live in this miserable way, and exposed them to starvation on the failure of a single root crop? On the contrary, it was the same remorseless rapacity that robbed the Indian ryot of the fruits of his toil and left him to starve where nature offered plenty. A merciless banditti of tax-gatherers did not march through the land plundering and torturing, but the laborer was just as effectually stripped by as merciless a horde of landlords, among whom the soil had been divided as their absolute possession, regardless of any rights of those who lived upon it.

Consider the conditions of production under which this eight millions managed to live until the potato blight came. It was a condition to which the words used by Mr. Tennant in reference to India may as appropriately be applied—"the great spur to industry, that of security, was taken away." Cultivation was for the most part carried on by tenants at will, who, even if the rack-rents which they were forced to pay had permitted them, did not dare to make improvements which would have been but the signal for an increase of rent. Labor was thus applied in the most inefficient and wasteful manner, and labor was dissipated in aimless idleness that, with any security for its fruits, would have been applied unremittingly. But even under these conditions, it is a matter of fact that Ireland did more than support eight millions. For when her population was at its highest, Ireland was a food-exporting country. Even during the famine, grain and meat and butter and cheese were carted for exportation along roads lined with the starving and past trenches into which the dead were piled. For these exports of food, or at least for a great part of them, there was no return. So far as the people of Ireland were concerned, the food thus exported might as well have been burned up or thrown into the sea, or never produced. It went not as an exchange, but as a tribute—to pay the rent of absentee landlords; a levy wrung from producers by those who in no wise contributed to production.

Had this food been left to those who raised it; had the cultivators of the soil been permitted to retain and use the capital their labor produced; had security stimulated industry and permitted the adoption of economical methods, there would have been enough to support in bounteous comfort the largest population Ireland ever had, and the potato blight might have come and gone without stinting a single human being of a full meal. For it was not the imprudence "of Irish peasants," as English economists coldly say, which induced them to make the potato the staple of their food. Irish emigrants, when they can get other things, do not live upon the potato, and certainly in the United States the prudence of the Irish character, in endeavoring to lay by something for a rainy day, is remarkable. They lived on the potato, because rack-rents stripped everything else from them. The truth is, that the poverty and misery of Ireland have never been fairly attributable to over-population.

McCulloch, writing in 1838, says, in Note **IV** to "Wealth of Nations:"

"The wonderful density of population in Ireland is the immediate cause of the abject poverty and depressed condition of the great bulk of the people. It is not too much to say that there are at present more than double the persons in Ireland it is, with its existing means of production, able either fully to employ or to maintain in a moderate state of comfort."

As in 1841 the population of Ireland was given as 8,175,124, we may set it down in 1838 as about eight millions. Thus, to change McCulloch's negative into an affirmative, Ireland would, according to the over-population theory, have been able to employ fully and maintain in a moderate state of comfort something less than four million persons. Now, in the early part of the preceding century, when Dean Swift wrote his "Modest Proposal," the population of Ireland was about two millions. As neither the means nor the arts of production had perceptibly advanced in Ireland during the interval, then—if the abject poverty and depressed condition of the Irish people in 1838 were attributable to over-population—there should, upon McCulloch's own admission, have been in Ireland in 1727 more than full employment, and much more than a moderate state of comfort, for the whole two millions. Yet, instead of this being the case, the abject poverty and depressed condition of the Irish people in 1727 were such, that, with burning, blistering irony, Dean Swift proposed to relieve surplus population by cultivating a taste for roasted babies, and bringing yearly to the shambles, as dainty food for the rich, 100,000 Irish infants!

It is difficult for one who has been looking over the literature of Irish misery, as while writing this chapter I have been doing, to speak in decorous terms of the complacent attribution of Irish want and suffering to over-population which are to be found even in the works of such high-minded men as Mill and Buckle. I know of nothing better calculated to make the blood boil than the cold accounts of the grasping, grinding tyranny to which the Irish people have been subjected, and to which, and not to any inability of the land to support its population, Irish pauperism and Irish famine are to be attributed; and were it not for the enervating effect which the history of the world proves to be everywhere the result of abject poverty, it would be difficult to resist something like a feeling of contempt for a race who, stung by such wrongs, have only occasionally murdered a landlord!

Whether over-population ever did cause pauperism and starvation, may be an open question; but the pauperism and starvation of Ireland can no more be attributed to this cause than can the slave trade be attributed to the over-population of Africa, or the destruction of Jerusalem to the inability of subsistence to keep pace with reproduction. Had Ireland been by nature a grove of bananas and bread-fruit, had her coasts been lined by the guano-deposits of the Chinchas, and the sun of lower latitudes warmed into more abundant life her moist soil, the social conditions that have prevailed there would still have brought forth poverty and starvation. How could there fail to be pauperism and famine in a country where rack-rents wrested from the cultivator of the soil all the produce of his labor except just enough to maintain life in good seasons; where tenure at will forbade improvements and removed incentive to any but the most wasteful and poverty-stricken culture; where the tenant dared not accumulate capital, even if he could get it, for fear the landlord would demand it in the rent; where in fact he was an abject slave, who, at the nod of a human being like himself, might at any time be driven from his miserable mud cabin, a houseless, homeless, starving wanderer, forbidden even to pluck the spontaneous fruits of the earth, or to trap a wild hare to satisfy his hunger? No matter how sparse the population, no matter what the natural resources, are not pauperism and starvation necessary consequences in a land where the producers of wealth are compelled to work under conditions which deprive them of hope, of self-respect, of energy, of thrift; where absentee landlords drain away without return at least a fourth of the net produce of the soil, and when, besides them, a starving industry must support resident landlords, with their horses and hounds, agents, jobbers, middlemen and bailiffs, an alien state church to insult religious prejudices, and an army of policemen and soldiers to overawe and hunt down any opposition to the iniquitous system? Is it not impiety far worse than atheism to charge upon natural laws misery so caused?

What is true in these three cases will be found upon examination true of all cases. So far as our knowledge of facts goes, we may safely deny that the increase of population has ever yet pressed upon subsistence in such a way as to produce vice and misery; that increase of numbers has ever yet decreased the relative production of food. The famines of India, China, and Ireland can no more be credited to over-population than the famines of sparsely populated Brazil. The vice and misery that come of want can no more be attributed to the niggardliness of Nature than can the six millions slain by the sword of Genghis Khan, Tamerlane's pyramid of skulls, or the extermination of the ancient Britons or of the aboriginal inhabitants of the West Indies.

CHAPTER III.

IF we turn from an examination of the facts brought forward in illustration of the Malthusian theory to consider the analogies by which it is supported, we shall find the same inconclusiveness.

The strength of the reproductive force in the animal and vegetable kingdoms—such facts as that a single pair of salmon might, if preserved from their natural enemies for a few years, fill the ocean; that a pair of rabbits would, under the same circumstances, soon overrun a continent; that many plants scatter their seeds by the hundred fold, and some insects deposit thousands of eggs; and that everywhere through these kingdoms each species constantly tends to press, and when not limited by the number of its enemies, evidently does press, against the limits of subsistence—is constantly cited, from Malthus down to the text-books of the present day, as showing that population likewise tends to press against subsistence, and, when unrestrained by other means, its natural increase must necessarily result in such low wages and want, or, if that will not suffice, and the increase still goes on, in such actual starvation, as will keep it within the limits of subsistence.

But is this analogy valid? It is from the vegetable and animal kingdoms that man's food is drawn, and hence the greater strength of the reproductive force in the vegetable and animal kingdoms than in man simply proves the power of subsistence to increase faster than population. Does not the fact that all of the things which furnish man's subsistence have the power to multiply many fold—some of them many thousand fold, and some of them many million or even billion fold—while he is only doubling his numbers, show that, let human beings increase to the full extent of their reproductive power, the increase of population can never exceed subsistence? This is clear when it is remembered that though in the vegetable and animal kingdoms each species, by virtue of its reproductive power, naturally and necessarily presses against the conditions which limit its further increase, yet these conditions are nowhere fixed and final. No species reaches the ultimate limit of soil, water, air, and sunshine; but the actual limit of each is in the existence of other species, its rivals, its enemies, or its food. Thus the conditions which limit the existence of such of these species as afford him subsistence man can extend (in some cases his mere appearance will extend them), and thus the reproductive forces of the species which supply his wants, instead of wasting themselves against their former limit, start forward in his service at a pace which his powers of increase cannot rival. If he but shoot hawks, food-birds will increase, if he but trap foxes the wild rabbits will multiply; the honey bee moves with the pioneer, and on the organic matter with which man's presence fills the rivers, fishes feed.

Even if any consideration of final causes be excluded; even if it be not permitted to suggest that the high and constant reproductive force in vegetables and animals has been ordered to enable them to subserve the uses of man, and that therefore the pressure of the lower forms of life against subsistence does not tend to show that it must likewise be so with man, "the roof and crown of things;" yet there still remains a distinction between man and all other forms of life that destroys the analogy.

Of all living things, man is the only one who can give play to the reproductive forces, more powerful than his own, which supply him with food. Beast, insect, bird, and fish take only what they find. Their increase is at the expense of their food, and when they have reached the existing limits of food, their food must increase before they can increase. But unlike that of any other living thing, the increase of man involves the increase of his food. If bears instead of men had been shipped from Europe to the North American continent, there would now be no more bears than in the time of Columbus, and possibly fewer, for bear food would not have been increased nor the conditions of bear life extended, by the bear immigration, but probably the reverse. But within the limits of the United States alone, there are now forty-five millions of men where then there were only a few hundred thousand, and yet there is now within that territory much more food per capita for the forty-five millions than there was then for the few hundred thousand. It is not the increase of food that has caused this increase of men; but the increase of men that has brought about the increase of food. There is more food, simply because there are more men.

Here is a difference between the animal and the man. Both the jay-hawk and the man eat chickens, but the more jay-hawks the fewer chickens, while the more men the more chickens. Both the seal and the man eat salmon, but when a seal takes a salmon there is a salmon the less, and were seals to increase past a certain point salmon must diminish; while by placing the spawn of the salmon under favorable conditions man can so increase the number of salmon as more than to make up for all he may take, and thus, no matter how much men may increase, their increase need never outrun the supply of salmon.

In short, while all through the vegetable and animal

kingdoms the limit of subsistence is independent of the thing subsisted, with man the limit of subsistence is, within the final limits of earth, air, water, and sunshine, dependent·upon man himself. And this being the case, the analogy which it is sought to draw between the lower forms of life and man manifestly fails. While vegetables and animals do press against the limits of subsistence, man cannot press against the limits of his subsistence until the limits of the globe are reached. Observe, this is not merely true of the whole, but of all the parts. As we cannot reduce the level of the smallest bay or harbor without reducing the level not merely of the ocean with which it communicates, but of all the seas and oceans of the world, so the limit of subsistence in any particular place is not the physical limit of that place, but the physical limit of the globe. Fifty square miles of soil will in the present state of the productive arts yield subsistence for only some thousands of people, but on the fifty square miles which comprise the city of London some three and a half millions of people are maintained, and subsistence increases as population increases. So far as the limit of subsistence is concerned, London may grow to a population of a hundred millions, or five hundred millions, or a thousand millions, for she draws for subsistence upon the whole globe, and the limit which subsistence sets to her growth in population is the limit of the globe to furnish food for its inhabitants.

But here will arise another idea from which the Malthusian theory derives great support—that of the diminishing productiveness of land. As conclusively proving the law of diminishing productiveness it is said in the current treatises that were it not true that beyond a certain point land yields less and less to additional applications of labor and capital, increasing population would not cause any extension of cultivation, but that all the increased supplies needed could and would be raised without taking into cultivation any fresh ground. Assent to this seems to involve assent to the doctrine that the difficulty of obtaining subsistence must increase with increasing population.

But I think the necessity is only in seeming. If the proposition be analyzed it will be seen to belong to a class that depend for validity upon an implied or suggested qualification—a truth relatively, which taken absolutely becomes a non-truth. For that man cannot exhaust or lessen the powers of nature follows from the indestructibility of matter and the persistence of force. Production and consumption are only relative terms. Speaking absolutely, man neither produces nor consumes. The whole human race, were they to labor to infinity, could not make this rolling sphere one atom heavier or one atom lighter, could not add to or diminish by one iota the sum of the forces whose everlasting circling produces all motion and sustains all life. As the water that we take from the ocean must again return to the ocean, so the food we take from the reservoirs of nature is, from the moment we take it, on its way back to those reservoirs. What we draw from a limited extent of land may temporarily reduce the productiveness of that land, because the return may be to other land, or may be divided between that land and other land, or, perhaps, all land; but this possibility lessens with increasing area, and ceases when the whole globe is considered. That the earth could maintain a thousand billions of people as easily as a thousand millions is a necessary deduction from the manifest truths that, at least so far as our agency is concerned, matter is eternal and force must forever continue to act. Life does not use up the forces that maintain life. We come into the material universe bringing nothing; we take nothing away when we depart. The human being, physically considered, is but a transient form of matter, a changing mode of motion. The matter remains and the force persists. Nothing is lessened, nothing is weakened. And from this it follows that the limit to the population of the globe can be only the limit of space.

Now this limitation of space—this danger that the human race may increase beyond the possibility of finding elbow room—is so far off as to have for us no more practical interest than the recurrence of the glacial period or the final extinguishment of the sun. Yet remote and shadowy as it is, it is this possibility which gives to the Malthusian theory its apparently self-evident character. But if we follow it, even this shadow will disappear. It, also, springs from a false analogy. That vegetable and animal life tend to press against the limits of space does not prove the same tendency in human life.

Granted that man is only a more highly developed animal; that the ring-tailed monkey is a distant relative who has gradually developed acrobatic tendencies, and the hump-backed whale a far-off connection who in early life took to the sea—granted that back of these he is kin to the vegetable, and is still subject to the same laws as plants, fishes, birds, and beasts. Yet there is still this difference between man and all other animals—he is the only animal whose desires increase as they are fed; the only animal that is never satisfied. The wants of every other living thing are uniform and fixed. The ox of to-day aspires to no more than did the ox when man first yoked him. The sea gull of the English Channel, who poises himself above the swift steamer, wants no better food or lodging than the gulls who circled round as the keels of Cæsar's galleys first grated on a British beach. Of all that nature offers them, be it ever so abundant, all living things save man can take, and care for, only enough to supply wants which are definite and fixed. The only use they can make of additional supplies or additional opportunities is to multiply.

But not so with man.   No sooner are his animal wants satisfied than new wants arise.   Food he wants first, as does the beast; shelter next, as does the beast; and these given, his reproductive instincts assert their sway, as do those of the beast.   But here man and beast part company.   The beast never goes further; the man has but set his feet on the first step of an infinite progression—a progression upon which the beast never enters; a progression away from and above the beast.

The demand for quantity once satisfied, he seeks quality.   The very desires that he has in common with the beast become extended, refined, exalted.   It is not merely hunger, but taste, that seeks gratification in food; in clothes, he seeks not merely comfort, but adornment; the rude shelter becomes a house; the undiscriminating sexual attraction begins to transmute itself into subtile influences, and the hard and common stock of animal life to blossom and to bloom into shapes of delicate beauty.   As power to gratify his wants increases, so does aspiration grow.   Held down to lower levels of desire, Lucullus will sup with Lucullus; twelve boars turn on spits that Antony's mouthful of meat may be done to a turn; every kingdom of Nature be ransacked to add to Cleopatra's charms, and marble colonnades and hanging gardens and pyramids that rival the hills arise.   Passing into higher forms of desire, that which slumbered in the plant and fitfully stirred in the beast, awakes in the man.   The eyes of the mind are opened, and he longs to know.   He braves the scorching heat of the desert and the icy blasts of the polar sea, but not for food; he watches all night, but it is to trace the circling of the eternal stars.   He adds toil to toil, to gratify a hunger no animal has felt; to assuage a thirst no beast can know.

Out upon nature, in upon himself, back through the mists that shroud the past, forward into the darkness that overhangs the future, turns the restless desire that arises when the animal wants slumber in satisfaction. Beneath things, he seeks the law; he would know how the globe was forged and the stars were hung, and trace to their origins the springs of life. And, then, as the man develops his nobler nature, there arises the desire higher yet—the passion of passions, the hope of hopes— the desire that he, even he, may somehow aid in making life better and brighter, in destroying want and sin, sorrow and shame. He masters and curbs the animal; he turns his back upon the feast and renounces the place of power; he leaves it to others to accumulate wealth, to gratify pleasant tastes, to bask themselves in the warm sunshine of the brief day. He works for those he never saw and never can see; for a fame, or maybe but for a scant justice, that can only come long after the clods have rattled upon his coffin lid. He toils in the advance, where it is cold, and there is little cheer from men, and the stones are sharp and the brambles thick. Amid the scoffs of the present and the sneers that stab like knives, he builds for the future; he cuts the trail that progressive humanity may hereafter broaden into a highroad. Into higher, grander spheres desire mounts and beckons, and a star that rises in the east leads him on. Lo! the pulses of the man throb with the yearnings of the god— he would aid in the process of the suns!

Is not the gulf too wide for the analogy to span? Give more food, open fuller conditions of life, and the vegetable or animal can but multiply; the man will develop. In the one the expansive force can but extend existence in new numbers; in the other, it will inevitably tend to extend existence in higher forms and wider powers. Man is an animal; but he is an animal plus something else. He is the mythic earth-tree, whose roots are in the ground, but whose topmost branches may blossom in the heavens!

Whichever **way it** be turned, the reasoning by which

this theory of the constant tendency of population to press against the limits of subsistence is supported shows an unwarranted assumption, an undistributed middle, as the logicians would say. Facts do not warrant it, analogy does not countenance it. It is a pure chimera of the imagination, such as those that for a long time prevented men from recognizing the rotundity and motion of the earth. It is just such a theory as that underneath us everything not fastened to the earth must fall off; as that a ball dropped from the mast of a ship in motion must fall behind the mast; as that a live fish placed in a vessel full of water will displace no water. It is as unfounded, if not as grotesque, as an assumption we can imagine Adam might have made had he been of an arithmetical turn of mind and figured on the growth of his first baby from the rate of its early months. From the fact that at birth it weighed ten pounds and in eight months thereafter twenty pounds, he might, with the arithmetical knowledge which some sages have supposed him to possess, have ciphered out a result quite as striking as that of Mr. Malthus; namely, that by the time it got to be ten years old it would be as heavy as an ox, at twelve as heavy as an elephant, and at thirty would weigh no less than 175,716,339,548 tons.

The fact is, there is no more reason for us to trouble ourselves about the pressure of population upon subsistence than there was for Adam to worry himself about the rapid growth of his baby. So far as an inference is really warranted by facts and suggested by analogy, it is that the law of population includes such beautiful adaptations as investigation has already shown in other natural laws, and that we are no more warranted in assuming that the instinct of reproduction, in the natural development of society, tends to produce misery and vice, than we should be in assuming that the force of gravitation must hurl the moon to the earth and the earth to the

sun, or than in assuming from the contraction of water
with reductions of temperature down to thirty-two
degrees that rivers and lakes must freeze to the bottom
with every frost, and the temperate regions of earth be
thus rendered uninhabitable by even moderate winters.
That, besides the positive and prudential checks of Malthus, there is a third check which comes into play with
the elevation of the standard of comfort and the development of the intellect, is pointed to by many well-known
facts.   The proportion of births is notoriously greater in
new settlements, where the struggle with nature leaves
little opportunity for intellectual life, and among the
poverty-bound classes of older countries, who in the
midst of wealth are deprived of all its advantages and reduced to all but an animal existence, than it is among
the classes to whom the increase of wealth has brought
independence, leisure, comfort, and a fuller and more
varied life.   This fact, long ago recognized in the
homely adage, "a rich man for luck, and a poor man for
children," was noted by Adam Smith, who says it is not
uncommon to find a poor half-starved Highland woman
has been the mother of twenty-three or twenty-four children, and is everywhere so clearly perceptible that it is
only necessary to allude to it.

If the real law of population is thus indicated, as I
think it must be, then the tendency to increase, instead
of being always uniform, is strong where a greater population would give increased comfort, and where the perpetuity of the race is threatened by the mortality induced by adverse conditions; but weakens just as the
higher development of the individual becomes possible
and the perpetuity of the race is assured.   In other
words, the law of population accords with and is subordinate to the law of intellectual development, and any
danger that human beings may be brought into a world
where they cannot be provided for arises not from the

ordinances of nature, but from social mal-adjustments that in the midst of wealth condemn men to want. The truth of this will, I think, be conclusively demonstrated when, after having cleared the ground, we trace out the true laws of social growth. But it would disturb the natural order of the argument to anticipate them now. If I have succeeded in maintaining a negative—in showing that the Malthusian theory is not proved by the reasoning by which it is supported—it is enough for the present. In the next chapter I propose to take the affirmative and show that it is disproved by facts.

CHAPTER IV.

So deeply rooted and thoroughly entwined with the reasonings of the current political economy is this doctrine that increase of population tends to reduce wages and produce poverty, so completely does it harmonize with many popular notions, and so liable is it to recur in different shapes, that I have thought it necessary to meet and show in some detail the insufficiency of the arguments by which it is supported, before bringing it to the test of facts; for the general acceptance of this theory adds a most striking instance to the many which the history of thought affords of how easily men ignore facts when blindfolded by a preaccepted theory.

To the supreme and final test of facts we can easily bring this theory. Manifestly the question whether increase of population necessarily tends to reduce wages and cause want, is simply the question whether it tends to reduce the amount of wealth that can be produced by a given amount of labor.

This is what the current doctrine holds. The accepted theory is, that the more that is required from nature the less generously does she respond, so that doubling the application of labor will not double the product; and hence, increase of population must tend to reduce wages and deepen poverty, or, in the phrase of Malthus, must result in vice and misery. To quote the language of John Stuart Mill:

"A greater number of people cannot, in any given state of civilization, be collectively so well provided for as a smaller. The niggardliness of nature, not the injustice of society, is the cause of the penalty attached to over-population. An unjust distribution of wealth does not aggravate the evil, but, at most, causes it be somewhat earlier felt. It is in vain to say that all mouths which the increase of mankind calls into existence bring with them hands. The new mouths require as much food as the old ones, and the hands do not produce as much. If all instruments of production were held in joint property by the whole people, and the produce divided with perfect equality among them, and if in a society thus constituted, industry were as energetic and the produce as ample as at the present time, there would be enough to make all the existing population extremely comfortable; but when that population had doubled itself, as, with existing habits of the people, under such an encouragement, it undoubtedly would in little more than twenty years, what would then be their condition? Unless the arts of production were in the same time improved in an almost unexampled degree, the inferior soils which must be resorted to, and the more laborious and scantily remunerative cultivation which must be employed on the superior soils, to procure food for so much larger a population, would, by an insuperable necessity, render every individual in the community poorer than before. If the population continued to increase at the same rate, a time would soon arrive when no one would have more than mere necessaries, and, soon after, a time when no one would have a sufficiency of those, and the further increase of population would be arrested by death." *

All this I deny. I assert that the very reverse of these propositions is true. I assert that in any given state of civilization a greater number of people can collectively be better provided for than a smaller. I assert that the injustice of society, not the niggardliness of nature, is the cause of the want and misery which the current theory attributes to over-population. I assert that the new mouths which an increasing population calls into existence require no more food than the old ones, while the hands they bring with them can in the natural order of things produce more. I assert that, other things being equal, the greater the population, the greater the com-

* Principles of Political Economy, Book I., Chap. XIII., Sec. 2.

fort which an equitable distribution of wealth would give to each individual. I assert that in a state of equality the natural increase of population would constantly tend to make every individual richer instead of poorer.

I thus distinctly join issue, and submit the question to the test of facts.

But observe (for even at the risk of repetition I wish to warn the reader against a confusion of thought that is observable even in writers of great reputation), that the question of fact into which this issue resolves itself is not in what stage of population is most subsistence produced? but in what stage of population is there exhibited the greatest power of producing wealth? For the power of producing wealth in any form is the power of producing subsistence—and the consumption of wealth in any form, or of wealth-producing power, is equivalent to the consumption of subsistence. I have, for instance, some money in my pocket. With it I may buy either food or cigars or jewelry or theater tickets, and just as I expend my money do I determine labor to the production of food, of cigars, of jewelry, or of theatrical representations. A set of diamonds has a value equal to so many barrels of flour—that is to say, it takes on the average as much labor to produce the diamonds as it would to produce so much flour. If I load my wife with diamonds, it is as much an exertion of subsistence-producing power as though I had devoted so much food to purposes of ostentation. If I keep a footman, I take a possible plowman from the plow. The breeding and maintenance of a race-horse require care and labor which would suffice for the breeding and maintenance of many work-horses. The destruction of wealth involved in a general illumination or the firing of a salute is equivalent to the burning up of so much food; the keeping of a regiment of soldiers, or of a war-ship and her crew, is the diversion to unproductive uses of labor that could produce subsistence for many thousands of people. Thus the power of any population to produce the necessaries of life is not to be measured by the necessaries of life actually produced, but by the expenditure of power in all modes.

There is no necessity for abstract reasoning. The question is one of simple fact. Does the relative power of producing wealth decrease with the increase of population?

The facts are so patent that it is only necessary to call attention to them. We have, in modern times, seen many communities advance in population. Have they not at the same time advanced even more rapidly in wealth? We see many communities still increasing in population. Are they not also increasing their wealth still faster? Is there any doubt that while England has been increasing her population at the rate of two per cent. per annum, her wealth has been growing in still greater proportion? Is it not true that while the population of the United States has been doubling every twenty-nine* years her wealth has been doubling at much shorter intervals? Is it not true that under similar conditions—that is to say, among communities of similar people in a similar stage of civilization—the most densely populated community is also the richest? Are not the more densely populated Eastern States richer in proportion to population than the more sparsely populated Western or Southern States? Is not England, where population is even denser than in the Eastern States of the Union, also richer in proportion? Where will you find wealth devoted with the most lavishness to non-productive use—costly buildings, fine furniture, luxurious equipages, statues, pictures, pleasure gardens and yachts? Is it not where population is densest rather

---

* The rate up to 1860 was 35 per cent. each decade.

than where it is sparsest? Where will you find in largest
proportion those whom the general production suffices to
keep without productive labor on their part—men of income and of elegant leisure, thieves, policemen, menial
servants, lawyers, men of letters, and the like? Is it not
where population is dense rather than where it is sparse?
Whence is it that capital overflows for remunerative investment? Is it not from densely populated countries to
sparsely populated countries? These things conclusively
show that wealth is greatest where population is densest;
that the production of wealth to a given amount of labor
increases as population increases. These things are apparent wherever we turn our eyes. On the same level of
civilization, the same stage of the productive arts, government, etc., the most populous countries are always
the most wealthy.

Let us take a particular case, and that a case which of
all that can be cited seems at first blush best to support
the theory we are considering—the case of a community
where, while population has largely increased, wages
have greatly decreased, and it is not a matter of dubious
inference but of obvious fact that the generosity of
nature has lessened. That community is California.
When upon the discovery of gold the first wave of immigration poured into California it found a country in
which nature was in the most generous mood. From
the river banks and bars the glittering deposits of thousands of years could be taken by the most primitive appli-
ances, in amounts which made an ounce ($16) per day
only ordinary wages. The plains, covered with nutri-
tious grasses, were alive with countless herds of horses
and cattle, so plenty that any traveler was at liberty to
shift his saddle to a fresh steed, or to kill a bullock if he
needed a steak, leaving the hide, its only valuable part,
for the owner. From the rich soil which came first
under cultivation, the mere plowing and sowing brought

crops that in older countries, if procured at all, can only be procured by the most thorough manuring and cultivation. In early California, amid this profusion of nature, wages and interest were higher than anywhere else in the world.

This virgin profusion of nature has been steadily giving way before the greater and greater demands which an increasing population has made upon it. Poorer and poorer diggings have been worked, until now no diggings worth speaking of can be found, and gold mining requires much capital, large skill, and elaborate machinery, and involves great risks. "Horses cost money," and cattle bred on the sage-brush plains of Nevada are brought by railroad across the mountains and killed in San Francisco shambles, while farmers are beginning to save their straw and look for manure, and land is in cultivation which will hardly yield a crop three years out of four without irrigation. At the same time wages and interest have steadily gone down. Many men are now glad to work for a week for less than they once demanded for the day, and money is loaned by the year for a rate which once would hardly have been thought extortionate by the month. Is the connection between the reduced productiveness of nature and the reduced rate of wages that of cause and effect? Is it true that wages are lower because labor yields less wealth? On the contrary! Instead of the wealth-producing power of labor being less in California in 1879 than in 1849, I am convinced that it is greater. And, it seems to me, that no one who considers how enormously during these years the efficiency of labor in California has been increased by roads, wharves, flumes, railroads, steamboats, telegraphs, and machinery of all kinds; by a closer connection with the rest of the world; and by the numberless economies resulting from a larger population, can doubt that the return which labor receives from nature in California is

on the whole much greater now than it was in the days of
unexhausted placers and virgin soil—the increase in the
power of the human factor having more than compensated for the decline in the power of the natural factor.
That this conclusion is the correct one is proved by many
facts which show that the consumption of wealth is now
much greater, as compared with the number of laborers,
than it was then.   Instead of a population composed almost exclusively of men in the prime of life, a large proportion of women and children are now supported, and
other non-producers have increased in much greater ratio
than the population; luxury has grown far more than
wages have fallen; where the best houses were cloth and
paper shanties, are now mansions whose magnificence
rivals European palaces; there are liveried carriages on
the streets of San Francisco and pleasure yachts on her
bay; the class who can live sumptuously on their incomes
has steadily grown; there are rich men beside whom the
richest of the earlier years would seem little better than
paupers—in short, there are on every hand the most
striking and conclusive evidences that the production
and consumption of wealth have increased with even
greater rapidity than the increase of population, and that
if any class obtains less it is solely because of the greater
inequality of distribution.

What is obvious in this particular instance is obvious
where the survey is extended. The richest countries
are not those where nature is most prolific; but those
where labor is most efficient—not Mexico, but Massachusetts; not Brazil, but England. The countries where
population is densest and presses hardest upon the capabilities of nature, are, other things being equal, the
countries where the largest proportion of the produce
can be devoted to luxury and the support of non-producers, the countries where capital overflows, the countries that upon exigency, such as war, can stand the

greatest drain. That the production of wealth must, in proportion to the labor employed, be greater in a densely populated country like England than in new countries where wages and interest are higher, is evident from the fact that, though a much smaller proportion of the population is engaged in productive labor, a much larger surplus is available for other purposes than that of supplying physical needs. In a new country the whole available force of the community is devoted to production—there is no well man who does not do productive work of some kind, no well woman exempt from household tasks. There are no paupers or beggars, no idle rich, no class whose labor is devoted to ministering to the convenience or caprice of the rich, no purely literary or scientific class, no criminal class who live by preying upon society, no large class maintained to guard society against them. Yet with the whole force of the community thus devoted to production, no such consumption of wealth in proportion to the whole population takes place, or can be afforded, as goes on in the old country; for, though the condition of the lowest class is better, and there is no one who cannot get a living, there is no one who gets much more—few or none who can live in anything like what would be called luxury, or even comfort, in the older country. That is to say, that in the older country the consumption of wealth in proportion to population is greater, although the proportion of labor devoted to the production of wealth is less—or that fewer laborers produce more wealth; for wealth must be produced before it can be consumed.

It may, however, be said, that the superior wealth of older countries is due not to superior productive power, but to the accumulations of wealth which the new country has not yet had time to make.

It will be well for a moment to consider this idea of accumulated wealth. The truth is, that wealth can be accumulated but to a slight degree, and that communities really live, as the vast majority of individuals live, from hand to mouth. Wealth will not bear much accumulation; except in a few unimportant forms it will not keep. The matter of the universe, which, when worked up by labor into desirable forms, constitutes wealth, is constantly tending back to its original state. Some forms of wealth will last for a few hours, some for a few days, some for a few months, some for a few years; and there are very few forms of wealth that can be passed from one generation to another. Take wealth in some of its most useful and permanent forms—ships, houses, railways, machinery. Unless labor is constantly exerted in preserving and renewing them, they will almost immediately become useless. Stop labor in any community, and wealth would vanish almost as the jet of a fountain vanishes when the flow of water is shut off. Let labor again exert itself, and wealth will almost as immediately reappear. This has been long noticed where war or other calamity has swept away wealth, leaving population unimpaired. There is not less wealth in London to-day because of the great fire of 1666; nor yet is there less wealth in Chicago because of the great fire of 1870. On those fire-swept acres have arisen, under the hand of labor, more magnificent buildings, filled with greater stocks of goods; and the stranger who, ignorant of the history of the city, passes along those stately avenues would not dream that a few years ago all lay so black and bare. The same principle—that wealth is constantly re-created—is obvious in every new city. Given the same population and the same efficiency of labor, and the town of yesterday will possess and enjoy as much as the town founded by the Romans. No one who has seen Melbourne or San Francisco can doubt that if the population of England were transported to New Zealand, leaving all accumulated wealth behind, New Zealand would soon be as rich as England is now; or, conversely, that if the population of England were reduced to the sparseness of the present population of New Zealand, in spite of accumulated wealth, they would soon be as poor. Accumulated wealth seems to play just about such a part in relation to the social organism as accumulated nutriment does to the physical organism. Some accumulated wealth is necessary, and to a certain extent it may be drawn upon in exigencies; but the wealth produced by past generations can no more account for the consumption of the present than the dinners he ate last year can supply a man with present strength.

But without these considerations, which I allude to more for their general than for their special bearing, it is evident that superior accumulations of wealth can account for greater consumption of wealth only in cases where accumulated wealth is decreasing, and that wherever the volume of accumulated wealth is maintained, and even more obviously where it is increasing, a greater consumption of wealth must imply a greater production of wealth. Now, whether we compare different communities with each other, or the same community at different times, it is obvious that the progressive state, which is marked by increase of population, is also marked by an increased consumption and an increased accumulation of wealth, not merely in the aggregate, but per capita. And hence, increase of population, so far as it has yet anywhere gone, does not mean a reduction, but an increase in the average production of wealth.

And the reason of this is obvious. For, even if the increase of population does reduce the power of the natural factor of wealth, by compelling a resort to poorer soils, etc., it yet so vastly increases the power of the human factor as more than to compensate. Twenty men working together will, where nature is niggardly, produce more than twenty times the wealth that one man can produce where nature is most bountiful. The denser the population the more minute becomes the subdivision of labor, the greater the economies of production and distribution, and, hence, the very reverse of the Malthusian doctrine is true; and, within the limits in which we have reason to suppose increase would still go on, in any given state of civilization a greater number of people can produce a larger proportionate amount of wealth, and more fully supply their wants, than can a smaller number.

Look simply at the facts. Can anything be clearer than that the cause of the poverty which festers in the centers of civilization is not in the weakness of the productive forces? In countries where poverty is deepest, the forces of production are evidently strong enough, if fully employed, to provide for the lowest not merely comfort but luxury. The industrial paralysis, the commercial depression which curses the civilized world to-day, evidently springs from no lack of productive power. Whatever be the trouble, it is clearly not in the want of ability to produce wealth.

It is this very fact—that want appears where productive power is greatest and the production of wealth is largest—that constitutes the enigma which perplexes the civilized world, and which we are trying to unravel. Evidently the Malthusian theory, which attributes want to the decrease of productive power, will not explain it. That theory is utterly inconsistent with all the facts. It is really a gratuitous attribution to the laws of God of results which, even from this examination, we may infer really spring from the mal-adjustments of men—an inference which, as we proceed, will become a demonstration. For we have yet to find what *does* produce poverty amid advancing wealth.

BOOK III.

THE LAWS OF DISTRIBUTION.

The machines that are first invented to perform any particular movement are always the most complex, and succeeding artists generally discover that with fewer wheels, with fewer principles of motion than had originally been employed, the same effects may be more easily produced. The first philosophical systems, in the same manner, are always the most complex, and a particular connecting chain, or principle, is generally thought necessary to unite every two seemingly disjointed appearances; but it often happens that one great connecting principle is afterward found to be sufficient to bind together all the discordant phenomena that occur in a whole species of things.—*Adam Smith, Essay on the Principles which Lead and Direct Philosophical Inquiries, as Illustrated by the History of Astronomy.*

CHAPTER I.

The preceding examination has, I think, conclusively shown that the explanation currently given, in the name of political economy, of the problem we are attempting to solve, is no explanation at all.

That with material progress wages fail to increase, but rather tend to decrease, cannot be explained by the theory that the increase of laborers constantly tends to divide into smaller portions the capital sum from which wages are paid. For, as we have seen, wages do not come from capital, but are the direct produce of labor. Each productive laborer, as he works, creates his wages, and with every additional laborer there is an addition to the true wages fund—an addition to the common stock of wealth, which, generally speaking, is considerably greater than the amount he draws in wages.

Nor, yet, can it be explained by the theory that nature yields less to the increasing drafts which an increasing population make upon her; for the increased efficiency of labor makes the progressive state a state of continually increasing production per capita, and the countries of densest population, other things being equal, are always the countries of greatest wealth.

So far, we have only increased the perplexities of the problem. We have overthrown a theory which did, in some sort of fashion, explain existing facts; but in doing so have only made existing facts seem more inexplicable. It is as though, while the Ptolemaic theory was yet in its strength, it had been proved simply that the sun and stars do not revolve about the earth. The phenomena of day and night, and of the apparent motion of the celestial bodies, would yet remain unexplained, inevitably to reinstate the old theory unless a better one took its place. Our reasoning has led us to the conclusion that each productive laborer produces his own wages, and that increase in the number of laborers should increase the wages of each; whereas, the apparent facts are that there are many laborers who cannot obtain remunerative employment, and that increase in the number of laborers brings diminution of wages. We have, in short, proved that wages ought to be highest where in reality they are lowest.

Nevertheless, even in doing this we have made some progress. Next to finding what we look for, is to discover where it is useless to look. We have at least narrowed the field of inquiry. For this, at least, is now clear—that the cause which, in spite of the enormous increase of productive power, confines the great body of producers to the least share of the product upon which they will consent to live, is not the limitation of capital, nor yet the limitation of the powers of nature which respond to labor. As it is not, therefore, to be found in the laws which bound the production of wealth, it must be sought in the laws which govern distribution. To them let us turn.

It will be necessary to review in its main branches the whole subject of the distribution of wealth. To discover the cause which, as population increases and the productive arts advance, deepens the poverty of the lowest class, we must find the law which determines what part of the produce is distributed to labor as wages. To find the law of wages, or at least to make sure when we have found it, we must also determine the laws which fix the part of the produce which goes to capital and the part which goes to land owners, for as land, labor, and capital join in producing wealth, it is between these three that the produce must be divided. What is meant by the produce or production of a community is the sum of the wealth produced by that community—the general fund from which, as long as previously existing stock is not lessened, all consumption must be met and all revenues drawn. As I have already explained, production does not merely mean the making of things, but includes the increase of value gained by transporting or exchanging things. There is a produce of wealth in a purely commercial community, as there is in a purely agricultural or manufacturing community; and in the one case, as in the others, some part of this produce will go to capital, some part to labor, and some part, if land have any value, to the owners of land. As a matter of fact, a portion of the wealth produced is constantly going to the replacement of capital, which is constantly consumed and constantly replaced. But it is not necessary to take this into account, as it is eliminated by considering capital as continuous, which, in speaking or thinking of it, we habitually do. When we speak of the produce, we mean, therefore, that part of the wealth produced above what is necessary to replace the capital consumed in production; and when we speak of interest, or the return to capital, we mean what goes to capital after its replacement or maintenance.

It is, further, a matter of fact, that in every community which has passed the most primitive stage some portion of the produce is taken in taxation and consumed by government. But it is not necessary, in seeking the laws of distribution, to take this into consideration. We may consider taxation either as not existing, or as by so much reducing the produce. And so, too, of what is taken from the produce by certain forms of mon-

opoly, which will be considered in a subsequent chapter
(Chap. IV), and which exercise powers analogous to taxation.   After we have discovered the laws of distribution
we can then see what bearing, if any, taxation has upon
them.

We must discover these laws of distribution for ourselves—or, at least, two out of the three.   For, that they
are not, at least as a whole, correctly apprehended by the
current political economy, may be seen, irrespective of
our preceding examination of one of them, in any of
the standard treatises.

This is evident, in the first place, from the terminology employed.

In all politico-economic works we are told that the
three factors in production are land, labor, and capital,
and that the whole produce is primarily distributed into
three corresponding parts.   Three terms, therefore, are
needed, each of which shall clearly express one of these
parts to the exclusion of the others.   Rent, as defined,
clearly enough expresses the first of these parts—that
which goes to the owners of land.   Wages, as defined,
clearly enough expresses the second—that part which
constitutes the return to labor.   But as to the third
term—that which should express the return to capital—
there is in the standard works a most puzzling ambiguity
and confusion.

Of words in common use, that which comes nearest to
exclusively expressing the idea of return for the use of
capital, is interest, which, as commonly used, implies
the return for the use of capital, exclusive of any labor
in its use or management, and exclusive of any risk, except such as may be involved in the security.   The word
profits, as commonly used, is almost synonymous with
revenue; it means a gain, an amount received in excess
of an amount expended, and frequently includes receipts
that are properly rent; while it nearly always includes

receipts which are properly wages, as well as compensations for the risk peculiar to the various uses of capital. Unless extreme violence is done to the meaning of the word, it cannot, therefore, be used in political economy to signify that share of the produce which goes to capital, in contradistinction to those parts which go to labor and to land owners.

Now, all this is recognized in the standard works on political economy. Adam Smith well illustrates how wages and compensation for risk largely enter into profits, pointing out how the large profits of apothecaries and small retail dealers are in reality wages for their labor, and not interest on their capital; and how the great profits sometimes made in risky businesses, such as smuggling and the lumber trade, are really but compensations for risk, which, in the long run, reduce the returns to capital so used to the ordinary, or below the ordinary, rate. Similar illustrations are given in most of the subsequent works, where profit is formally defined in its common sense, with, perhaps, the exclusion of rent. In all these works, the reader is told that profits are made up of three elements—wages of superintendence, compensation for risk, and *interest*, or the return for the use of capital.

Thus, neither in its common meaning nor in the meaning expressly assigned to it in the current political economy, can profits have any place in the discussion of the distribution of wealth between the three factors of production. Either in its common meaning or in the meaning expressly assigned to it, to talk about the distribution of wealth into rent, wages, and profits is like talking of the division of mankind into men, women, and human beings.

Yet this, to the utter bewilderment of the reader, is what is done in all the standard works. After formally decomposing profits into wages of superintendence, compensation for risk, and interest—the net return for the use of capital—they proceed to treat of the distribution of wealth between the rent of land, the wages of labor, and the PROFITS of capital.

I doubt not that there are thousands of men who have vainly puzzled their brains over this confusion of terms, and abandoned the effort in despair, thinking that as the fault could not be in such great thinkers, it must be in their own stupidity. If it is any consolation to such men they may turn to Buckle's "History of Civilization," and see how a man who certainly got a marvelously clear idea of what he read, and who had read carefully the principal economists from Smith down, was inextricably confused by this jumble of profits and interest. For Buckle (Vol. 1, Chap. II, and notes) persistently speaks of the distribution of wealth into rent, wages, interest, *and* profits.

And this is not to be wondered at. For, after formally decomposing profits into wages of superintendence, insurance, and interest, these economists, in assigning causes which fix the general rate of profit, speak of things which evidently affect only that part of profits which they have denominated interest; and then, in speaking of the rate of interest, either give the meaningless formula of supply and demand, or speak of causes which affect the compensation for risk; evidently using the word in its common sense, and not in the economic sense they have assigned to it, from which compensation for risk is eliminated. If the reader will take up John Stuart Mill's "Principles of Political Economy," and compare the chapter on Profits (Book II, Chap. 15) with the chapter on Interest (Book III, Chap. 23), he will see the confusion thus arising exemplified in the case of the most logical of English economists, in a more striking manner than I would like to characterize.

Now, such men have not been led into such confusion of thought without a cause. If they, one after another, have followed Dr. Adam Smith, as boys play "follow my leader," jumping where he jumped, and falling where he fell, it has been that there was a fence where he jumped and a hole where he fell.

The difficulty from which this confusion has sprung is in the preaccepted theory of wages. For reasons which I have before assigned, it has seemed to them a self-evident truth that the wages of certain classes of laborers depended upon the ratio between capital and the number of laborers. But there are certain kinds of reward for exertion to which this theory evidently will not apply, so the term wages has in use been contracted to include only wages in the narrow common sense. This being the case, if the term interest were used, as consistently with their definitions it should have been used, to represent the third part of the division of the produce, all rewards of personal exertion, save those of what are commonly called wage-workers, would clearly have been left out. But by treating the division of wealth as between rent, wages, and profits, instead of between rent, wages, and interest, this difficulty is glossed over, all wages which will not fall under the preaccepted law of wages being vaguely grouped under profits, as wages of superintendence.

To read carefully what economists say about the distribution of wealth is to see that, though they correctly define it, wages, as they use it in this connection, is what logicians would call an undistributed term—it does not mean all wages, but only some wages—viz., the wages of manual labor paid by an employer. So other wages are thrown over with the return to capital, and included under the term profits, and any clear distinction between the returns to capital and the returns to human exertion thus avoided. The fact is that the current political economy fails to give any clear and consistent account of the distribution of wealth. The law of rent *is* clearly stated,

pensatie for risk, and interest—the net return for the
use of cpital—they proceed to treat of the distribution
of wealh between the rent of land, the wages of labor,
and the ROFITS of capital.

I doug not that there are thousands of men who have
vainly pzzled their brains over this confusion of terms,
and abarloned the effort in despair, thinking that as the
fault coıd not be in such great thinkers, it must be in
their owstupidity. If it is any consolation to such men
they ma turn to Buckle's "History of Civilization," and
see how .man who certainly got a marvelously clear idea
of what t read, and who had read carefully the principal
economis from Smith down, was inextricably confused
by this jmble of profits and interest. For Buckle (Vol.
1, Chap. [, and notes) persistently speaks of the dis-
tributioıwf wealth into rent, wages, interest, *and* profits.

And tis is not to be wondered at. For, after
formally ecomposing profits into wages of superintendence, insrance, and interest, these economists, in r-
signing cases which fix the general rate of prof**
of thingsvhich evidently affect only that par'
which thy have denominated interest; r
speaking f the rate of interest, either gir
less formła of supply and demand, or
which affst the compensation for ri
the word ı its common sense, and
sense theyhave assigned to it, fr-
for risk isliminated. If the
Stuart Ml's "Principles
compare tè chapter on
the chaptc on Intere·
the confuən thus r
most logid of F
manner thn I ⊢

  Now, suh r
of thought

have followed Dr. Adam Smith, as boys play 'follow my leader," jumping where he jumped, and f.ling where he fell, it has been that there was a fen³ where he jumped and a hole where he fell.

The difficulty from which this confusion ᴛs sprung is in the preaccepted theory of wages.   For rᴇsons which I have before assigned, it has seemed to ɪem a self-evident truth that the wages of certain classᴇ of laborers depended upon the ratio between capital aᴅ the number of laborers.   But there are certain kins of reward for exertion to which this theory evideɪly will not apply, so the term wages has in use been ɔntracted to include only wages in the narrow common ᴇnse.   This being the case, if the term interest were usᴇ, as consistently with their definitions it should have ᴇen used, to representᴜ the third part of **the** diᵥⁱ˙ ˙ᶠ **he** produᴄe, all rewards of personal exertion. of wℎ ᵗ· commonly called **wage-worke**ʳ⁻ ᵎ ℎ˙ left ⁻˙ᵗ⁻ .**But by** treating oᶠ tw ᵊnt, wages, and pᵘ .ᴅ of ᵎ

is ℊᴵ all

ᵥ of

ɴder ɡes of

the dis-
correctly
ℊᴜɪon, is what
⌐it does not
ᴵ the wages of
ᵊr wages arᴇ
ᵑd inclᵤ

but it stands unrelated. The rest is a confused and incoherent jumble.

The very arrangement of these works shows this confusion and inconclusiveness of thought. In no politico-economic treatise that I know of are these laws of distribution brought together, so that the reader can take them in at a glance and recognize their relation to each other; but what is said about each one is enveloped in a mass of political and moral reflections and dissertations. And the reason is not far to seek. To bring together the three laws of distribution as they are now taught, is to show at a glance that they lack necessary relation.

The laws of the distribution of wealth are obviously laws of proportion, and must be so related to each other that any two being given the third may be inferred. For to say that one of the three parts of a whole is increased or decreased, is to say that one or both of the other parts is, reversely, decreased or increased. If Tom, Dick, and Harry are partners in business, the agreement which fixes the share of one in the profits must at the same time fix either the separate or the joint shares of the other two. To fix Tom's share at forty per cent. is to leave but sixty per cent. to be divided between Dick and Harry. To fix Dick's share at forty per cent. and Harry's share at thirty-five per cent. is to fix Tom's share at twenty-five per cent.

But between the laws of the distribution of wealth, as laid down in the standard works, there is no such relation. If we fish them out and bring them together, we find them to be as follows:

Wages are determined by the ratio between the amount of capital devoted to the payment and subsistence of labor and the number of laborers seeking employment.

Rent is determined by the margin of cultivation; all lands yielding as rent that part of their produce which exceeds what an equal application of labor and capital could procure from the poorest land in use.

Interest is determined by the equation between the demands of borrowers and the supply of capital offered by lenders. Or, if we take what is given as the law of profits, it is determined by wages, falling as wages rise and rising as wages fall—or, to use the phrase of Mill, by the cost of labor to the capitalist.

The bringing together of these current statements of the laws of the distribution of wealth shows at a glance that they lack the relation to each other which the true laws of distribution must have. They do not correlate and co-ordinate. Hence, at least two of these three laws are either wrongly apprehended or wrongly stated. This tallies with what we have already seen, that the current apprehension of the law of wages, and, inferentially, of the law of interest, will not bear examination. Let us, then, seek the true laws of the distribution of the produce of labor into wages, rent, and interest. The proof that we have found them will be in their correlation—that they meet, and relate, and mutually bound each other.

With profits this inquiry has manifestly nothing to do. We want to find what it is that determines the division of their joint produce between land, labor, and capital; and profits is not a term that refers exclusively to any one of these three divisions. Of the three parts into which profits are divided by political economists—namely, compensation for risk, wages of superintendence, and return for the use of capital—the latter falls under the term interest, which includes all the returns for the use of capital, and excludes everything else; wages of superintendence falls under the term wages, which includes all returns for human exertion, and excludes everything else; and compensation for risk has no place whatever, as risk is eliminated when all the transactions of a community are taken together. I shall, therefore, consistently with the definitions of political economists, use the term .

interest as signifying that part of the produce which goes to capital.

To recapitulate:

Land, labor, and capital are the factors of production. The term land includes all natural opportunities or forces; the term labor, all human exertion; and the term capital, all wealth used to produce more wealth. In returns to these three factors is the whole produce distributed. That part which goes to land owners as payment for the use of natural opportunities is called rent; that part which constitutes the reward of human exertion is called wages; and that part which constitutes the return for the use of capital is called interest. These terms mutually exclude each other. The income of any individual may be made up from any one, two, or all three of these sources; but in the effort to discover the laws of distribution we must keep them separate.

Let me premise the inquiry which we are about to undertake by saying that the miscarriage of political economy, which I think has now been abundantly shown, can, it seems to me, be traced to the adoption of an erroneous standpoint. Living and making their observations in a state of society in which a capitalist generally rents land and hires labor, and thus seems to be the undertaker or first mover in production, the great cultivators of the science have been led to look upon capital as the prime factor in production, land as its instrument, and labor as its agent or tool. This is apparent on every page—in the form and course of their reasoning, in the character of their illustrations, and even in their choice of terms. Everywhere capital is the starting point, the capitalist the central figure. So far does this go that both Smith and Ricardo use the term "natural wages" to express the minimum upon which laborers can live; whereas, unless injustice is natural, all that the laborer produces should rather be held as his natural wages. This habit of look-ing upon capital as the employer of labor has led both to the theory that wages depend upon the relative abun-dance of capital, and to the theory that interest varies inversely with wages, while it has led away from truths that but for this habit would have been apparent. In short, the misstep which, so far as the great laws of dis-tribution are concerned, has led political economy into the jungles, instead of upon the mountain tops, was taken when Adam Smith, in his first book, left the standpoint indicated in the sentence, "The produce of labor constitutes the natural recompense or wages of labor," to take that in which capital is considered as employing labor and paying wages.

But when we consider the origin and natural sequence of things, this order is reversed; and capital instead of first is last; instead of being the employer of labor, it is in reality employed by labor. There must be land be-fore labor can be exerted, and labor must be exerted before capital can be produced. Capital is a result of labor, and is used by labor to assist it in further produc-tion. Labor is the active and initial force, and labor is therefore the employer of capital. Labor can be exerted only upon land, and it is from land that the matter which it transmutes into wealth must be drawn. Land therefore is the condition precedent, the field and ma-terial of labor. The natural order is land, labor, capital; and, instead of starting from capital as our initial point, we should start from land.

There is another thing to be observed. Capital is not a necessary factor in production. Labor exerted upon land can produce wealth without the aid of capital, and in the necessary genesis of things must so produce wealth before capital can exist. Therefore the law of rent and the law of wages must correlate each other and form a perfect whole without reference to the law of

capital, as otherwise these laws would not fit the cases
which can readily be imagined, and which to some degree
actually exist, in which capital takes no part in production.   And as capital is, as is often said, but stored-up
labor, it is but a form of labor, a subdivision of the general term labor; and its law must be subordinate to, and
independently correlate with, the law of wages, so as to
fit cases in which the whole produce is divided between
labor and capital, without any deduction for rent.   To
resort to the illustration before used: The division of the
produce between land, labor and capital must be as it
would be between Tom, Dick, and Harry, if Tom and
Dick were the original partners, and Harry came in but
as an assistant to and sharer with Dick.

CHAPTER II

RENT AND THE LAW OF RENT.

The term rent, in its economic sense—that is, when used, as I am using it, to distinguish that part of the produce which accrues to the owners of land or other natural capabilities by virtue of their ownership—differs in meaning from the word rent as commonly used. In some respects this economic meaning is narrower than the common meaning; in other respects it is wider.

It is narrower in this: In common speech, we apply the word rent to payments for the use of buildings, machinery, fixtures, etc., as well as to payments for the use of land or other natural capabilities; and in speaking of the rent of a house or the rent of a farm, we do not separate the price for the use of the improvements from the price for the use of the bare land. But in the economic meaning of rent, payments for the use of any of the products of human exertion are excluded, and of the lumped payments for the use of houses, farms, etc., only that part is rent which constitutes the consideration for the use of the land—that part paid for the use of buildings or other improvements being properly interest, as it is a consideration for the use of capital.

It is wider in this: In common speech we speak of rent only when owner and user are distinct persons. But in the economic sense there is also rent where the same person is both owner and user. Where owner and user are thus the same person, whatever part of his income he might obtain by letting the land to another is rent, while the return for his labor and capital are that part of his

income which they would yield him did he hire instead
of owning the land.   Rent is also expressed in a selling
price.   When land is purchased, the payment which is
made for the ownership, or right to perpetual use, is rent
commuted or capitalized.   If I buy land for a small price
and hold it until I can sell it for a large price, I have
become rich, not by wages for my labor or by interest
upon my capital, but by the increase of rent.   Rent, in
short, is the share in the wealth produced which the exclusive right to the use of natural capabilities gives to
the owner.   Wherever land has an exchange value there
is rent in the economic meaning of the term.   Wherever
land having a value is used, either by owner or hirer,
there is rent actual; wherever it is not used, but still has
a value, there is rent potential.   It is this capacity of
yielding rent which gives value to land.   Until its ownership will confer some advantage, land has no value.*

Thus rent or land value does not arise from the productiveness or utility of land.   It in no wise represents
any help or advantage given to production, but simply
the power of securing a part of the results of production.
No matter what are its capabilities, land can yield no
rent and have no value until some one is willing to give
labor or the results of labor for the privilege of using it;
and what any one will thus give depends not upon the
capacity of the land, but upon its capacity as compared
with that of land that can be had for nothing.   I may
have very rich land, but it will yield no rent and have no
value so long as there is other land as good to be had
without cost.   But when this other land is appropriated,
and the best land to be had for nothing is inferior, either
in fertility, situation, or other quality, my land will begin

* In speaking of the value of land I use and shall use the words
as referring to the value of the bare land.   When I wish to speak of
the value of land and improvements I shall use those words.

to have a value and yield rent. And though the productiveness of my land may decrease, yet if the productiveness of the land to be had without charge decreases
in greater proportion, the rent I can get, and couse-
quently the value of my land, will steadily increase.
Rent, in short, is the price of monopoly, arising from the
reduction to individual ownership of natural elements
which human exertion can neither produce nor increase.

If one man owned all the land accessible to any community, he could, of course, demand any price or condition for its use that he saw fit; and, as long as his ownership was acknowledged, the other members of the community would have but death or emigration as the alternative to submission to his terms. This has been the
case in many communities; but in the modern form of
society, the land, though generally reduced to individual ownership, is in the hands of too many different persons to permit the price which can be obtained for its
use to be fixed by mere caprice or desire. While each
individual owner tries to get all he can, there is a limit
to what he can get, which constitutes the market price
or market rent of the land, and which varies with different lands and at different times. The law, or relation,
which, under these circumstances of free competition
among all parties, the condition which in tracing out the
principles of political economy is always to be assumed,
determines what rent or price can be got by the owner,
is styled the law of rent. This fixed with certainty, we
have more than a starting point from which the laws
which regulate wages and interest may be traced. For,
as the distribution of wealth is a division, in ascertaining
what fixes the share of the produce which goes as rent,
we also ascertain what fixes the share which is left for
wages, where there is no co-operation of capital; and what
fixes the joint share left for wages and interest, where
capital does co-operate in production.

Fortunately, as to the law of rent there is no necessity for discussion. Authority here coincides with common sense,* and the accepted dictum of the current political economy has the self-evident character of a geometric axiom. This accepted law of rent, which John Stuart Mill denominates the *pons asinorum* of political economy, is sometimes styled "Ricardo's law of rent," from the fact that, although not the first to announce it, he first brought it prominently into notice.† It is:

The rent of land is determined by the excess of its produce over that which the same application can secure from the least productive land in use.

This law, which of course applies to land used for other purposes than agriculture, and to all natural agencies, such as mines, fisheries, etc., has been exhaustively explained and illustrated by all the leading economists since Ricardo. But its mere statement has all the force of a self-evident proposition, for it is clear that the effect of competition is to make the lowest reward for which labor and capital will engage in production, the highest that they can claim; and hence to enable the owner of more productive land to appropriate in rent all

---

* I do not mean to say that the accepted law of rent has never been disputed. In all the nonsense that in the present disjointed condition of the science has been printed as political economy, it would be hard to find anything that has not been disputed. But I mean to say that it has the sanction of all economic writers who are really to be regarded as authority. As John Stuart Mill says (Book II., Chap. XVI.), "there are few persons who have refused their assent to it, except from not having thoroughly understood it. The loose and inaccurate way in which it is often apprehended by those who affect to refute it is very remarkable." An observation which has received many later exemplifications.

† According to McCulloch the law of rent was first stated in a pamphlet by Dr. James Anderson of Edinburgh in 1777, and simultaneously in the beginning of this century by Sir Edward West, Mr. Malthus, and Mr. Ricardo.

the return above that required to recompense labor and capital at the ordinary rate—that is to say, what they can obtain upon the least productive land in use, or at the least productive point, where, of course, no rent is paid.

Perhaps it may conduce to a fuller understanding of the law of rent to put it in this form: The ownership of a natural agent of production will give the power of appropriating so much of the wealth produced by the exertion of labor and capital upon it as exceeds the return which the same application of labor and capital could secure in the least productive occupation in which they freely engage.

This, however, amounts to precisely the same thing, for there is no occupation in which labor and capital can engage which does not require the use of land; and, furthermore, the cultivation or other use of land will always be carried to as low a point of remuneration, all things considered, as is freely accepted in any other pursuit. Suppose, for instance, a community in which part of the labor and capital is devoted to agriculture and part to manufactures. The poorest land cultivated yields an average return which we will call 20, and 20 therefore will be the average return to labor and capital, as well in manufactures as in agriculture. Suppose that from some permanent cause the return in manufactures is now reduced to 15. Clearly, the labor and capital engaged in manufactures will turn to agriculture; and the process will not stop until, either by the extension of cultivation to inferior lands or to inferior points on the same land, or by an increase in the relative value of manufactured products, owing to the diminution of production—or, as a matter of fact, by both processes—the yield to labor and capital in both pursuits has, all things considered, been brought again to the same level, so that whatever be the final point of productiveness at which manufactures are still carried on, whether it be 18 or 17 or 16, cultivation will also be extended to that point. And, thus, to say that rent will be the excess in productiveness over the yield at the margin, or lowest point, of cultivation, is the same thing as to say that it will be the excess of produce over what the same amount of labor and capital obtains in the least remunerative occupation.

The law of rent is, in fact, but a deduction from the law of competition, and amounts simply to the assertion that as wages and interest tend to a common level, all that part of the general production of wealth which exceeds what the labor and capital employed could have secured for themselves, if applied to the poorest natural agent in use, will go to land owners in the shape of rent. It rests, in the last analysis, upon the fundamental principle, which is to political economy what the attraction of gravitation is to physics—that men will seek to gratify their desires with the least exertion.

This, then, is the law of rent. Although many standard treatises follow too much the example of Ricardo, who seems to view it merely in its relation to agriculture, and in several places speaks of manufactures yielding no rent, when, in truth, manufactures and exchange yield the highest rents, as is evinced by the greater value of land in manufacturing and commercial cities, thus hiding the full importance of the law, yet, ever since the time of Ricardo, the law itself has been clearly apprehended and fully recognized. But not so its corollaries. Plain as they are, the accepted doctrine of wages (backed and fortified not only as has been hitherto explained, but by considerations whose enormous weight will be seen when the logical conclusion toward which we are tending is reached) has hitherto prevented their recognition.*

* Buckle (Chap. II., History of Civilization) recognizes the necessary relation between rent, interest, and wages, but evidently never worked it out.

Yet, is it not as plain as the simplest geometrical demon. stration, that the corollary of the law of rent is the law of wages, where the division of the produce is simply between rent and wages; or the law of wages and interest taken together, where the division is into rent, wages, and interest? Stated reversely, the law of rent is necessarily the law of wages and interest taken together, for it is the assertion, that no matter what be the production which results from the application of labor and capital, these two factors will receive in wages and interest only such part of the produce as they could have produced on land free to them without the payment of rent—that is, the least productive land or point in use. For, if, of the produce, all over the amount which labor and capital could secure from land for which no rent is paid must go to land owners as rent, then all that can be claimed by labor and capital as wages and interest is the amount which they could have secured from land yielding no rent.

Or to put it in algebraic form:

As Produce = Rent + Wages + Interest,

Therefore, Produce − Rent = Wages + Interest.

Thus wages and interest do not depend upon the produce of labor and capital, but upon what is left after rent is taken out; or, upon the produce which they could obtain without paying rent—that is, from the poorest land in use. And hence, no matter what be the increase in productive power, if the increase in rent keeps pace with it, neither wages nor interest can increase.

The moment this simple relation is recognized, a flood of light streams in upon what was before inexplicable, and seemingly discordant facts range themselves under an obvious law. The increase of rent which goes on in progressive countries is at once seen to be the key which explains why wages and interest fail to increase with increase of productive power. For the wealth produced in every community is divided into two parts by what

may be called the rent line, which is fixed by the margin
of cultivation, or the return which labor and capital could
obtain from such natural opportunities as are free to
them without the payment of rent. From the part of
the produce below this line wages and interest must be
paid. All that is above goes to the owners of land.
Thus, where the value of land is low, there may be a
small production of wealth, and yet a high rate of wages
and interest, as we see in new countries. And, where the
value of land is high, there may be a very large production of wealth, and yet a low rate of wages and interest,
as we see in old countries. And, where productive power
increases, as it is increasing in all progressive countries,
wages and interest will be affected, not by the increase,
but by the manner in which rent is affected. If the
value of land increases proportionately, all the increased
production will be swallowed up by rent, and wages and
interest will remain as before. If the value of land increases in greater ratio than productive power, rent will
swallow up even more than the increase; and while the
produce of labor and capital will be much larger, wages
and interest will fall. It is only when the value of land
fails to increase as rapidly as productive power, that wages
and interest can increase with the increase of productive
power. All this is exemplified in actual fact.

CHAPTER III.

Having made sure of the law of rent, we have obtained as its necessary corollary the law of wages, where the division is between rent and wages; and the law of wages and interest taken together, where the division is between the three factors. What proportion of the produce is taken as rent must determine what proportion is left for wages, if but land and labor are concerned; or to be divided between wages and interest, if capital joins in the production.

But without reference to this deduction, let us seek each of these laws separately and independently. If, when obtained in this way, we find that they correlate, our conclusions will have the highest certainty.

And, inasmuch as the discovery of the law of wages is the ultimate purpose of our inquiry, let us take up first the subject of interest.

I have already referred to the difference in meaning between the terms profits and interest. It may be worth while, further, to say that interest, as an abstract term in the distribution of wealth, differs in meaning from the word as commonly used, in this: That it includes all returns for the use of capital, and not merely those that pass from borrower to lender; and that it excludes compensation for risk, which forms so great a part of what is commonly called interest. Compensation for risk is evidently only an equalization of return between different employments of capital. What we want to find is, what fixes the general rate of interest proper? The different rates of compensation for risk added to this will give the current rates of commercial interest.

Now, it is evident that the greatest differences in what is ordinarily called interest are due to differences in risk; but it is also evident that between different countries and different times there are also considerable variations in the rate of interest proper. In California at one time two per cent. a month would not have been considered extravagant interest on security on which loans could now be effected at seven or eight per cent. per annum, and though some part of the difference may be due to an increased sense of general stability, the greater part is evidently due to some other general cause. In the United States generally the rate of interest has been higher than in England; and in the newer States of the Union higher than in the older States; and the tendency of interest to sink as society progresses is well marked and has long been noticed. What is the law which will bind all these variations together and exhibit their cause?

It is not worth while to dwell more than has hitherto incidentally been done upon the failure of the current political economy to determine the true law of interest. Its speculations upon this subject have not the definiteness and coherency which have enabled the accepted doctrine of wages to withstand the evidence of fact, and do not require the same elaborate review. That they run counter to the facts is evident. That interest does not depend on the productiveness of labor and capital is proved by the general fact that where labor and capital are most productive interest is lowest. That it does not depend reversely upon wages (or the cost of labor), lowering as wages rise, and increasing as wages fall, is proved by the general fact that interest is high when and where wages are high, and low when and where wages are low.

Let us begin at the beginning. The nature and functions of capital have already been sufficiently shown, but even at the risk of something like a digression, let us endeavor to ascertain the cause of interest before consid. ering its law. For in addition to aiding our inquiry by giving us a firmer and clearer grasp of the subject now in hand, it may lead to conclusions whose practical im. portance will be hereafter apparent.

What is the reason and justification of interest? Why should the borrower pay back to the lender more than he received? These questions are worth answering, not merely from their speculative, but from their practical importance. The feeling that interest is the robbery of industry is widespread and growing, and on both sides of the Atlantic shows itself more and more in popular literature and in popular movements. The expounders of the current political economy say that there is no conflict between labor and capital, and oppose as injurious to labor, as well as to capital, all schemes for restricting the reward which capital obtains; yet in the same works the doctrine is laid down that wages and interest bear to each other an inverse relation, and that interest will be low or high as wages are high or low.* Clearly, then, if this doctrine is correct, the only objection that from the standpoint of the laborer can be logically made to any scheme for the reduction of interest is that it will not work, which is manifestly very weak ground while ideas of the omnipotence of legislatures are yet so widespread; and though such an objection may lead to the abandonment of any one particular scheme, it will not prevent the search for another.

Why should interest be? Interest, we are told, in all the standard works, is the reward of abstinence. But, manifestly, this does not sufficiently account for it. Abstinence is not an active, but a passive quality; it is not a

---

* This is really said of profits, but with the evident meaning of returns to capital.

doing—it is simply a not doing.   Abstinence in itself produces nothing.   Why, then, should any part of what is produced be claimed for it?   If I have a sum of money which I lock up for a year, I have exercised as much abstinence as though I had loaned it.   Yet, though in the latter case I will expect it to be returned to me with an additional sum by way of interest, in the former I will have but the same sum, and no increase.   But the abstinence is the same.   If it be said that in lending it I do the borrower a service, it may be replied that he also does me a service in keeping it safely—a service that under some conditions may be very valuable, and for which I would willingly pay, rather than not have it; and a service which, as to some forms of capital, may be even more obvious than as to money.   For there are many forms of capital which will not keep, but must be constantly renewed; and many which are onerous to maintain if one has no immediate use for them.   So, if the accumulator of capital helps the user of capital by loaning it to him, does not the user discharge the debt in full when he hands it back?   Is not the secure preservation, the maintenance, the re-creation of capital, a complete offset to the use?   Accumulation is the end and aim of abstinence.   Abstinence can go no further and accomplish no more; nor of itself can it even do this.   If we were merely to abstain from using it, how much wealth would disappear in a year!   And how little would be left at the end of two years!   Hence, if more is demanded for abstinence than the safe return of capital, is not labor wronged?   Such ideas as these underlie the widespread opinion that interest can accrue only at the expense of labor, and is in fact a robbery of labor which in a social condition based on justice would be abolished.

The attempts to refute these views do not appear to me always successful.   For instance, as it illustrates the usual reasoning, take Bastiat's oft-quoted illustration of the plane. One carpenter, James, at the expense of ten days' labor, makes himself a plane, which will last in use for 290 of the 300 working days of the year. William, another carpenter, proposes to borrow the plane for a year, offering to give back at the end of that time, when the plane will be worn out, a new plane equally as good. James objects to lending the plane on these terms, urging that if he merely gets back a plane he will have nothing to compensate him for the loss of the advantage which the use of the plane during the year would give him. William, admitting this, agrees not merely to return a plane, but, in addition, to give James a new plank. The agreement is carried out to mutual satisfaction. The plane is used up during the year, but at the end of the year James receives as good a one, and a plank in addition. He lends the new plane again and again, until finally it passes into the hands of his son, "who still continues to lend it," receiving a plank each time. This plank, which represents interest, is said to be a natural and equitable remuneration, as by giving it in return for the use of the plane, William "obtains the power which exists in the tool to increase the productiveness of labor," and is no worse off than he would have been had he not borrowed the plane; while James obtains no more than he would have had if he had retained and used the plane instead of lending it.

Is this really so? It will be observed that it is not affirmed that James could make the plane and William could not, for that would be to make the plank the reward of superior skill. It is only that James had abstained from consuming the result of his labor until he had accumulated it in the form of a plane—which is the essential idea of capital.

Now, if James had not lent the plane he could have used it for 290 days, when it would have been worn out, and he would have been obliged to take the remaining ten days of the working year to make a new plane. If William had not borrowed the plane he would have taken ten days to make himself a plane, which he could have used for the remaining 290 days. Thus, if we take a plank to represent the fruits of a day's labor with the aid of a plane, at the end of the year, had no borrowing taken place, each would have stood with reference to the plane as he commenced, James with a plane, and William with none, and each would have had as the result of the year's work 290 planks. If the condition of the borrowing had been what William first proposed, the return of a new plane, the same relative situation would have been secured. William would have worked for 290 days, and taken the last ten days to make the new plane to return to James. James would have taken the first ten days of the year to make another plane which would have lasted for 290 days, when he would have received a new plane from William. Thus, the simple return of the plane would have put each in the same position at the end of the year as if no borrowing had taken place. James would have lost nothing to the gain of William, and William would have gained nothing to the loss of James. Each would have had the return his labor would otherwise have yielded—viz., 290 planks, and James would have had the advantage with which he started, a new plane.

But when, in addition to the return of a plane, a plank is given, James at the end of the year will be in a better position than if there had been no borrowing, and William in a worse. James will have 291 planks and a new plane, and William 289 planks and no plane. If William now borrows the plank as well as the plane on the same terms as before, he will at the end of the year have to return to James a plane, two planks and a fraction of a plank; and if this difference be again borrowed, and so on, is it not evident that the income of the one will progressively decline, and that of the other will progress-ively increase, until at length, if the operation be con-tinued, the time will come when, as the result of the original lending of a plane, James will obtain the whole result of William's labor—that is to say, William will be-come virtually his slave?

Is interest, then, natural and equitable? There is nothing in this illustration to show it to be. Evidently what Bastiat (and many others) assigns as the basis of interest, "the power which exists in the tool to increase the productiveness of labor," is neither in justice nor in fact the basis of interest. The fallacy which makes Bastiat's illustration pass as conclusive with those who do not stop to analyze it, as we have done, is that with the loan of the plane they associate the transfer of the increased productive power which a plane gives to labor. But this is really not involved. The essential thing which James loaned to William was not the increased power which labor acquires from using planes. To sup-pose this, we should have to suppose that the making and using of planes was a trade secret or a patent right, when the illustration would become one of monopoly, not of capital. The essential thing which James loaned to William was not the privilege of applying his labor in a more effective way, but the use of the concrete result of ten days' labor. If "the power which exists in tools to increase the productiveness of labor" were the cause of interest, then the rate of interest would increase with the march of invention. This is not so. Nor yet will I be expected to pay more interest if I borrow a fifty-dollar sewing machine than if I borrow fifty dollars' worth of needles; if I borrow a steam engine than if I borrow a pile of bricks of equal value. Capital, like wealth, is interchangeable. It is not one thing; it is anything to that value within the circle of exchange. Nor yet does the improvement of tools add to the reproductive power of capital; it adds to the productive power of labor.

And I am inclined to think that if all wealth consisted of such things as planes, and all production was such as that of carpenters—that is to say, if wealth consisted but of the inert matter of the universe, and production of working up this inert matter into different shapes, that interest would be but the robbery of industry, and could not long exist. This is not to say that there would be no accumulation, for though the hope of increase is a motive for turning wealth into capital, it is not the motive, or, at least, not the main motive, for accumulating. Children will save their pennies for Christmas; pirates will add to their buried treasure; Eastern princes will accumulate hoards of coin; and men like Stewart or Vanderbilt, having become once possessed of the passion of accumulating, would continue as long as they could to add to their millions, even though accumulation brought no increase. Nor yet is it to say that there would be no borrowing or lending, for this, to a large extent, would be prompted by mutual convenience. If William had a job of work to be immediately begun and James one that would not commence until ten days thereafter, there might be a mutual advantage in the loan of the plane, though no plank should be given.

But all wealth is not of the nature of planes, or planks, or money, which has no reproductive power; nor is all production merely the turning into other forms of this inert matter of the universe. It is true that if I put away money, it will not increase. But suppose, instead, I put away wine. At the end of a year I will have an increased value, for the wine will have improved in quality. Or supposing that in a country adapted to them, I set out bees; at the end of a year I will have more swarms of bees, and the honey which they have made. Or, supposing, where there is a range, I turn out sheep, or hogs, or cattle; at the end of the year I will, upon the average, also have an increase.

Now what gives the increase in these cases is something which, though it generally requires labor to utilize it, is yet distinct and separable from labor—the active power of nature; the principle of growth, of reproduction, which everywhere characterizes all the forms of that mysterious thing or condition which we call life. And it seems to me that it is this which is the cause of interest, or the increase of capital over and above that due to labor. There are, so to speak, in the movements which make up the everlasting flux of nature, certain vital currents, which will, if we use them, aid us, with a force independent of our own efforts, in turning matter into the forms we desire—that is to say, into wealth.

While many things might be mentioned which, like money, or planes, or planks, or engines, or clothing, have no innate power of increase, yet other things are included in the terms wealth and capital which, like wine, will of themselves increase in quality up to a certain point; or, like bees or cattle, will of themselves increase in quantity; and certain other things, such as seeds, which, though the conditions which enable them to increase may not be maintained without labor, yet will, when these conditions are maintained, yield an increase, or give a return over and above that which is to be attributed to labor.

Now the interchangeability of wealth necessarily involves an average between all the species of wealth of any special advantage which accrues from the possession of any particular species, for no one would keep capital in one form when it could be changed into a more advantageous form. No one, for instance, would grind wheat into flour and keep it on hand for the convenience of those who desire from time to time to exchange wheat or its equivalent for flour, unless he could by such exchange secure an increase equal to that which, all things considered, he could secure by planting his wheat. No

one, if he could keep them, would exchange a flock of
sheep now for their net weight in mutton to be returned
next year; for by keeping the sheep he would not only
have the same amount of mutton next year, but also the
lambs and the fleeces. No one would dig an irrigating
ditch, unless those who by its aid are enabled to utilize
the reproductive forces of nature would give him such
a portion of the increase they receive as to make his capital yield him as much as theirs. And so, in any circle of exchange, the power of increase which the reproductive or vital force of nature gives to some species of
capital must average with all; and he who lends, or uses
in exchange, money, or planes, or bricks, or clothing, is
not deprived of the power to obtain an increase, any
more than if he had lent or put to a reproductive use so
much capital in a form capable of increase.

There is also in the utilization of the variations in the
powers of nature and of man which is effected by exchange, an increase which somewhat resembles that produced by the vital forces of nature. In one place, for
instance, a given amount of labor will secure 200 in
vegetable food or 100 in animal food. In another place,
these conditions are reversed, and the same amount of
labor will produce 100 in vegetable food or 200 in animal. In the one place, the relative value of vegetable
to animal food will be as two to one, and in the other as
one to two; and, supposing equal amounts of each to be required, the same amount of labor will in either place secure
150 of both. But by devoting labor in the one place to
the procurement of vegetable food, and in the other, to
the procurement of animal food, and exchanging to the
quantity required, the people of each place will be enabled by the given amount of labor to procure 200
of both, less the losses and expenses of exchange; so
that in each place the produce which is taken from
use and devoted to exchange brings back an increase.

Thus Whittington's cat, sent to a far country where cats are scarce and rats are plenty, returns in bales of goods and bags of gold.

Of course, labor is necessary to exchange, as it is to the utilization of the reproductive forces of nature, and the produce of exchange, as the produce of agriculture, is clearly the produce of labor; but yet, in the one case as in the other, there is a distinguishable force co-operating with that of labor, which makes it impossible to measure the result solely by the amount of labor expended, but renders the amount of capital and the time it is in use integral parts in the sum of forces. Capital aids labor in all of the different modes of production, but there is a distinction between the relations of the two in such modes of production as consist merely of changing the form or place of matter, as planing boards or mining coal; and such modes of production as avail themselves of the reproductive forces of nature, or of the power of increase arising from differences in the distribution of natural and human powers, such as the raising of grain or the exchange of ice for sugar. In production of the first kind, labor alone is the efficient cause; when labor stops, production stops. When the carpenter drops his plane as the sun sets, the increase of value, which he with his plane is producing, ceases until he begins his labor again the following morning. When the factory bell rings for closing, when the mine is shut down, production ends until work is resumed. The intervening time, so far as regards production, might as well be blotted out. The lapse of days, the change of seasons is no element in the production that depends solely upon the amount of labor expended. But in the other modes of production to which I have referred, and in which the part of labor may be likened to the operations of lumbermen who throw their logs into the stream, leaving it to the current to carry them to the boom of the sawmill many miles below, time *is* an element. The seed in the ground germinates and grows while the farmer sleeps or plows new fields, and the ever-flowing currents of air and ocean bear Whittington's cat toward the rat-tormented ruler in the regions of romance.

To recur now to Bastiat's illustration. It is evident that if there is any reason why William at the end of the year should return to James more than an equally good plane, it does not spring, as Bastiat has it, from the increased power which the tool gives to labor, for that, as I have shown, is not an element; but it springs from the element of time—the difference of a year between the lending and return of the plane. Now, if the view is confined to the illustration, there is nothing to suggest how this element should operate, for a plane at the end of the year has no greater value than a plane at the beginning. But if we substitute for the plane a calf, it is clearly to be seen that to put James in as good a position as if he had not lent, William at the end of the year must return, not a calf, but a cow. Or, if we suppose that the ten days' labor had been devoted to planting corn, it is evident that James would not have been fully recompensed if at the end of the year he had received simply so much planted corn, for during the year the planted corn would have germinated and grown and multiplied; and so if the plane had been devoted to exchange, it might during the year have been turned over several times, each exchange yielding an increase to James. Now, therefore, as James' labor might have been applied in any of those ways—or what amounts to the same thing, some of the labor devoted to making planes might have been thus transferred—he will not make a plane for William to use for the year unless he gets back more than a plane. And William can afford to give back more than a plane, because the same general average of the advantages of labor applied in different modes will enable him to obtain from his labor an ad-vantage from the element of time. It is this general averaging, or as we may say, "pooling" of advantages, which necessarily takes place where the exigencies of society require the simultaneous carrying on of the differ-ent modes of production, which gives to the possession of wealth incapable in itself of increase an advantage simi-lar to that which attaches to wealth used in such a way as to gain from the element of time. And, in the last analysis, the advantage which is given by the lapse of time springs from the generative force of nature and the varying powers of nature and of man.

Were the quality and capacity of matter everywhere uniform, and all productive power in man, there would be no interest. The advantage of superior tools might at times be transferred on terms resembling the payment of interest, but such transactions would be irregular and intermittent—the exception, not the rule. For the power of obtaining such returns would not, as now, inhere in the possession of capital, and the advantage of time would operate only in peculiar circumstances. That I, having a thousand dollars, can certainly let it out at in-terest, does not arise from the fact that there are others, not having a thousand dollars, who will gladly pay me for the use of it, if they can get it no other way; but from the fact that the capital which my thousand dollars represents has the power of yielding an increase to whomsoever has it, even though he be a millionaire. For the price which anything will bring does not depend upon what the buyer would be willing to give rather than go without it, so much as upon what the seller can other-wise get. For instance, a manufacturer who wishes to retire from business has machinery to the value of $100,-000. If he cannot, should he sell, take this $100,000 and invest it so that it will yield him interest, it will be immaterial to him, risk being eliminated, whether he obtains the whole price at once or in installments, and if the purchaser has the requisite capital, which we must suppose in order that the transaction may rest on its own merits, it will be immaterial whether he pay at once or after a time.　If the purchaser has not the required capital, it may be to his convenience that payments should be delayed, but it would be only in exceptional circumstances that the seller would ask, or the buyer would consent, to pay any premium on this account; nor in such cases would this premium be properly interest.　For interest is not properly a payment made for the use of capital, but a return accruing from the increase of capital.　If the capital did not yield an increase, the cases would be few and exceptional in which the owner would get a premium.　William would soon find out if it did not pay him to give a plank for the privilege of deferring payment on James' plane.

In short, when we come to analyze production we find it to fall into three modes—viz:

ADAPTING, or changing natural products either in form or in place so as to fit them for the satisfaction of human desire.

GROWING, or utilizing the vital forces of nature, as by raising vegetables or animals.

EXCHANGING, or utilizing, so as to add to the general sum of wealth, the higher powers of those natural forces which vary with locality, or of those human forces which vary with situation, occupation, or character.

In each of these three modes of production capital may aid labor—or, to speak more precisely, in the first mode capital may aid labor, but is not absolutely necessary; in the others capital must aid labor, or is necessary.

Now, while by adapting capital in proper forms we may increase the effective power of labor to impress upon matter the character of wealth, as when we adapt wood and iron to the form and use of a plane; or iron, coal, water, and oil to the form and use of a steam engine; or stone, clay, timber, and iron to that of a building, yet the characteristic of this use of capital is, that the benefit is in the use.   When, however, we employ capital in the second of these modes, as when we plant grain in the ground, or place animals on a stock farm, or put away wine to improve with age, the benefit arises, not from the use, but from the increase.   And so, when we employ capital in the third of these modes, and instead of using a thing we exchange it, the benefit is in the increase or greater value of the things received in return.

Primarily, the benefits which arise from use go to labor, and the benefits which arise from increase, to capital. But, inasmuch as the division of labor and the interchangeability of wealth necessitate and imply an averaging of benefits, in so far as these different modes of production correlate with each other, the benefits that arise from one will average with the benefits that arise from the others, for neither labor nor capital will be devoted to any mode of production while any other mode which is open to them will yield a greater return.   That is to say, labor expended in the first mode of production will get, not the whole return, but the return minus such part as is necessary to give to capital such an increase as it could have secured in the other modes of production, and capital engaged in the second and third modes will obtain, not the whole increase, but the increase minus what is sufficient to give to labor such reward as it could have secured if expended in the first mode.

Thus interest springs from the power of increase which the reproductive forces of nature, and the in effect analogous capacity for exchange, give to capital.   It is not an arbitrary, but a natural thing; it is not the result of a particular social organization, but of laws of the universe which underlie society.   It is, therefore, just.

They who talk about abolishing interest fall into an error similar to that previously pointed out as giving its plausibility to the doctrine that wages are drawn from capital. When they thus think of interest, they think only of that which is paid by the user of capital to the owner of capital. But, manifestly, this is not all interest, but only some interest. Whoever uses capital and obtains the increase it is capable of giving receives interest. If I plant and care for a tree until it comes to maturity, I receive, in its fruit, interest upon the capital I have thus accumulated—that is, the labor I have expended. If I raise a cow, the milk which she yields me, morning and evening, is not merely the reward of the labor then exerted; but interest upon the capital which my labor, expended in raising her, has accumulated in the cow. And so, if I use my own capital in directly aiding production, as by machinery, or in indirectly aiding production, in exchange, I receive a special and distinguishable advantage from the reproductive character of capital, which is as real, though perhaps not as clear, as though I had lent my capital to another and he had paid me interest.

CHAPTER IV.

The belief that interest is the robbery of industry is, I
am persuaded, in large part due to a failure to discrim-
inate between what is really capital and what is not, and
between profits which are properly interest and profits
which arise from other sources than the use of capital.
In the speech and literature of the day every one is
styled a capitalist who possesses what, independent of
his labor, will yield him a return, while whatever is thus
received is spoken of as the earnings or takings of capital, and we everywhere hear of the conflict of labor and
capital. Whether there is, in reality, any conflict between labor and capital, I do not yet ask the reader to
make up his mind; but it will be well here to clear away
some misapprehensions which confuse the judgment.

Attention has already been called to the fact that land
values, which constitute such an enormous part of what
is commonly called capital, are not capital at all; and
that rent, which is as commonly included in the receipts
of capital, and which takes an ever-increasing portion of
the produce of an advancing community, is not the earnings of capital, and must be carefully separated from interest. It is not necessary now to dwell further upon
this point. Attention has likewise been called to the
fact that the stocks, bonds, etc., which constitute another great part of what is commonly called capital,
are not capital at all; but, in some of their shapes, these
evidences of indebtedness so closely resemble capital,

and in some cases actually perform, or seem to perform, the functions of capital, while they yield a return to their owners which is not only spoken of as interest, but has every semblance of interest, that it is worth while, before attempting to clear the idea of interest from some other ambiguities that beset it, to speak again of these at greater length.

Nothing can be capital, let it always be remembered, that is not wealth—that is to say, nothing can be capital that does not consist of actual, tangible things, not the spontaneous offerings of nature, which have in themselves, and not by proxy, the power of directly or indirectly ministering to human desire.

Thus, a government bond is not capital, nor yet is it the representative of capital. The capital that was once received for it by the government has been consumed unproductively—blown away from the mouths of cannon, used up in war ships, expended in keeping men marching and drilling, killing and destroying. The bond cannot represent capital that has been destroyed. It does not represent capital at all. It is simply a solemn declaration that the government will, some time or other, take by taxation from the then existing stock of the people, so much wealth, which it will turn over to the holder of the bond; and that, in the meanwhile, it will, from time to time, take, in the same way, enough to make up to the holder the increase which so much capital as it some day promises to give him would yield him were it actually in his possession. The immense sums which are thus taken from the produce of every modern country to pay interest on public debts are not the earnings or increase of capital—are not really interest in the strict sense of the term, but are taxes levied on the produce of labor and capital, leaving so much less for wages and so much less for real interest.

But, supposing the bonds have been issued for the

deepening of a river bed, the construction of lighthouses, or the erection of a public market; or supposing, to embody the same idea while changing the illustration, they have been issued by a railroad company. Here they do represent capital, existing and applied to productive uses, and like stock in a dividend paying company may be considered as evidences of the ownership of capital. But they can be so considered only in so far as they actually represent capital, and not as they have been issued in excess of the capital used. Nearly all our railroad companies and other incorporations are loaded down in this way. Where one dollar's worth of capital has been really used, certificates for two, three, four, five, or even ten, have been issued, and upon this fictitious amount interest or dividends are paid with more or less regularity. Now, what, in excess of the amount due as interest to the real capital invested, is thus earned by these companies and thus paid out, as well as the large sums absorbed by managing rings and never accounted for, is evidently not taken from the aggregate produce of the community on account of the services rendered by capital—it is not interest. If we are restricted to the terminology of economic writers who decompose profits into interest, insurance, and wages of superintendence, it must fall into the category of wages of superintendence.

But while wages of superintendence clearly enough include the income derived from such personal qualities as skill, tact, enterprise, organizing ability, inventive power, character, etc., to the profits we are speaking of there is another contributing element, which can only arbitrarily be classed with these—the element of monopoly.

When James I. granted to his minion the exclusive privilege of making gold and silver thread, and prohibited, under severe penalties, every one else from making such thread, the income which Buckingham enjoyed in consequence did not arise from the interest upon the capital invested in the manufacture, nor from the skill, etc., of those who really conducted the operations, but from what he got from the king—viz., the exclusive privilege—in reality the power to levy a tax for his own purposes upon all the users of such thread. From a similar source comes a large part of the profits which are commonly confounded with the earnings of capital. Receipts from the patents granted for a limited term of years for the purpose of encouraging invention are clearly attributable to this source, as are the returns derived from monopolies created by protective tariffs under the pretense of encouraging home industry. But there is another far more insidious and far more general form of monopoly. In the aggregation of large masses of capital under a common control there is developed a new and essentially different power from that power of increase which is a general characteristic of capital and which gives rise to interest. While the latter is, so to speak, constructive in its nature, the power which, as aggregation proceeds, rises upon it is destructive. It is a power of the same kind as that which James granted to Buckingham, and it is often exercised with as reckless a disregard, not only of the industrial, but of the personal rights of individuals. A railroad company approaches a small town as a highwayman approaches his victim. The threat, "If you do not accede to our terms we will leave your town two or three miles to one side!" is as efficacious as the "Stand and deliver," when backed by a cocked pistol. For the threat of the railroad company is not merely to deprive the town of the benefits which the railroad might give; it is to put it in a far worse position than if no railroad had been built. Or if, where there is water communication, an opposition boat is put on; rates are reduced until she is forced off, and then the public are compelled to pay the cost of the operation, just as the Rohillas were obliged to pay the forty lacs with which Surajah Dowlah hired of Warren Hastings an English force to assist him in desolating their country and decimating their people. And just as robbers unite to plunder in concert and divide the spoil, so do the trunk lines of railroad unite to raise rates and pool their earnings, or the Pacific roads form a combination with the Pacific Mail Steamship Company by which toll gates are virtually established on land and ocean. And just as Buckingham's creatures, under authority of the gold thread patent, searched private houses, and seized papers and persons for purposes of lust and extortion, so does the great telegraph company which, by the power of associated capital deprives the people of the United States of the full benefits of a beneficent invention, tamper with correspondence and crush out newspapers which offend it.

It is necessary only to allude to these things, not to dwell on them. Every one knows the tyranny and rapacity with which capital when concentrated in large amounts is frequently wielded to corrupt, to rob, and to destroy. What I wish to call the reader's attention to is that profits thus derived are not to be confounded with the legitimate returns of capital as an agent of production. They are for the most part to be attributed to a maladjustment of forces in the legislative department of government, and to a blind adherence to ancient barbarisms and the superstitious reverence for the technicalities of a narrow profession in the administration of law; while the general cause which in advancing communities tends, with the concentration of wealth, to the concentration of power, is the solution of the great problem we are seeking for, but have not yet found.

Any analysis will show that much of the profits which are, in common thought, confounded with interest are in reality due, not to the power of capital, but to the power of concentrated capital, or of concentrated capital

acting upon bad social adjustments. And it will also
show that what are clearly and properly wages of superintendence are very frequently confounded with the
earnings of capital.

And, so, profits properly due to the elements of risk
are frequently confounded with interest. Some people
acquire wealth by taking chances which to the majority
of people must necessarily bring loss. Such are many
forms of speculation, and especially that mode of
gambling known as stock dealing. Nerve, judgment,
the possession of capital, skill in what in lower forms of
gambling are known as the arts of the confidence man
and blackleg, give advantage to the individual; but,
just as at a gaming table, whatever one gains some one
else must lose.

Now, taking the great fortunes that are so often referred to as exemplifying the accumulative power of capital—the Dukes of Westminster and Marquises of Bute,
the Rothschilds, Astors, Stewarts, Vanderbilts, Goulds,
Stanfords, and Floods—it is upon examination readily
seen that they have been built up, in greater or less part,
not by interest, but by elements such as we have been
reviewing.

How necessary it is to note the distinctions to which I
have been calling attention is shown in current discussions, where the shield seems alternately white or black
as the standpoint is shifted from one side to the other.
On the one hand we are called upon to see, in the existence of deep poverty side by side with vast accumulations of wealth, the aggressions of capital on labor, and
in reply it is pointed out that capital aids labor, and
hence we are asked to conclude that there is nothing
unjust or unnatural in the wide gulf between rich and
poor; that wealth is but the reward of industry, intelligence, and thrift; and poverty but the punishment of
indolence, ignorance, and imprudence.

CHAPTER V.

Let us turn now to the law of interest, keeping in mind two things to which attention has heretofore been called—viz:

First—That it is not capital which employs labor, but labor which employs capital.

Second—That capital is not a fixed quantity, but can always be increased or decreased, (1) by the greater or less application of labor to the production of capital, and (2) by the conversion of wealth into capital, or capital into wealth, for capital being but wealth applied in a certain way, wealth is the larger and inclusive term.

It is manifest that under conditions of freedom the maximum that can be given for the use of capital will be the increase it will bring, and the minimum or zero will be the replacement of capital; for above the one point the borrowing of capital would involve a loss, and below the other, capital could not be maintained.

Observe, again: It is not, as is carelessly stated by some writers, the increased efficiency given to labor by the adaptation of capital to any special form or use which fixes this maximum, but the average power of increase which belongs to capital generally. The power of applying itself in advantageous forms is a power of labor, which capital as capital cannot claim nor share. A bow and arrows will enable an Indian to kill, let us say, a buffalo every day, while with sticks and stones he could hardly kill one in a week; but the weapon maker of the tribe could not claim from the hunter six out of every

seven buffaloes killed as a return for the use of a bow
and arrows; nor will capital invested in a woolen factory
yield to the capitalist the difference between the produce
of the factory and what the same amount of labor could
have obtained with the spinning-wheel and handloom.
William when he borrows a plane from James does not
in that obtain the advantage of the increased efficiency of
labor when using a plane for the smoothing of boards over
what it has when smoothing them with a shell or flint.
The progress of knowledge has made the advantage involved in the use of planes a common property and power
of labor.   What he gets from James is merely such advantage as the element of a year's time will give to the
possession of so much capital as is represented by the
plane.

Now, if the vital forces of nature which give an advantage to the element of time be the cause of interest,
it would seem to follow that this maximum rate of interest would be determined by the strength of these forces
and the extent to which they are engaged in production.
But while the reproductive force of nature seems to vary
enormously, as, for instance, between the salmon, which
spawns thousands of eggs, and the whale, which brings
forth a single calf at intervals of years; between the rab-
bit and the elephant, the thistle and the gigantic redwood, it appears from the way the natural balance is
maintained that there is an equation between the reproductive and destructive forces of nature, which in effect
brings the principle of increase to a uniform point.   This
natural balance man has within narrow limits the power
to disturb, and by the modification of natural conditions
may avail himself at will of the varying strength of the
reproductive force in nature.   But when he does so,
there arises from the wide scope of his desires another
principle which brings about in the increase of wealth a
similar equation and balance to that which is effected in

nature between the different forms of life. This equation exhibits itself through values. If, in a country
adapted to both, I go to raising rabbits and you to raising horses, my rabbits may, until the natural limit is
reached, increase faster than your horses. But my capital will not increase faster, for the effect of the varying
rates of increase will be to lower the value of rabbits as
compared with horses, and to increase the value of horses
as compared with rabbits.

Though the varying strength of the vital forces of
nature is thus brought to uniformity, there may be a difference in the different stages of social development as to
the proportionate extent to which, in the aggregate production of wealth, these vital forces are enlisted. But
as to this, there are two remarks to be made. In the
first place, although in such a country as England the
part taken by manufactures in the aggregate wealth production has very much increased as compared with the
part taken by agriculture, yet it is to be noticed that to
a very great extent this is true only of the political or
geographical division, and not of the industrial community. For industrial communities are not limited by
political divisions, or bounded by seas or mountains.
They are limited only by the scope of their exchanges,
and the proportion which in the industrial economy of
England agriculture and stock-raising bear to maufac-
tures is averaged with Iowa and Illinois, with Texas and
California, with Canada and India, with Queensland and
the Baltic—in short, with every country to which the
world-wide exchanges of England extend. In the next
place, it is to be remarked that although in the progress
of civilization the tendency is to the relative increase of
manufactures, as compared with agriculture, and consequently to a proportionately less reliance upon the
reproductive forces of nature, yet this is accompanied
by a corresponding extension of exchanges, and hence a

greater calling in of the power of increase which thus arises. So these tendencies, to a great extent, and, probably, so far as we have yet gone, completely, balance each other, and preserve the equilibrium which fixes the average increase of capital, or the normal rate of interest.

Now, this normal point of interest, which lies between the necessary maximum and the necessary minimum of the return to capital, must, wherever it rests, be such that all things (such as the feeling of security, desire for accumulation, etc.) considered, the reward of capital and the reward of labor will be equal—that is to say, will give an equally attractive result for the exertion or sacrifice involved. It is impossible, perhaps, to formulate this point, as wages are habitually estimated in quantity and interest in a ratio; but if we suppose a given quantity of wealth to be the produce of a given amount of labor, co-operating for a stated time with a certain amount of capital, the proportion in which the produce would be divided between the labor and the capital would afford a comparison. There must be such a point at, or rather, about, which the rate of interest must tend to settle; since, unless such an equilibrium were effected, labor would not accept the use of capital, or capital would not be placed at the disposal of labor. For labor and capital are but different forms of the same thing—human exertion. Capital is produced by labor; it is, in fact, but labor impressed upon matter—labor stored up in matter, to be released again as needed, as the heat of the sun stored up in coal is released in the furnace. The use of capital in production is, therefore, but a mode of labor. As capital can be used only by being consumed, its use is the expenditure of labor, and for the maintenance of capital, its production by labor must be commensurate with its consumption in aid of labor. Hence the principle that, under circumstances which permit free competition, operates to bring wages to a common standard and profits to a substantial equality—the principle that men will seek to gratify their desires with the least exer_ tion—operates to establish and maintain this equilibrium between wages and interest.

This natural relation between interest and wages—tnis equilibrium at which both will represent equal returns to equal exertions—may be stated in a form which suggests a relation of opposition; but this opposition is only apparent. In a partnership between Dick and Harry, the statement that Dick receives a certain proportion of the profits implies that the portion of Harry is less or greater as Dick's is greater or less; but where, as in this case, each gets only what he adds to the common fund, the increase of the portion of the one does not decrease what the other receives.

And this relation fixed, it is evident that interest and wages must rise and fall together, and that interest cannot be increased without increasing wages; nor wages lowered without depressing interest. For if wages fall, interest must also fall in proportion, else it becomes more profitable to turn labor into capital than to apply it directly; while, if interest falls, wages must likewise proportionately fall, or else the increment of capital would be checked.

We are, of course, not speaking of particular wages and particular interest, but of the general rate of wages and the general rate of interest, meaning always by interest the return which capital can secure, less insurance and wages of superintendence. In a particular case, or a particular employment, the tendency of wages and interest to an equilibrium may be impeded; but between the general rate of wages and the general rate of interest, this tendency must be prompt to act. For though in a particular branch of producton the line may be clearly drawn between those who furnish labor and those who furnish capital, yet even in communities where there is the sharpest distinction between the general class laborers and the general class capitalists, these two classes shade off into each other by imperceptible gradations, and on the extremes where the two classes meet in the same persons, the interaction which restores equilibrium, or rather prevents its disturbance, can go on without obstruction, whatever obstacles may exist where the separation is complete. And, furthermore, it must be remembered, as has before been stated, that capital is but a portion of wealth, distinguished from wealth generally only by the purpose to which it is applied, and, hence, the whole body of wealth has upon the relations of capital and labor the same equalizing effect that a fly-wheel has upon the motion of machinery, taking up capital when it is in excess and giving it out again when there is a deficiency, just as a jeweler may give his wife diamonds to wear when he has a superabundant stock, and put them in his showcase again when his stock becomes reduced. Thus any tendency on the part of interest to rise above the equilibrium with wages must immediately beget not only a tendency to direct labor to the production of capital, but also the application of wealth to the uses of capital; while any tendency of wages to rise above the equilibrium with interest must in like manner beget not only a tendency to turn labor from the production of capital, but also to lessen the proportion of capital by diverting from a productive to a non-productive use some of the articles of wealth of which capital is composed.

To recapitulate: There is a certain relation or ratio between wages and interest, fixed by causes, which, if not absolutely permanent, slowly change, at which enough labor will be turned into capital to supply the capital which, in the degree of knowledge, state of the arts, density of population, character of occupations, variety, extent and rapidity of exchanges, will be demanded for production, and this relation or ratio the interaction of labor and capital constantly maintains; hence interest must rise and fall with the rise and fall of wages.

To illustrate: The price of flour is determined by the price of wheat and cost of milling. The cost of milling varies slowly and but little, the difference being, even at long intervals, hardly perceptible; while the price of' wheat varies frequently and largely. Hence we correctly say that the price of flour is governed by the price of wheat. Or, to put the proposition in the same form as the preceding: There is a certain relation or ratio between the value of wheat and the value of flour, fixed by the cost of milling, which relation or ratio the interaction between the demand for flour and the supply of wheat constantly maintains; hence the price of flour must rise and fall with the rise and fall of the price of wheat.

Or, as, leaving the connecting link, the price of wheat, to inference, we say that the price of flour depends upon the character of the seasons, wars, etc., so may we put the law of interest in a form which directly connects it with the law of rent, by saying that the general rate of interest will be determined by the return to capital upon the poorest land to which capital is freely applied—that is to say, upon the best land open to it without the payment of. rent. Thus we bring the law of interest into a form which shows it to be a corollary of the law of rent.

We may prove this conclusion in another way: For that interest must decrease as rent increases, we can plainly see if we eliminate wages. To do this, we must, to be sure, imagine a universe organized on totally different principles. Nevertheless, we may imagine what Carlyle would call a fool's paradise, where the production of wealth went on without the aid of labor, and solely by the reproductive force of capital—where sheep bore ready-made clothing on their backs, cows presented butter and cheese, and oxen, when they got to the proper point of fatness, carved themselves into beefsteaks and roasting ribs; where houses grew from the seed, and a jackknife thrown upon the ground would take root and in due time bear a crop of assorted cutlery. Imagine certain capitalists transported, with their capital in appropriate forms, to such a place. Manifestly, they would get, as the return for their capital, the whole amount of wealth it produced only so long as none of its produce was demanded as rent. When rent arose, it would come out of the produce of capital, and as it increased, the return to the owners of capital must necessarily diminish. If we imagine the place where capital possessed this power of producing wealth without the aid of labor to be of limited extent, say an island, we shall see that as soon as capital had increased to the limit of the island to support it, the return to capital must fall to a trifle above its minimum of mere replacement, and the land owners would receive nearly the whole produce as rent, for the only alternative capitalists would have would be to throw their capital into the sea. Or, if we imagine such an island to be in communication with the rest of the world, the return to capital would settle at the rate of return in other places. Interest there would be neither higher nor lower than anywhere else. Rent would obtain the whole of the superior advantage, and the land of such an island would have a great value.

To sum up, the law of interest is this:

The relation between wages and interest is determined by the average power of increase which attaches to capital from its use in reproductive modes. As rent arises, interest will fall as wages fall, or will be determined by the margin of cultivation.

I have endeavored at this length to trace out and illustrate the law of interest more in deference to the existing terminology and modes of thought than from the real necessities of our inquiry, were it unembarrassed by be-fogging discussions. In truth, the primary division of wealth in distribution is dual, not tripartite. Capital is but a form of labor, and its distinction from labor is in reality but a subdivision, just as the division of labor into skilled and unskilled would be. In our examination we have reached the same point as would have been attained had we simply treated capital as a form of labor, and sought the law which divides the produce between rent and wages; that is to say, between the possessors of the two factors, natural substances and powers, and human exertion—which two factors by their union produce all wealth.

CHAPTER VI

We have by inference already obtained the law of wages. But to verify the deduction and to strip the subject of all ambiguities, let us seek the law from an independent starting point.

There is, of course, no such thing as a common rate of wages, in the sense that there is at any given time and place a common rate of interest. Wages, which include all returns received from labor, not only vary with the differing powers of individuals, but, as the organization of society becomes elaborate, vary largely as between occupations. Nevertheless, there is a certain general relation between all wages, so that we express a clear and well-understood idea when we say that wages are higher or lower in one time or place than in another. In their degrees, wages rise and fall in obedience to a common law. What is this law?

The fundamental principle of human action—the law that is to political economy what the law of gravitation is to physics—is that men seek to gratify their desires with the least exertion. Evidently, this principle must bring to an equality, through the competition it induces, the reward gained by equal exertions under similar circumstances. When men work for themselves, this equalization will be largely affected by the equation of prices; and between those who work for themselves and those who work for others, the same tendency to equalization will operate. Now, under this principle, what, in conditions of freedom, will be the terms at which one man can hire others to work for him? Evidently, they will be fixed by what the men could make if laboring for themselves. The principle which will prevent him from having to give anything above this, except what is necessary to induce the change, will also prevent them from taking less. Did they demand more, the competition of others would prevent them from getting employment. Did he offer less, none would accept the terms, as they could obtain greater results by working for themselves. Thus, although the employer wishes to pay as little as possible, and the employee to receive as much as possible, wages will be fixed by the value or produce of such labor to the laborers themselves. If wages are temporarily carried either above or below this line, a tendency to carry them back at once arises.

But the result, or the earnings of labor, as is readily seen in those primary and fundamental occupations in which labor first engages, and which, even in the most highly developed condition of society, still form the base of production, does not depend merely upon the intensity or quality of the labor itself. Wealth is the product of two factors, land and labor, and what a given amount of labor will yield will vary with the powers of the natural opportunities to which it is applied. This being the case, the principle that men seek to gratify their desires with the least exertion will fix wages at the produce of such labor at the point of highest natural productiveness open to it. Now, by virtue of the same principle, the highest point of natural productiveness open to labor under existing conditions will be the lowest point at which production continues, for men, impelled by a supreme law of the human mind to seek the satisfaction of their desires with the least exertion, will not expend labor at a lower point of productiveness while a higher is open to them. Thus the wages which an employer must pay will be measured by the lowest point of natural productiveness to which production extends, and wages will rise or fall as this point rises or falls.

To illustrate: In a simple state of society, each man, as is the primitive mode, works for himself—some in hunting, let us say, some in fishing, some in cultivating the ground. Cultivation, we will suppose, has just begun, and the land in use is all of the same quality, yielding a similar return to similar exertions. Wages, therefore—for, though there is neither employer nor employed, there are yet wages—will be the full produce of labor, and, making allowance for the difference of agreeableness, risk, etc., in the three pursuits, they will be on the average equal in each—that is to say, equal exertions will yield equal results. Now, if one of their number wishes to employ some of his fellows to work for him instead of for themselves, he must pay wages fixed by this full, average produce of labor.

Let a period of time elapse. Cultivation has extended, and, instead of land of the same quality, embraces lands of different qualities. Wages, now, will not be as before, the average produce of labor. They will be the average produce of labor at the margin of cultivation, or the point of lowest return. For, as men seek to satisfy their desires with the least possible exertion, the point of lowest return in cultivation must yield to labor a return equivalent to the average return in hunting and fishing.* Labor will no longer yield equal returns to equal exertions, but those who expend their labor on the superior land will obtain a greater produce for the same exertion than those who cultivate the inferior land. Wages, however, will still be equal, for this excess which the cultivators of the superior land receive is in reality rent, and if land has been subjected to individual ownership will give it a value. Now, if, under these changed circumstances, one member of this community wishes to hire others to work for him, he will have to pay only

---

* This equalization will be effected by the equation of prices.

what the labor yields at the lowest point of cultivation. If thereafter the margin of cultivation sinks to points of lower and lower productiveness, so must wages sink; if, on the contrary, it rises, so also must wages rise; for, just as a free body tends to take the shortest route to the earth's center, so do men seek the easiest mode to the gratification of their desires.

Here, then, we have the law of wages, as a deduction from a principle most obvious and most universal. That wages depend upon the margin of cultivation—that they will be greater or less as the produce which labor can obtain from the highest natural opportunities open to it is greater or less, flows from the principle that men will seek to satisfy their wants with the least exertion.

Now, if we turn from simple social states to the complex phenomena of highly civilized societies, we shall find upon examination that they also fall under this law.

In such societies, wages differ widely, but they still bear a more or less definite and obvious relation to each other. This relation is not invariable, as at one time a philosopher of repute may earn by his lectures many fold the wages of the best mechanic, and at another can hardly hope for the pay of a footman; as in a great city occupations may yield relatively high wages, which in a new settlement would yield relatively low wages; yet these variations between wages may, under all conditions, and in spite of arbitrary divergences caused by custom, law, etc., be traced to certain circumstances. In one of his most interesting chapters Adam Smith thus enumerates the principal circumstances "which make up for a small pecuniary gain in some employments and counterbalance a great one in others: First, the agreeableness or disagreeableness of the employments themselves. Secondly, the easiness and cheapness, or the difficulty and expense of learning them. Thirdly, the constancy or inconstancy of employment in them. Fourthly, the small or great trust which must be reposed in them. Fifthly, the probability or improbability of success in them." * It is not necessary to dwell in detail on these causes of variation in wages between different employments. They have been admirably explained and illustrated by Adam Smith and the economists who have followed him, who have well worked out the details, even if they have failed to apprehend the main law.

The effect of all the circumstances which give rise to the differences between wages in different occupations may be included as supply and demand, and it is perfectly correct to say that the wages in different occupations will vary relatively according to differences in the supply and demand of labor—meaning by demand the call which the community as a whole makes for services of the particular kind, and by supply the relative amount of labor which, under the existing conditions, can be determined to the performance of those particular services. But though this is true as to the relative differences of wages, when it is said, as is commonly said, that the general rate of wages is determined by supply and demand, the words are meaningless. For supply and demand are but relative terms. The supply of labor can only mean labor offered in exchange for labor or the produce of labor, and the demand for labor can only mean labor or the produce of labor offered in exchange for labor. Supply is thus demand, and demand supply, and, in the whole community, one must be co-extensive with the other. This is clearly apprehended by the current political economy in relation to sales, and the reasoning of Ricardo, Mill, and others, which proves that alterations in supply and demand cannot produce a general rise or fall of

---

* This last, which is analogous to the element of risk in profits, accounts for the high wages of successful lawyers, physicians, contractors, actors, etc.

values, though they may cause a rise or fall in the value of a particular thing, is as applicable to labor. What conceals the absurdity of speaking generally of supply and demand in reference to labor is the habit of considering the demand for labor as springing from capital and as something distinct from labor; but the analysis to which this idea has been heretofore subjected has sufficiently shown its fallacy. It is indeed evident from the mere statement, that wages can never permanently exceed the produce of labor, and hence that there is no fund from which wages can for any time be drawn, save that which labor constantly creates.

But, though all the circumstances which produce the differences in wages between occupations may be considered as operating through supply and demand, they, or rather, their effects, for sometimes the same cause operates in both ways, may be separated into two classes, according as they tend only to raise apparent wages or as they tend to raise real wages—that is, to increase the average reward for equal exertion. The high wages of some occupations much resemble what Adam Smith compares them to, the prizes of a lottery, in which the great gain of one is made up from the losses of many others. This is not only true of the professions by means of which Dr. Smith illustrates the principle, but is largely true of the wages of superintendence in mercantile pursuits, as shown by the fact that over ninety per cent. of the mercantile firms that commence business ultimately fail. The higher wages of those occupations which can be prosecuted only in certain states of the weather, or are otherwise intermittent and uncertain, are also of this class; while differences that arise from hardship, discredit, unhealthiness, etc., imply differences of sacrifice, the increased compensation for which only preserves the level of equal returns for equal exertions. All these differences are, in fact, equalizations, arising from circumstances which, to use the words of Adam Smith, "make up for a small pecuniary gain in some employments and counterbalance a great one in others." But, besides these merely apparent differences, there are real differences in wages between occupations, which are caused by the greater or less rarity of the qualities required—greater abilities or skill, whether natural or acquired, commanding on the average greater wages. Now, these qualities, whether natural or acquired, are essentially analogous to differences in strength and quickness in manual labor, and as in manual labor the higher wages paid the man who can do more would be based upon wages paid to those who can do only the average amount, so wages in the occupations requiring superior abilities and skill must depend upon the common wages paid for ordinary abilities and skill.

It is, indeed, evident from observation, as it must be from theory, that whatever be the circumstances which produce the differences of wages in different occupations, and although they frequently vary in relation to each other, producing, as between time and time, and place and place, greater or less relative differences, yet the rate of wages in one occupation is always dependent on the rate in another, and so on, down, until the lowest and widest stratum of wages is reached, in occupations where the demand is more nearly uniform and in which there is the greatest freedom to engage.

For, although barriers of greater or less difficulty may exist, the amount of labor which can be determined to any particular pursuit is nowhere absolutely fixed. All mechanics could act as laborers, and many laborers could readily become mechanics; all storekeepers could act as shopmen, and many shopmen could easily become storekeepers; many farmers would, upon inducement, become hunters or miners, fishermen or sailors, and many hunters, miners, fishermen, and sailors know enough of farming to turn their hands to it on demand. In each occupation there are men who unite it with others, or who alternate between occupations, while the young men who are constantly coming in to fill up the ranks of labor are drawn in the direction of the strongest inducements and least resistances. And further than this, all the gradations of wages shade into each other by imperceptible degrees, instead of being separated by clearly defined gulfs. The wages, even of the poorer paid mechanics, are generally higher than the wages of simple laborers, but there are always some mechanics who do not, on the whole, make as much as some laborers; the best paid lawyers receive much higher wages than the best paid clerks, but the best paid clerks make more than some lawyers, and in fact the worst paid clerks make more than the worst paid lawyers. Thus, on the verge of each occupation, stand those to whom the inducements between one occupation and another are so nicely balanced that the slightest change is sufficient to determine their labor in one direction or another. Thus, any increase or decrease in the demand for labor of a certain kind cannot, except temporarily, raise wages in that occupation above, nor depress them below, the relative level with wages in other occupations, which is determined by the circumstances previously adverted to, such as relative agreeableness or continuity of employment, etc. Even, as experience shows, where artificial barriers are imposed to this interaction, such as limiting laws, guild regulations, the establishment of caste, etc., they may interfere with, but cannot prevent, the maintenance of this equilibrium. They operate only as dams, which pile up the water of a stream above its natural level, but cannot prevent its overflow.

Thus, although they may from time to time alter in relation to each other, as the circumstances which determine relative levels change, yet it is evident that wages in all strata must ultimately depend upon wages in the lowest and widest stratum—the general rate of wages rising or falling as these rise or fall.

Now, the primary and fundamental occupations, upon which, so to speak, all others are built up, are evidently those which procure wealth directly from nature; hence the law of wages in them must be the general law of wages. And, as wages in such occupations clearly depend upon what labor can produce at the lowest point of natural productiveness to which it is habitually applied; therefore, wages generally depend upon the margin of cultivation, or, to put it more exactly, upon the highest point of natural productiveness to which labor is free to apply itself without the payment of rent.

So obvious is this law that it is often apprehended without being recognized. It is frequently said of such countries as California and Nevada that cheap labor would enormously aid their development, as it would enable the working of the poorer but most extensive deposits of ore. A relation between low wages and a low point of production is perceived by those who talk in this way, but they invert cause and effect. It is not low wages which will cause the working of low-grade ore, but the extension of production to the lower point which will diminish wages. If wages could be arbitrarily forced down, as has sometimes been attempted by statute, the poorer mines would not be worked so long as richer mines could be worked. But if the margin of production were arbitrarily forced down, as it might be, were the superior natural opportunities in the ownership of those who chose rather to wait for future increase of value than to permit them to be used now, wages would necessarily fall.

The demonstration is complete. The law of wages we have thus obtained is that which we previously obtained as the corollary of the law of rent, and it completely harmonizes with the law of interest. It is, that:

Wages depend upon the margin of production, or upon the produce which labor can obtain at the highest point of natural productiveness open to it without the payment of rent.

This law of wages accords with and explains universal facts that without its apprehension seem unrelated and contradictory. It shows that:

Where land is free and labor is unassisted by capital, the whole produce will go to labor as wages.

Where land is free and labor is assisted by capital, wages will consist of the whole produce, less that part necessary to induce the storing up of labor as capital.

Where land is subject to ownership and rent arises, wages will be fixed by what labor could secure from the highest natural opportunities open to it without the payment of rent.

Where natural opportunities are all monopolized, wages may be forced by the competition among laborers to the minimum at which laborers will consent to reproduce.

This necessary minimum of wages (which by Smith and Ricardo is denominated the point of "natural wages," and by Mill supposed to regulate wages, which will be higher or lower as the working classes consent to reproduce at a higher or lower standard of comfort) is, however, included in the law of wages as previously stated, as it is evident that the margin of production cannot fall below that point at which enough will be left as wages to secure the maintenance of labor.

Like Ricardo's law of rent of which it is the corollary, this law of wages carries with it its own proof and becomes self-evident by mere statement. For it is but an application of the central truth that is the foundation of economic reasoning—that men will seek to satisfy their desires with the least exertion. The average man will not work for an employer for less, all things considered, than he can earn by working for himself; nor yet will he work for himself for less than he can earn by working for an employer, and hence the return which labor can secure from such natural opportunities as are free to it must fix the wages which labor everywhere gets. That is to say, the line of rent is the necessary measure of the line of wages. In fact, the accepted law of rent depends for its recognition upon a previous, though in many cases it seems to be an unconscious, acceptance of this law of wages. What makes it evident that land of a particular quality will yield as rent the surplus of its produce over that of the least productive land in use, is the apprehension of the fact that the owner of the higher quality of land can procure the labor to work his land by the payment of what that labor could produce if exerted upon land of the poorer quality.

In its simpler manifestations, this law of wages is recognized by people who do not trouble themselves about political economy, just as the fact that a heavy body would fall to the earth was long recognized by those who never thought of the law of gravitation. It does not require a philosopher to see that if in any country natural opportunities were thrown open which would enable laborers to make for themselves wages higher than the lowest now paid, the general rate of wages would rise; while the most ignorant and stupid of the placer miners of early California knew that as the placers gave out or were monopolized, wages must fall. It requires no finespun theory to explain why wages are so high relatively to production in new countries where land is yet unmonopolized. The cause is on the surface. One man will not work for another for less than his labor will really yield, when he can go upon the next quarter section and take up a farm for himself. It is only as land becomes monopolized and these natural opportunities are shut off from labor, that laborers are obliged to compete with each other for employment, and it becomes possible for the farmer to hire hands to do his work while he maintains himself on the difference between what their labor produces and what he pays them for it.

Adam Smith himself saw the cause of high wages where land was yet open to settlement, though he failed to appreciate the importance and connection of the fact. In treating of the Causes of the Prosperity of New Colonies (Chapter VII, Book IV, "Wealth of Nations,") he says:

"Every colonist gets more land than he can possibly cultivate. He has no rent and scarce any taxes to pay. * * He is eager, therefore, to collect laborers from every quarter and to pay them the most liberal wages. But these liberal wages, joined to the plenty and cheapness of land, soon make these laborers leave him in order to become landlords themselves, and to reward with equal liberality other laborers who soon leave them for the same reason they left their first masters."

This chapter contains numerous expressions which, like the opening sentence in the chapter on The Wages of Labor, show that Adam Smith failed to appreciate the true laws of the distribution of wealth only because he turned away from the more primitive forms of society to look for first principles amid complex social manifestations, where he was blinded by a pre-accepted theory of the functions of capital, and, as it seems to me, by a vague acceptance of the doctrine which, two years after his death, was formulated by Malthus. And it is impossible to read the works of the economists who since the time of Smith have endeavored to build up and elucidate the science of political economy without seeing how, over and over again, they stumble over the law of wages without once recognizing it. Yet, "if it were a dog it would bite them!" Indeed, it is difficult to resist the impression that some of them really saw this law of wages, but, fearful of the practical conclusions to which it would lead, preferred to ignore and cover it up, rather than use it as the key to problems which without it are so perplexing. A great truth to an age which has rejected and trampled on it, is not a word of peace, but a sword!

Perhaps it may be well to remind the reader, before closing this chapter, of what has been before stated—that I am using the word wages not in the sense of a quantity, but in the sense of a proportion. When I say that wages fall as rent rises, I do not mean that the quantity of wealth obtained by laborers as wages is necessarily less, but that the proportion which it bears to the whole produce is necessarily less. The proportion may diminish while the quantity remains the same or even increases. If the margin of cultivation descends from the productive point which we will call 25, to the productive point we will call 20, the rent of all lands that before paid rent will increase by this difference, and the proportion of the whole produce which goes to laborers as wages will to the same extent diminish; but if, in the meantime, the advance of the arts or the economies that become possible with greater population have so increased the productive power of labor that at 20 the same exertion will produce as much wealth as before at 25, laborers will get as wages as great a quantity as before, and the relative fall of wages will not be noticeable in any diminution of the necessaries or comforts of the laborer, but only in the increased value of land and the greater incomes and more lavish expenditure of the rent-receiving class.

CHAPTER VII

The conclusions we have reached as to the laws which govern the distribution of wealth recast a large and most important part of the science of political economy, as at present taught, overthrowing some of its most highly elaborated theories and shedding a new light on some of its most important problems. Yet, in doing this, no disputable ground has been occupied; not a single fundamental principle advanced that is not already recognized.

The law of interest and the law of wages which we have substituted for those now taught are necessary deductions from the great law which alone makes any science of political economy possible—the all-compelling law that is as inseparable from the human mind as attraction is inseparable from matter, and without which it would be impossible to previse or calculate upon any human action, the most trivial or the most important. This fundamental law, that men seek to gratify their desires with the least exertion, becomes, when viewed in its relation to one of the factors of production, the law of rent; in relation to another, the law of interest; and in relation to a third, the law of wages. And in accepting the law of rent, which, since the time of Ricardo, has been accepted by every economist of standing, and which, like a geometrical axiom, has but to be understood to compel assent, the law of interest and law of wages, as I have stated them, are inferentially accepted, as its necessary sequences. In fact, it is only relatively that they can be called sequences, as in the recognition of the law of rent they too must be recognized. For on what depends the recognition of the law of rent? Evidently upon the recognition of the fact that the effect of competition is to prevent the return to labor and capital being anywhere greater than upon the poorest land in use. It is in seeing this that we see that the owner of land will be able to claim as rent all of its produce which exceeds what would be yielded to an equal application of labor and capital on the poorest land in use.

The harmony and correlation of the laws of distribution as we have now apprehended them are in striking contrast with the want of harmony which characterizes these laws as presented by the current political economy. Let us state them side by side:

The Current Statement.	*The True Statement.*
RENT depends on the margin of cultivation, rising as it falls and falling as it rises.	RENT depends on the margin of cultivation, rising as it falls and falling as it rises.
WAGES depend upon the ratio between the number of laborers and the amount of capital devoted to their employment.	WAGES depend on the margin of cultivation, falling as it falls and rising as it rises.
INTEREST depends upon the equation between the supply of and demand for capital; or, as is stated of profits, upon wages (or the cost of labor), rising as wages fall, and falling as wages rise.	INTEREST (its ratio with wages being fixed by the net power of increase which attaches to capital) depends on the margin of cultivation, falling as it falls and rising as it rises.

In the current statement the laws of distribution have no common center, no mutual relation; they are not the correlating divisions of a whole, but measures of different qualities. In the statement we have given, they spring from one point, support and supplement each other, and form the correlating divisions of a complete whole.

CHAPTER VIII.

THE STATICS OF THE PROBLEM THUS EXPLAINED.

We have now obtained a clear, simple, and consistent theory of the distribution of wealth, which accords with first principles and existing facts, and which, when understood, will commend itself as self-evident.

Before working out this theory, I have deemed it necessary to show conclusively the insufficiency of current theories; for, in thought, as in action, the majority of men do but follow their leaders, and a theory of wages which has not merely the support of the highest names, but is firmly rooted in common opinions and prejudices, will, until it has been proved untenable, prevent any other theory from being even considered, just as the theory that the earth was the center of the universe prevented any consideration of the theory that it revolves on its own axis and circles round the sun, until it was clearly shown that the apparent movements of the heavenly bodies could not be explained in accordance with the theory of the fixity of the earth.

There is in truth a marked resemblance between the science of political economy, as at present taught, and the science of astronomy, as taught previous to the recognition of the Copernican theory. The devices by which the current political economy endeavors to explain the social phenomena that are now forcing themselves upon the attention of the civilized world may well be compared to the elaborate system of cycles and epicycles constructed by the learned to explain the celestial phenomena in a manner according with the dogmas of authority and the rude impressions and prejudices of the un-learned. And, just as the observations which showed that this theory of cycles and epicycles could not explain all the phenomena of the heavens cleared the way for the consideration of the simpler theory that supplanted it, so will a recognition of the inadequacy of the current theories to account for social phenomena clear the way for the consideration of a theory that will give to polit-ical economy all the simplicity and harmony which the Copernican theory gave to the science of astronomy.

But at this point the parallel ceases. That "the fixed and steadfast earth" should be really whirling through space with inconceivable velocity is repugnant to the first apprehensions of men in every state and situation; but the truth I wish to make clear is naturally perceived, and has been recognized in the infancy of every people, being obscured only by the complexities of the civilized state, the warpings of selfish interests, and the false di-rection which the speculations of the learned have taken. To recognize it, we have but to come back to first prin-ciples and heed simple perceptions. Nothing can be clearer than the proposition that the failure of wages to increase with increasing productive power is due to the increase of rent.

Three things unite to production—labor, capital, and land.

Three parties divide the produce—the laborer, the capitalist, and the land owner.

If, with an increase of production the laborer gets no more and the capitalist no more it is a necessary infer-ence that the land owner reaps the whole gain.

And the facts agree with the inference. Though neither wages nor interest anywhere increase as material progress goes on, yet the invariable accompaniment and mark of material progress is the increase of rent—the rise of land values.

The increase of rent explains why wages and interest do not increase. The cause which gives to the land holder is the cause which denies to the laborer and capitalist. That wages and interest are higher in new than in old countries is not, as the standard economists say, because nature makes a greater return to the application of labor and capital, but because land is cheaper, and, therefore, as a smaller proportion of the return is taken by rent, labor and capital can keep for their share a larger proportion of what nature does return. It is not the total produce, but the net produce, after rent has been taken from it, that determines what can be divided as wages and interest. Hence, the rate of wages and interest is everywhere fixed, not so much by the productiveness of labor as by the value of land. Wherever the value of land is relatively low, wages and interest are relatively high; wherever land is relatively high, wages and interest are relatively low.

If production had not passed the simple stage in which all labor is directly applied to the land and all wages are paid in its produce, the fact that when the land owner takes a larger portion the laborer must put up with a smaller portion could not be lost sight of.

But the complexities of production in the civilized state, in which so great a part is borne by exchange, and so much labor is bestowed upon materials after they have been separated from the land, though they may to the unthinking disguise, do not alter the fact that all production is still the union of the two factors, land and labor, and that rent (the share of the land holder) cannot be increased except at the expense of wages (the share of the laborer) and interest (the share of capital). Just as the portion of the crop, which in the simpler forms of industrial organization the owner of agricultural land receives at the end of the harvest as his rent, lessens the amount left to the cultivator as wages and

interest, so does the rental of land on which a manufacturing or commercial city is built lessen the amount
which can be divided as wages and interest between the
laborer and capital there engaged in the production and
exchange of wealth.

In short, the value of land depending wholly upon the
power which its ownership gives of appropriating wealth
created by labor, the increase of land values is always at
the expense of the value of labor.   And, hence, that the
increase of productive power does not increase wages, is
because it does increase the value of land.   Rent swal-
lows up the whole gain and pauperism accompanies
progress.

It is unnecessary to refer to facts.   They will suggest
themselves to the reader.   It is the general fact, observable everywhere, that as the value of land increases, so
does the contrast between wealth and want appear.   It is
the universal fact, that where the value of land is highest, civilization exhibits the greatest luxury side by side
with the most piteous destitution.   To see human beings
in the most abject, the most helpless and hopeless condition, you must go, not to the unfenced prairies and the
log cabins of new clearings in the backwoods, where man
single-handed is commencing the struggle with nature,
and land is yet worth nothing, but to the great cities,
where the ownership of a little patch of ground is a
fortune.

BOOK IV.

EFFECT OF MATERIAL PROGRESS UPON THE DISTRIBUTION OF WEALTH.

Hitherto, it is questionable if all the mechanical inventions yet made have lightened the day's toil of any human being.—*John Stuart Mill.*

———

Do ye hear the children weeping, O my brothers,
 Ere the sorrow comes with years?
They are leaning their young heads against their mothers,
 And *that* cannot stop their tears.
The young lambs are bleating in the meadows;
 The young birds are chirping in the nest;
The young fawns are playing with the shadows;
 The young flowers are blowing toward the west—
But the young, young children, O, my brothers,
 They are weeping bitterly!
They are weeping in the playtime of the others,
 In the country of the free.

—Mrs. Browning.

CHAPTER I.

In identifying rent as the receiver of the increased production which material progress gives, but which labor fails to obtain; in seeing that the antagonism of interests is not between labor and capital, as is popularly believed, but is in reality between labor and capital on the one side and land ownership on the other, we have reached a conclusion that has most important practical bearings. But it is not worth while to dwell on them now, for we have not yet fully solved the problem which was at the outset proposed. To say that wages remain low because rent advances is like saying that a steamboat moves because its wheels turn around. The further question is, What causes rent to advance? What is the force or necessity that, as productive power increases, distributes a greater and greater proportion of the produce as rent?

The only cause pointed out by Ricardo as advancing rent is the increase of population, which by requiring larger supplies of food necessitates the extension of cultivation to inferior lands, or to points of inferior production on the same lands, and in current works of other authors attention is so exclusively directed to the extension of production from superior to inferior lands as the cause of advancing rents that Mr. Carey (followed by Professor Perry and others) has imagined that he has overthrown the Ricardian theory of rent by denying that the progress of agriculture is from better to worse lands.*

---

* As to this, it may be worth while to say: (1) That the general fact, as shown by the progress of agriculture in the newer States of

Now, while it is unquestionably true that the increasing pressure of population which compels a resort to inferior points of production will raise rents, and does raise rents, I do not think that all the deductions commonly made from this principle are valid, nor yet that it fully accounts for the increase of rent as material progress goes on. There are evidently other causes which conspire to raise rent, but which seem to have been wholly or partially hidden by the erroneous views as to the functions of capital and genesis of wages which have been current. To see what these are, and how they operate, let us trace the effect of material progress upon the distribution of wealth.

The changes which constitute or contribute to material progress are three: (1) increase in population; (2) improvements in the arts of production and exchange; and (3) improvements in knowledge, education, government, police, manners, and morals, so far as they increase the power of producing wealth. Material progress, as commonly understood, consists of these three elements or directions of progression, in all of which the progressive nations have for some time past been advancing, though in different degrees. As, considered in the light of ma-

---

the Union and by the character of the land left out of cultivation in the older, is that the course of cultivation *is* from the better to the worse qualities of land. (2) That, whether the course of production be from the absolutely better to the absolutely worse lands or the reverse (and there is much to indicate that better or worse in this connection merely relates to our knowledge, and that future advances may discover compensating qualities in portions of the earth now esteemed most sterile), it is always, and from the nature of the human mind, *must* always tend to be, from land under existing conditions deemed better, to land under existing conditions deemed worse. (3) That Ricardo's law of rent does not depend upon the direction of the extension of cultivation, but upon the proposition that if land of a certain quality will yield something, land of a better quality will yield more.

terial forces or economies, the increase of knowledge, the betterment of government, etc., have the same effect as improvements in the arts, it will not be necessary in this view to consider them separately.   What bearing intellectual or moral progress, merely as such, has upon our problem we may hereafter consider.   We are at present dealing with material progress, to which these things contribute only as they increase wealth-producing power, and shall see their effects when we see the effect of improvements in the arts.

To ascertain the effects of material progress upon the distribution of wealth, let us, therefore, consider the effects of increase of population apart from improvement in the arts, and then the effect of improvement in the arts apart from increase of population.

CHAPTER II.

The manner in which increasing population advances rent, as explained and illustrated in current treatises, is that the increased demand for subsistence forces production to inferior soil or to inferior productive points. Thus, if, with a given population, the margin of cultivation is at 30, all lands of productive power over 30 will pay rent. If the population be doubled, an additional supply is required, which cannot be obtained without an extension of cultivation that will cause lands to yield rent that before yielded none. If the extension be to 20, then all the land between 20 and 30 will yield rent and have a value, and all land over 30 will yield increased rent and have increased value.

It is here that the Malthusian doctrine receives from the current elucidations of the theory of rent the support of which I spoke when enumerating the causes that have combined to give that doctrine an almost undisputed sway in current thought. According to the Malthusian theory, the pressure of population against subsistence becomes progressively harder as population increases, and although two hands come into the world with every new mouth, it becomes, to use the language of John Stuart Mill, harder and harder for the new hands to supply the new mouths. According to Ricardo's theory of rent, rent arises from the difference in productiveness of the lands in use, and as explained by Ricardo and the economists who have followed him, the advance in rents which, experience shows, accompanies increasing population, is caused by the inability of procuring more food except at a greater cost, which thus forces the margin of population to lower and lower points of production, commensurately increasing rent. Thus the two theories, as I have before explained, are made to harmonize and blend, the law of rent becoming but a special application of the more general law propounded by Malthus, and the advance of rents with increasing population a demonstration of its resistless operation. I refer to this incidentally, because it now lies in our way to see the misapprehension which has enlisted the doctrine of rent in the support of a theory to which it in reality gives no countenance. The Malthusian theory has been already disposed of, and the cumulative disproof which will prevent the recurrence of a lingering doubt will be given when it is shown, further on, that the phenomena attributed to the pressure of population against subsistence would, under existing conditions, manifest themselves were population to remain stationary.

The misapprehension to which I now refer, and which, to a proper understanding of the effect of increase of population upon the distribution of wealth, it is necessary to clear up, is the presumption, expressed or implied in all the current reasoning upon the subject of rent in connection with population, that the recourse to lower points of production involves a smaller aggregate produce in proportion to the labor expended; though that this is not always the case is clearly recognized in connection with agricultural improvements, which, to use the words of Mill, are considered "as a partial relaxation of the bonds which confine the increase of population." But it is not involved even where there is no advance in the arts, and the recourse to lower points of production is clearly the result of the increased demand of an increased population. For increased population, of itself, and

without any advance in the arts, implies an increase in
the productive power of labor. The labor of 100 men,
other things being equal, will produce much more than
one hundred times as much as the labor of one man, and
the labor of 1,000 men much more than ten times as
much as the labor of 100 men; and, so, with every additional pair of hands which increasing population brings,
there is a more than proportionate addition to the productive power of labor. Thus, with an increasing population, there may be a recourse to lower natural powers
of production, not only without any diminution in the
average production of wealth as compared to labor, but
without any diminution at the lowest point. If population be doubled, land of but 20 productiveness may
yield to the same amount of labor as much as land
of 30 productiveness could before yield. For it must
not be forgotten (what often *is* forgotten) that the
productiveness either of land or labor is not to be measured in any one thing, but in all desired things. A
settler and his family may raise as much corn on land
a hundred miles away from the nearest habitation
as they could raise were their land in the center of a
populous district. But in the populous district they
could obtain with the same labor as good a living from
much poorer land, or from land of equal quality could
make as good a living after paying a high rent, because
in the midst of a large population their labor would have
become more effective; not, perhaps, in the production
of corn, but in the production of wealth generally—or
the obtaining of all the commodities and services which
are the real object of their labor.

But even where there is a diminution in the productiveness of labor at the lowest point—that is to say,
where the increasing demand for wealth has driven production to a lower point of natural productiveness than
the addition to the power of labor from increasing popu-

lation suffices to make up for—it does not follow that the aggregate production, as compared with the aggregate labor, has been lessened.

Let us suppose land of diminishing qualities. The best would naturally be settled first, and as population increased production would take in the next lower quality, and so on. But, as the increase of population, by permitting greater economies, adds to the effectiveness of labor, the cause which brought each quality of land successively into cultivation would at the same time increase the amount of wealth that the same quality of labor could produce from it. But it would also do more than this—it would increase the power of producing wealth on all the superior lands already in cultivation. If the relations of quantity and quality were such that increasing population added to the effectiveness of labor faster than it compelled a resort to less productive qualities of land, though the margin of cultivation would fall and rent would rise, the minimum return to labor would increase. That is to say, though wages as a proportion would fall, wages as a quantity would rise. The average production of wealth would increase. If the relations were such that the increasing effectiveness of labor just compensated for the diminishing productiveness of the land as it was called into use, the effect of increasing population would be to increase rent by lowering the margin of cultivation without reducing wages as a quantity, and to increase the average production. If we now suppose population still increasing, but, between the poorest quality of land in use and the next lower quality, to be a difference so great that the increased power of labor which comes with the increased population that brings it into cultivation cannot compensate for it—the minimum return to labor will be reduced, and with the rise of rents, wages will fall, not only as a proportion, but as a quantity. But unless the descent in the quality of land is far more precipitous than we can well imagine, or than, I think, ever exists, the average production will still be increased, for the increased effectiveness which comes by reason of the increased population that compels resort to the inferior quality of land attaches to all labor, and the gain on the superior qualities of land will more than compensate for the diminished production on the quality last brought in. The aggregate wealth production, as compared with the aggregate expenditure of labor, will be greater, though its distribution will be more unequal.

Thus, increase of population, as it operates to extend production to lower natural levels, operates to increase rent and reduce wages as a proportion, and may or may not reduce wages as a quantity; while it seldom can, and probably never does, reduce the aggregate production of wealth as compared with the aggregate expenditure of labor, but on the contrary increases, and frequently largely increases it.

But while the increase of population thus increases rent by lowering the margin of cultivation, it is a mistake to look upon this as the only mode by which rent advances as population grows. Increasing population increases rent, without reducing the margin of cultivation; and notwithstanding the dicta of such writers as McCulloch, who assert that rent would not arise were there an unbounded extent of equally good land, increases it without reference to the natural qualities of land, for the increased powers of co-operation and exchange which come with increased population are equivalent to—nay, I think we can say without metaphor, that they give—an increased capacity to land.

I do not mean to say merely that, like an improvement in the methods or tools of production, the increased power which comes with increased population gives to the same labor an increased result, which is equivalent to an increase in the natural powers of land; but that it brings out a superior power in labor, which is localized on land—which attaches not to labor generally, but only to labor exerted on particular land; and which thus inheres in the land as much as any qualities of soil, climate, mineral deposit, or natural situation, and passes, as they do, with the possession of the land.

An improvement in the method of cultivation which, with the same outlay, will give two crops a year in place of one, or an improvement in tools and machinery which will double the result of labor, will manifestly, on a particular piece of ground, have the same effect on the produce as a doubling of the fertility of the land. But the difference is in this respect—the improvement in method or in tools can be utilized on any land; but the improvement in fertility can be utilized only on the particular land to which it applies. Now, in large part, the increased productiveness of labor which arises from increased population can be utilized only on particular land, and on particular land in greatly varying degrees.

Here, let us imagine, is an unbounded savannah, stretching off in unbroken sameness of grass and flower, tree and rill, till the traveler tires of the monotony. Along comes the wagon of the first immigrant. Where to settle he cannot tell—every acre seems as good as every other acre. As to wood, as to water, as to fertility, as to situation, there is absolutely no choice, and he is perplexed by the embarrassment of richness. Tired out with the search for one place that is better than another, he stops—somewhere, anywhere—and starts to make himself a home. The soil is virgin and rich, game is abundant, the streams flash with the finest trout. Nature is at her very best. He has what, were he in a populous district, would make him rich; but he is very poor. To say nothing of the mental craving, which would lead him to welcome the sorriest stranger, he labors under all the material disadvantages of solitude. He can get no temporary assistance for any work that requires a greater union of strength than that afforded by his own family, or by such help as he can permanently keep. Though he has cattle, he cannot often have fresh meat, for to get a beefsteak he must kill a bullock. He must be his own blacksmith, wagonmaker, carpenter, and cobbler—in short, a "jack of all trades and master of none." He cannot have his children schooled, for, to do so, he must himself pay and maintain a teacher. Such things as he cannot produce himself, he must buy in quantities and keep on hand, or else go without, for he cannot be constantly leaving his work and making a long journey to the verge of civilization; and when forced to do so, the getting of a vial of medicine or the replacement of a broken auger may cost him the labor of himself and horses for days. Under such circumstances, though nature is prolific, the man is poor. It is an easy matter for him to get enough to eat; but beyond this, his labor will suffice to satisfy only the simplest wants in the rudest way.

Soon there comes another immigrant. Although every quarter section of the boundless plain is as good as every other quarter section, he is not beset by any embarrassment as to where to settle. Though the land is the same, there is one place that is clearly better for him than any other place, and that is where there is already a settler and he may have a neighbor. He settles by the side of the first comer, whose condition is at once greatly improved, and to whom many things are now possible that were before impossible, for two men may help each other to do things that one man could never do.

Another immigrant comes, and, guided by the same attraction, settles where there are already two. Another, and another, until around our first comer there are a score of neighbors. Labor has now an effectiveness which, in the solitary state, it could not approach. If heavy work is to be done, the settlers have a log-rolling, and together accomplish in a day what singly would require years. When one kills a bullock, the others take part of it, returning when they kill, and thus they have fresh meat all the time. Together they hire a schoolmaster, and the children of each are taught for a fractional part of what similar teaching would have cost the first settler. It becomes a comparatively easy matter to send to the nearest town, for some one is always going. But there is less need for such journeys. A blacksmith and a wheelwright soon set up shops, and our settler can have his tools repaired for a small part of the labor it formerly cost him. A store is opened and he can get what he wants as he wants it; a post-office, soon added, gives him regular communication with the rest of the world. Then come a cobbler, a carpenter, a harness-maker, a doctor; and a little church soon arises. Satisfactions become possible that in the solitary state were impossible. There are gratifications for the social and the intellectual nature—for that part of the man that rises above the animal. The power of sympathy, the sense of companionship, the emulation of comparison and contrast, open a wider, and fuller, and more varied life. In rejoicing, there are others to rejoice; in sorrow, the mourners do not mourn alone. There are husking bees, and apple parings, and quilting parties. Though the ballroom be unplastered and the orchestra but a fiddle, the notes of the magician are yet in the strain, and Cupid dances with the dancers. At the wedding, there are others to admire and enjoy; in the house of death, there are watchers; by the open grave, stands human sympathy to sustain the mourners. Occasionally, comes a straggling lecturer to open up glimpses of the world of science, of literature, or of art; in election times, come stump speakers, and the citizen rises to a sense of dignity and power, as the cause of empires is tried before him in the struggle of John Doe and Richard Roe for his support and vote. And, by and by, comes the circus, talked of months before, and opening to children whose horizon has been the prairie, all the realms of the imagination—princes and princesses of fairy tale, mail-clad crusaders and turbaned Moors, Cinderella's fairy coach, and the giants of nursery lore; lions such as crouched before Daniel, or in circling Roman amphitheater tore the saints of God; ostriches who recall the sandy deserts; camels such as stood around when the wicked brethren raised Joseph from the well and sold him into bondage; elephants such as crossed the Alps with Hannibal, or felt the sword of the Maccabees; and glorious music that thrills and builds in the chambers of the mind as rose the sunny dome of Kubla Khan.

Go to our settler now, and say to him: "You have so many fruit trees which you planted; so much fencing, such a well, a barn, a house—in short, you have by your labor added so much value to this farm. Your land itself is not quite so good. You have been cropping it, and by and by it will need manure. I will give you the full value of all your improvements if you will give it to me, and go again with your family beyond the verge of settlement." He would laugh at you. His land yields no more wheat or potatoes than before, but it does yield far more of all the necessaries and comforts of life. His labor upon it will bring no heavier crops, and, we will suppose, no more valuable crops, but it will bring far more of all the other things for which men work. The presence of other settlers—the increase of population—has added to the productiveness, in these things, of labor bestowed upon it, and this added productiveness gives it a superiority over land of equal natural quality where there are as yet no settlers. If no land remains to be taken up, except such as is as far removed from population as was our settler's land when he first went upon it, the value or rent of this land will be measured by the whole of this added capability. If, however, as we have supposed, there is a continuous stretch of equal land, over which population is now spreading, it will not be necessary for the new settler to go into the wilderness, as did the first. He will settle just beyond the other settlers, and will get the advantage of proximity to them. The value or rent of our settler's land will thus depend on the advantage which it has, from being at the center of population, over that on the verge. In the one case, the margin of production will remain as before; in the other, the margin of production will be raised.

Population still continues to increase, and as it increases so do the economies which its increase permits, and which in effect add to the productiveness of the land. Our first settler's land, being the center of population, the store, the blacksmith's forge, the wheelwright's shop, are set up on it, or on its margin, where soon arises a village, which rapidly grows into a town, the center of exchanges for the people of the whole district. With no greater agricultural productiveness than it had at first, this land now begins to develop a productiveness of a higher kind. To labor expended in raising corn, or wheat, or potatoes, it will yield no more of those things than at first; but to labor expended in the subdivided branches of production which require proximity to other producers, and, especially, to labor expended in that final part of production, which consists in distribution, it will yield much larger returns. The wheat-grower may go further on, and find land on which his labor will produce as much wheat, and nearly as much wealth; but the artisan, the manufacturer, the storekeeper, the professional man, find that their labor expended here, at the center of exchanges, will yield them much more than if expended even at a little distance away from it; and this excess of productiveness for such purposes the land-owner can claim just as he could an excess in its wheat-producing power. And so our settler is able to sell in building lots a few of his acres for prices which it would not bring for wheat-growing if its fertility had been mul-tiplied many times. With the proceeds, he builds him-self a fine house, and furnishes it handsomely. That is to say, to reduce the transaction to its lowest terms, the people who wish to use the land build and furnish the house for him, on condition that he will let them avail themselves of the superior productiveness which the in-crease of population has given the land.

Population still keeps on increasing, giving greater and greater utility to the land, and more and more wealth to its owner. The town has grown into a city—a St. Louis, a Chicago or a San Francisco—and still it grows. Production is here carried on upon a great scale, with the best machinery and the most favorable facilities; the division of labor becomes extremely minute, wonderfully multiplying efficiency; exchanges are of such volume and rapidity that they are made with the minimum of friction and loss. Here is the heart, the brain, of the vast social organism that has grown up from the germ of the first settlement; here has developed one of the great gan-glions of the human world. Hither run all roads, hither set all currents, through all the vast regions round about. Here, if you have anything to sell, is the market; here, if you have anything to buy, is the largest and the choicest stock. Here intellectual activity is gathered into a focus, and here springs that stimulus which is born of the collision of mind with mind. Here are the great libraries, the storehouses and granaries of knowledge, the learned professors, the famous special-ists. Here are museums and art galleries, collections of philosophical apparatus, and all things rare, and valuable, and best of their kind. Here come great actors, and orators, and singers, from all over the world. Here, in short, is a center of human life, in all its varied mani-festations.

So enormous are the advantages which this land now offers for the application of labor that instead of one man with a span of horses scratching over acres, you may count in places thousands of workers to the acre, work-ing tier on tier, on floors raised one above the other, five, six, seven and eight stories from the ground, while un-derneath the surface of the earth engines are throbbing with pulsations that exert the force of thousands of horses.

All these advantages attach to the land; it is on this land and no other that they can be utilized, for here is the center of population—the focus of exchanges, the market place and workshop of the highest forms of in-dustry. The productive powers which density of popu-lation has attached to this land are equivalent to the multiplication of its original fertility by the hundred fold and the thousand fold. And rent, which measures the difference between this added productiveness and that of the least productive land in use, has increased accord-ingly. Our settler, or whoever has succeeded to his right to the land, is now a millionaire. Like another Rip Van Winkle, he may have lain down and slept; still he is rich—not from anything he has done, but from the increase of population. There are lots from which for every foot of frontage the owner may draw more than an average mechanic can earn; there are lots that will sell for more than would suffice to pave them with gold coin. In the principal streets are towering buildings, of granite, marble, iron, and plate glass, finished in the most expensive style, replete with every convenience. Yet they are not worth as much as the land upon which they rest—the same land, in nothing changed, which when our first settler came upon it had no value at all.

That this is the way in which the increase of population powerfully acts in increasing rent, whoever, in a progressive country, will look around him, may see for himself. The process is going on under his eyes. The increasing difference in the productiveness of the land in use, which causes an increasing rise in rent, results not so much from the necessities of increased population compelling the resort to inferior land, as from the increased productiveness which increased population gives to the lands already in use. The most valuable lands on the globe, the lands which yield the highest rent, are not lands of surpassing natural fertility, but lands to which a surpassing utility has been given by the increase of population.

The increase of productiveness or utility which increase of population gives to certain lands, in the way to which I have been calling attention, attaches, as it were, to the mere quality of extension. The valuable quality of land that has become a center of population is its superficial capacity—it makes no difference whether it is fertile, alluvial soil like that of Philadelphia; rich bottom land like that of New Orleans; a filled-in marsh like that of St. Petersburg, or a sandy waste like the greater part of San Francisco.

And where value seems to arise from superior natural qualities, such as deep water and good anchorage, rich deposits of coal and iron, or heavy timber, observation also shows that these superior qualities are brought out, rendered tangible, by population. The coal and iron fields of Pennsylvania, that to-day are worth enormous sums, were fifty years ago valueless. What is the efficient cause of the difference? Simply the difference in population. The coal and iron beds of Wyoming and Montana, which to-day are valueless, will, in fifty years from now, be worth millions on millions, simply because, in the meantime, population will have greatly increased.

It is a well provisioned ship, this on which we sail through space. If the bread and beef above decks seem to grow scarce, we but open a hatch and there is a new supply, of which before we never dreamed. And very great command over the services of others comes to those who as the hatches are opened are permitted to say, "This is mine!"

To recapitulate: The effect of increasing population upon the distribution of wealth is to increase rent, and consequently to diminish the proportion of the produce which goes to capital and labor, in two ways: First, By lowering the margin of cultivation. Second, By bringing out in land special capabilities otherwise latent, and by attaching special capabilities to particular lands.

I am disposed to think that the latter mode, to which little attention has been given by political economists, is really the more important. But this, in our inquiry, is not a matter of moment.

CHAPTER III.

Eliminating improvements in the arts, we have seen the effects of increase of population upon the distribution of wealth. Eliminating increase of population, let us now see what effect improvements in the arts of production have upon distribution.

We have seen that increase of population increases rent, rather by increasing the productiveness of labor than by decreasing it. If it can now be shown that, irrespective of the increase of population, the effect of improvements in methods of production and exchange is to increase rent, the disproof of the Malthusian theory— and of all the doctrines derived from or related to it— will be final and complete, for we shall have accounted for the tendency of material progress to lower wages and depress the condition of the lowest class, without recourse to the theory of increasing pressure against the means of subsistence.

That this is the case will, I think, appear on the slightest consideration.

The effect of inventions and improvements in the productive arts is to save labor—that is, to enable the same result to be secured with less labor, or a greater result with the same labor.

Now, in a state of society in which the existing power of labor served to satisfy all material desires, and there was no possibility of new desires being called forth by the opportunity of gratifying them, the effect of labor-saving improvements would be simply to reduce the amount of labor expended. But such a state of society, if it can anywhere be found, which I do not believe, exists only where the human most nearly approaches the animal. In the state of society called civilized, and which in this inquiry we are concerned with, the very reverse is the case. Demand is not a fixed quantity, that increases only as population increases. In each individual it rises with *his* power of getting the things demanded. Man is not an ox, who, when he has eaten his fill, lies down to chew the cud; he is the daughter of the horse leech, who constantly asks for more. "When I get some money," said Erasmus, "I will buy me some Greek books and afterward some clothes." The amount of wealth produced is nowhere commensurate with the desire for wealth, and desire mounts with every additional opportunity for gratification.

This being the case, the effect of labor-saving improvements will be to increase the production of wealth. Now, for the production of wealth, two things are required— labor and land. Therefore, the effect of labor-saving improvements will be to extend the demand for land, and wherever the limit of the quality of land in use is reached, to bring into cultivation lands of less natural productiveness, or to extend cultivation on the same lands to a point of lower natural productiveness. And thus, while the primary effect of labor-saving improvements is to increase the power of labor, the secondary effect is to extend cultivation, and, where this lowers the margin of cultivation, to increase rent. Thus, where land is entirely appropriated, as in England, or where it is either appropriated or is capable of appropriation as rapidly as it is needed for use, as in the United States, the ultimate effect of labor-saving machinery or improvements is to increase rent without increasing wages or interest.

It is important that this be fully understood, for it shows that effects attributed by current theories to increase of population are really due to the progress of invention, and explains the otherwise perplexing fact that labor-saving machinery everywhere fails to benefit laborers.

Yet, to grasp fully this truth, it is necessary to keep in mind what I have already more than once adverted to —the interchangeability of wealth. I refer to this again, only because it is so persistently forgotten or ignored by writers who speak of agricultural production as though it were to be distinguished from production in general, and of food or subsistence as though it were not included in the term wealth.

Let me ask the reader to bear in mind, what has already been sufficiently illustrated, that the possession or production of any form of wealth is virtually the possession or production of any other form of wealth for which it will exchange—in order that he may clearly see that it is not merely improvements which effect a saving in labor directly applied to land that tend to increase rent, but all improvements that in any way save labor.

That the labor of any individual is applied exclusively to the production of one form of wealth is solely the result of the division of labor. The object of labor on the part of any individual is not the obtainment of wealth in one particular form, but the obtainment of wealth in all the forms that consort with his desires. And, hence, an improvement which effects a saving in the labor required to produce one of the things desired, is, in effect, an increase in the power of producing all the other things. If it take half a man's labor to keep him in food, and the other half to provide him clothing and shelter, an improvement which would increase his power of producing food would also increase his power of providing clothing and shelter. If his desires for more or better food, and for more or better clothing and shelter, were equal, an improvement in one department of labor would be precisely equivalent to a like improvement in the other. If the improvement consisted in a doubling of the power of his labor in producing food, he would give one-third less labor to the production of food, and one-third more to the providing of clothing and shelter. If the improvement doubled his power to provide clothing and shelter he would give one-third less labor to the production of these things, and one-third more to the production of food. In either case, the result would be the same—he would be enabled with the same labor to get one-third more in quantity or quality of all the things he desired.

And, so, where production is carried on by the division of labor between individuals, an increase in the power of producing one of the things sought by production in the aggregate adds to the power of obtaining others, and will increase the production of the others, to an extent determined by the proportion which the saving of labor bears to the total amount of labor expended, and by the relative strength of desires. I am unable to think of any form of wealth, the demand for which would not be increased by a saving in the labor required to produce the others. Hearses and coffins have been selected as examples of things for which the demand is little likely to increase; but this is true only as to quantity. That increased power of supply would lead to a demand for more expensive hearses and coffins, no one can doubt who has noticed how strong is the desire to show regard for the dead by costly funerals.

Nor is the demand for food limited, as in economic reasoning is frequently, but erroneously, assumed. Subsistence is often spoken of as though it were a fixed quantity; but it is fixed only as having a definite minimum. Less than a certain amount will not keep a human being alive, and less than a somewhat larger amount will not keep a human being in good health. But, above this minimum, the subsistence which a human being can use may be increased almost indefinitely. Adam Smith says, and Ricardo indorses the statement, that the desire for food is limited in every man by the narrow capacity of the human stomach; but this, manifestly, is true only in the sense that when a man's belly is filled, hunger is satisfied. His demands for food have no such limit. The stomach of a Louis XIV., a Louis XV., or a Louis XVI., could not hold or digest more than the stomach of a French peasant of equal stature, yet, while a few rods of ground would supply the black bread and herbs which constituted the subsistence of the peasant, it took hundreds of thousands of acres to supply the demands of the king, who, besides his own wasteful use of the finest qualities of food, required immense supplies for his servants, horses and dogs. And in the common facts of daily life, in the unsatisfied, though perhaps latent, desires which each one has, we may see how every increase in the power of producing any form of wealth must result in an increased demand for land and the direct products of land. The man who now uses coarse food, and lives in a small house, will, as a rule, if his income be increased, use more costly food, and move to a larger house. If he grows richer and richer he will procure horses, servants, gardens and lawns, his demand for the use of land constantly increasing with his wealth. In the city where I write, is a man —but the type of men everywhere to be found—who used to boil his own beans and fry his own bacon, but who, now that he has got rich, maintains a town house that takes up a whole block and would answer for a first-class hotel, two or three country houses with extensive grounds, a large stud of racers, a breeding farm, private track, etc. It certainly takes at least a thousand times, it may be several thousand times, as much land to supply the demands of this man now as it did when he was poor.

And, so, every improvement or invention, no matter what it be, which gives to labor the power of producing more wealth, causes an increased demand for land and its direct products, and thus tends to force down the margin of cultivation, just as would the demand caused by an increased population. This being the case, every labor-saving invention, whether it be a steam plow, a telegraph, an improved process of smelting ores, a perfecting printing press, or a sewing machine, has a tendency to increase rent.

Or to state this truth concisely:

Wealth in all its forms being the product of labor applied to land or the products of land, any increase in the power of labor, the demand for wealth being unsatisfied, will be utilized in procuring more wealth, and thus increase the demand for land.

To illustrate this effect of labor-saving machinery and improvements, let us suppose a country where, as in all the countries of the civilized world, the land is in the possession of but a portion of the people. Let us suppose a permanent barrier fixed to further increase of population, either by the enactment and strict enforcement of an Herodian law, or from such a change in manners and morals as might result from an extensive circulation of Annie Besant's pamphlets. Let the margin of cultivation, or production, be represented by 20. Thus land or other natural opportunities which, from the application of labor and capital, will yield a return of 20, will just give the ordinary rate of wages and interest, without yielding any rent; while all lands yielding to equal applications of labor and capital more than 20 will yield the excess as rent. Population remaining fixed, let there be made inventions and improvements which will reduce by one-tenth the expenditure of labor and capital necessary to produce the same amount of wealth. Now, either one-tenth of the labor and capital may be freed, and production remain the same as before; or the same amount of labor and capital may be employed, and production be correspondingly increased. But the industrial organization, as in all civilized countries, is such that labor and capital, and especially labor, must press for employment on any terms—the industrial organization is such that mere laborers are not in a position to demand their fair share in the new adjustment, and that any reduction in the application of labor to production will, at first, at least, take the form, not of giving each laborer the same amount of produce for less work, but of throwing some of the laborers out of work and giving them none of the produce. Now, owing to the increased efficiency of labor secured by the new improvements, as great a return can be secured at the point of natural productiveness represented by 18, as before at 20. Thus, the unsatisfied desire for wealth, the competition of labor and capital for employment, would insure the extension of the margin of production, we will say to 18, and thus rent would be increased by the difference between 18 and 20, while wages and interest, in quantity, would be no more than before, and, in proportion to the whole produce, would be less. There would be a greater production of wealth, but land owners would get the whole benefit, subject to temporary deductions, which will be hereafter stated.

If invention and improvement still go on, the efficiency of labor will be still further increased, and the amount of labor and capital necessary to produce a given result further diminished. The same causes will lead to the utilization of this new gain in productive power for the production of more wealth; the margin of cultivation will be again extended, and rent will increase, both in proportion and amount, without any increase in wages and interest. And, so, as invention and improvement go on, constantly adding to the efficiency of labor, the margin of production will be pushed lower and lower, and rent constantly increased, though population should remain stationary.

I do not mean to say that the lowering of the margin of production would always exactly correspond with the increase in productive power, any more than I mean to say that the process would be one of clearly defined steps. Whether, in any particular case, the lowering of the margin of production lags behind or exceeds the increase in productive power, will depend, I conceive, upon what may be called the area of productiveness that can be utilized before cultivation is forced to the next lowest point. For instance, if the margin of cultivation be at 20, improvements which enable the same produce to be obtained with one-tenth less capital and labor will not carry the margin to 18, if the area having a productiveness of 19 is sufficient to employ all the labor and capital displaced from the cultivation of the superior lands. In this case, the margin of cultivation would rest at 19, and rents would be increased by the difference between 19 and 20, and wages and interest by the difference between 18 and 19. But if, with the same increase in productive power the area of productiveness between 20 and 18 should not be sufficient to employ all the displaced labor and capital, the margin of cultivation must, if the same amount of labor and capital press for employment, be carried lower than 18. In this case, rent would gain more than the increase in the product, and wages and interest would be less than before the improvements which increased productive power.

Nor is it precisely true that the labor set free by each

improvement will all be driven to seek employment in the production of more wealth. The increased power of satisfaction, which each fresh improvement gives to a certain portion of the community, will be utilized in demanding leisure or services, as well as in demanding wealth. Some laborers will, therefore, become idlers and some will pass from the ranks of productive to those of unproductive laborers—the proportion of which, as observation shows, tends to increase with the progress of society.

But, as I shall presently refer to a cause, as yet unconsidered, which constantly tends to lower the margin of cultivation, to steady the advance of rent, and even carry it beyond the proportion that would be fixed by the actual margin of cultivation, it is not worth while to take into account these perturbations in the downward movement of the margin of cultivation and the upward movement of rent. All I wish to make clear is that, without any increase in population, the progress of invention constantly tends to give a larger proportion of the produce to the owners of land, and a smaller and smaller proportion to labor and capital.

And, as we can assign no limits to the progress of invention, neither can we assign any limits to the increase of rent, short of the whole produce. For, if labor-saving inventions went on until perfection was attained, and the necessity of labor in the production of wealth was entirely done away with, then everything that the earth could yield could be obtained without labor, and the margin of cultivation would be extended to zero. Wages would be nothing, and interest would be nothing, while rent would take everything. For the owners of the land, being enabled without labor to obtain all the wealth that could be procured from nature, there would be no use for either labor or capital, and no possible way in which either could compel any share of the wealth produced. And no matter how small population might be, if anybody but the land owners continued to exist, it would be at the whim or by the mercy of the land owners —they would be maintained either for the amusement of the land owners, or, as paupers, by their bounty.

This point, of the absolute perfection of labor-saving inventions, may seem very remote, if not impossible of attainment; but it is a point toward which the march of invention is every day more strongly tending. And in the thinning out of population in the agricultural districts of Great Britain, where small farms are being converted into larger ones, and in the great machine-worked wheat-fields of California and Dakota, where one may ride for miles and miles through waving grain without seeing a human habitation, there are already suggestions of the final goal toward which the whole civilized world is hastening. The steam plow and the reaping machine are creating in the modern world latifundia of the same kind that the influx of slaves from foreign wars created in ancient Italy. And to many a poor fellow as he is shoved out of his accustomed place and forced to move on—as the Roman farmers were forced to join the proletariat of the great city, or sell their blood for bread in the ranks of the legions—it seems as though these labor-saving inventions were in themselves a curse, and we hear men talking of work, as though the wearying strain of the muscles were, in itself, a thing to be desired.

In what has preceded, I have, of course, spoken of inventions and improvements when generally diffused. It is hardly necessary to say that as long as an invention or an improvement is used by so few that they derive a special advantage from it, it does not, to the extent of this special advantage, affect the general distribution of wealth. So, in regard to the limited monopolies created by patent laws, or by the causes which give the same character to railroad and telegraph lines, etc. Although

generally mistaken for profits of capital, the special profits thus arising are really the returns of monopoly, as has
been explained in a previous chapter, and, to the extent
that they subtract from the benefits of an improvement,
do not primarily affect general distribution. For instance, the benefits of a railroad or similar improvement
in cheapening transportation are diffused or monopolized,
as its charges are reduced to a rate which will yield ordinary interest on the capital invested, or kept up to a
point which will yield an extraordinary return, or cover
the stealing of the constructors or directors. And, as is
well known, the rise in rent or land values corresponds
with the reduction in the charges.

As has before been said, in the improvements which
advance rent, are not only to be included the improvements which directly increase productive power, but also
such improvements in government, manners, and morals
as indirectly increase it. Considered as material forces,
the effect of all these is to increase productive power,
and, like improvements in the productive arts, their
benefit is ultimately monopolized by the possessors of
the land. A notable instance of this is to be found in
the abolition of protection by England. Free trade has
enormously increased the wealth of Great Britain, without lessening pauperism. It has simply increased rent.
And if the corrupt governments of our great American
cities were to be made models of purity and economy, the
effect would simply be to increase the value of land, not
to raise either wages or interest.

CHAPTER IV.

EFFECT OF THE EXPECTATION RAISED BY MATERIAL PROGRESS.

We have now seen that while advancing population tends to advance rent, so all the causes that in a progressive state of society operate to increase the productive power of labor tend, also, to advance rent, and not to advance wages or interest. The increased production of wealth goes ultimately to the owners of land in increased rent; and, although, as improvement goes on, advantages may accrue to individuals not land holders, which concentrate in their hands considerable portions of the increased produce, yet there is in all this improvement nothing which tends to increase the general return either to labor or to capital.

But there is a cause, not yet adverted to, which must be taken into consideration fully to explain the influence of material progress upon the distribution of wealth.

That cause is the confident expectation of the future enhancement of land values, which arises in all progressive countries from the steady increase of rent, and which leads to speculation, or the holding of land for a higher price than it would then otherwise bring.

We have hitherto assumed, as is generally assumed in elucidations of the theory of rent, that the actual margin of cultivation always coincides with what may be termed the necessary margin of cultivation—that is to say, we have assumed that cultivation extends to less productive points only as it becomes necessary from the fact that natural opportunities are at the more productive points fully utilized.

This, probably, is the case in stationary or very slowly progressing communities, but in rapidly progressing communities, where the swift and steady increase of rent gives confidence to calculations of further increase, it is not the case. In such communities, the confident expectation of increased prices produces, to a greater or less extent, the effects of a combination among land holders, and tends to the withholding of land from use, in expectation of higher prices, thus forcing the margin of cultivation farther than required by the necessities of production.

This cause must operate to some extent in all progressive communities, though in such countries as England, where the tenant system prevails in agriculture, it may be shown more in the selling price of land than in the agricultural margin of cultivation, or actual rent. But in communities like the United States, where the user of land generally prefers, if he can, to own it, and where there is a great extent of land to overrun, it operates with enormous power.

The immense area over which the population of the United States is scattered shows this. The man who sets out from the Eastern seaboard in search of the margin of cultivation, where he may obtain land without paying rent, must, like the man who swam the river to get a drink, pass for long distances through half-tilled farms, and traverse vast areas of virgin soil, before he reaches the point where land can be had free of rent— *i.e.*, by homestead entry or pre-emption. He (and, with him, the margin of cultivation) is forced so much farther than he otherwise need have gone, by the speculation which is holding these unused lands in expectation of increased value in the future. And when he settles, he will, in his turn, take up, if he can, more land than he can use, in the belief that it will soon become valuable; **and** so those who follow him are again forced farther on than the necessities of production require, carrying the margin of cultivation to still less productive, because still more remote points.

The same thing may be seen in every rapidly growing city. If the land of superior quality as to location were always fully used before land of inferior quality were resorted to, no vacant lots would be left as a city extended, nor would we find miserable shanties in the midst of costly buildings. These lots, some of them extremely valuable, are withheld from use, or from the full use to which they might be put, because their owners, not being able or not wishing to improve them, prefer, in expectation of the advance of land values, to hold them for a higher rate than could now be obtained from those willing to improve them. And, in consequence of this land being withheld from use, or from the full use of which it is capable, the margin of the city is pushed away so much farther from the center.

But when we reach the limits of the growing city—the actual margin of building, which corresponds to the margin of cultivation in agriculture—we shall not find the land purchasable at its value for agricultural purposes, as it would be were rent determined simply by present requirements; but we shall find that for a long distance beyond the city land bears a speculative value, based upon the belief that it will be required in the future for urban purposes, and that to reach the point at which land can be purchased at a price not based upon urban rent, we must go very far beyond the actual margin of urban use.

Or, to take another case of a different kind, instances similar to which may doubtless be found in every locality. There is in Marin County, within easy access of San Francisco, a fine belt of redwood timber. Naturally, this would be first used, before resorting for the supply of the San Francisco market to timber lands at a much

greater distance. But it yet remains uncut, and lumber
procured many miles beyond is daily hauled past it on
the railroad, because its owner prefers to hold for the
greater price it will bring in the future. Thus, by the
withholding from use of this body of timber, the margin
of production of redwood is forced so much farther up
and down the Coast Range. That mineral land, when
reduced to private ownership, is frequently withheld
from use while poorer deposits are worked, is well known,
and in new States it is common to find individuals who
are called "land poor"—that is, who remain poor, sometimes almost to deprivation, because they insist on holding land, which they themselves cannot use, at prices at
which no one else can profitably use it.

To recur now to the illustration we made use of in the
preceding chapter: With the margin of cultivation
standing at 20, an increase in the power of production
takes place, which renders the same result obtainable
with one-tenth less labor. For reasons before stated,
the margin of production must now be forced down, and
if it rests at 18, the return to labor and capital will be
the same as before, when the margin stood at 20.
Whether it will be forced to 18 or be forced lower depends
upon what I have called the area of productiveness which
intervenes between 20 and 18.   But if the confident expectation of a further increase of rents leads the land
owners to demand 3 rent for 20 land, 2 for 19, and 1 for
18 land, and to withhold their land from use until these
terms are complied with, the area of productiveness may
be so reduced that the margin of cultivation must fall to
17 or even lower; and thus, as the result of the increase
in the efficiency of labor, laborers would get less than
before, while interest would be proportionately reduced,
and rent would increase in greater ratio than the increase
in productive power.

Whether we formulate it as an extension of the **margin**

of production, or as a carrying of the rent line beyond the margin of production, the influence of speculation in land in increasing rent is a great fact which cannot be ignored in any complete theory of the distribution of wealth in progressive countries. It is the force, evolved by material progress, which tends constantly to increase rent in a greater ratio than progress increases production, and thus constantly tends, as material progress goes on and productive power increases, to reduce wages, not merely relatively, but absolutely. It is this expansive force which, operating with great power in new countries, brings to them, seemingly long before their time, the social diseases of older countries; produces "tramps" on virgin acres, and breeds paupers on half-tilled soil.

In short, the general and steady advance in land values in a progressive community necessarily produces that additional tendency to advance which is seen in the case of commodities when any general and continuous cause operates to increase their price. As, during the rapid depreciation of currency which marked the latter days of the Southern Confederacy, the fact that whatever was bought one day could be sold for a higher price the next, operated to carry up the prices of commodities even faster than the depreciation of the currency, so does the steady increase of land values, which material progress produces, operate still further to accelerate the increase. We see this secondary cause operating in full force in those manias of land speculation which mark the growth of new communities; but though these are the abnormal and occasional manifestations, it is undeniable that the cause steadily operates, with greater or less intensity, in all progressive societies.

The cause which limits speculation in commodities, the tendency of increasing price to draw forth additional supplies, cannot limit the speculative advance in land values, as land is a fixed quantity, which human agency can neither increase nor diminish; but there is neverthe-less a limit to the price of land, in the minimum required by labor and capital as the condition of engaging in pro-duction. If it were possible continuously to reduce wages until zero were reached, it would be possible con-tinuously to increase rent until it swallowed up the whole produce. But as wages cannot be permanently reduced below the point at which laborers will consent to work and reproduce, nor interest below the point at which capital will be devoted to production, there is a limit which restrains the speculative advance of rent. Hence speculation cannot have the same scope to ad-vance rent in countries where wages and interest are already near the minimum, as in countries where they are considerably above it. Yet that there is in all pro-gressive countries a constant tendency in the speculative advance of rent to overpass the limit where production would cease, is, I think, shown by recurring seasons of industrial paralysis—a matter which will be more fully examined in the next book.

BOOK V.

THE PROBLEM SOLVED.

To whomsoever the soil at any time belongs, to him belong the fruits of it. White parasols, and elephants mad with pride are the flowers of a grant of land.—*Sir Wm. Jones' translation of an Indian grant of land, found at Tanna.*

The widow is gathering nettles for her children's dinner; a perfumed seigneur, delicately lounging in the Œil de Bœuf, hath an alchemy whereby he will extract from her the third nettle, and call it rent.—*Carlyle.*

CHAPTER I.

Our long inquiry is ended. We may now marshal the results.

To begin with the industrial depressions, to account for which so many contradictory and self-contradictory theories are broached.

A consideration of the manner in which the speculative advance in land values cuts down the earnings of labor and capital and checks production leads, I think, irresistibly to the conclusion that this is the main cause of those periodical industrial depressions to which every civilized country, and all civilized countries together, seem increasingly liable.

I do not mean to say that there are not other proximate causes. The growing complexity and interdependence of the machinery of production, which makes each shock or stoppage propagate itself through a widening circle; the essential defect of currencies which contract when most needed, and the tremendous alternations in volume that occur in the simpler forms of commercial credit, which, to a much greater extent than currency in any form, constitute the medium or flux of exchanges; the protective tariffs which present artificial barriers to the interplay of productive forces, and other similar causes, undoubtedly bear important part in producing and continuing what are called hard times. But, both from the consideration of principles and the observation of phenomena, it is clear that the great initiatory cause is to be looked for in the speculative advance of land values.

In the preceding chapter I have shown that the speculative advance in land values tends to press the margin of cultivation, or production, beyond its normal limit, thus compelling labor and capital to accept of a smaller return, or (and this is the only way they can resist the tendency) to cease production. Now, it is not only natural that labor and capital should resist the crowding down of wages and interest by the speculative advance of rent, but they are driven to this in self-defense, inasmuch as there is a minimum of return below which labor cannot exist nor capital be maintained. Hence, from the fact of speculation in land, we may infer all the phenomena which mark these recurring seasons of industrial depression.

Given a progressive community, in which population is increasing and one improvement succeeds another, and land must constantly increase in value. This steady increase naturally leads to speculation in which future increase is anticipated, and land values are carried beyond the point at which, under the existing conditions of production, their accustomed returns would be left to labor and capital. Production, therefore, begins to stop. Not that there is necessarily, or even probably, an absolute diminution in production; but that there is what in a progressive community would be equivalent to an absolute diminution of production in a stationary community —a failure in production to increase proportionately, owing to the failure of new increments of labor and capital to find employment at the accustomed rates.

This stoppage of production at some points must necessarily show itself at other points of the industrial network, in a cessation of demand, which would again check production there, and thus the paralysis would communicate itself through all the interlacings of industry and commerce, producing everywhere a partial disjointing of production and exchange, and resulting in the phenomena that seem to show overproduction or overconsumption, according to the standpoint from which they are viewed.

The period of depression thus ensuing would continue until (1) the speculative advance in rents had been lost; or (2) the increase in the efficiency of labor, owing to the growth of population and the progress of improvement, had enabled the normal rent line to overtake the speculative rent line; or (3) labor and capital had become reconciled to engaging in production for smaller returns. Or, most probably, all three of these causes would cooperate to produce a new equilibrium, at which all the forces of production would again engage, and a season of activity ensue; whereupon rent would begin to advance again, a speculative advance again take place, production again be checked, and the same round be gone over.

In the elaborate and complicated system of production which is characteristic of modern civilization, where, moreover, there is no such thing as a distinct and independent industrial community, but geographically or politically separated communities blend and interlace their industrial organizations in different modes and varying measures, it is not to be expected that effect should be seen to follow cause as clearly and definitely as would be the case in a simpler development of industry, and in a community forming a complete and distinct industrial whole; but, nevertheless, the phenomena actually presented by these alternate seasons of activity and depression clearly correspond with those we have inferred from the speculative advance of rent.

Deduction thus shows the actual phenomena as resulting from the principle. If we reverse the process, it is as easy by induction to reach the principle by tracing up the phenomena.

These seasons of depression are always preceded by seasons of activity and speculation, and on all hands the connection between the two is admitted—the depression being looked upon as the reaction from the speculation, as the headache of the morning is the reaction from the debauch of the night. But as to the manner in which the depression results from the speculation, there are two classes or schools of opinion, as the attempts made on both sides of the Atlantic to account for the present industrial depression will show.

One school says that the speculation produced the depression by causing overproduction, and point to the warehouses filled with goods that cannot be sold at remunerative prices, to mills closed or working on half time, to mines shut down and steamers laid up, to money lying idly in bank vaults, and workmen compelled to idleness and privation. They point to these facts as showing that the production has exceeded the demand for consumption, and they point, moreover, to the fact that when government during war enters the field as an enormous consumer, brisk times prevail, as in the United States during the civil war and in England during the Napoleonic struggle.

The other school says that the speculation has produced the depression by leading to overconsumption, and point to full warehouses, rusting steamers, closed mills, and idle workmen as evidences of a cessation of effective demand, which, they say, evidently results from the fact that people, made extravagant by a fictitious prosperity, have lived beyond their means, and are now obliged to retrench—that is, to consume less wealth. They point, moreover, to the enormous consumption of wealth by wars, by the building of unremunerative railroads, by loans to bankrupt governments, etc., as extravagances which, though not felt at the time, just as the spendthrift does not at the moment feel the impairment of his fortune, must now be made up by a season of reduced consumption.

Now, each of these theories evidently expresses one side or phase of a general truth, but each of them evidently fails to comprehend the full truth. As an explanation of the phenomena, each is equally and utterly preposterous.

For while the great masses of men want more wealth than they can get, and while they are willing to give for it that which is the basis and raw material of wealth—their labor—how can there be overproduction? And while the machinery of production wastes and producers are condemned to unwilling idleness, how can there be overconsumption?

When, with the desire to consume more, there co-exist the ability and willingness to produce more, industrial and commercial paralysis cannot be charged either to overproduction or to overconsumption. Manifestly, the trouble is that production and consumption cannot meet and satisfy each other.

How does this inability arise? It is evidently and by common consent the result of speculation. But of speculation in what?

Certainly not of speculation in things which are the products of labor—in agricultural or mineral productions, or manufactured goods, for the effect of speculation in such things, as is well shown in current treatises that spare me the necessity of illustration, is simply to equalize supply and demand, and to steady the interplay of production and consumption by an action analogous to that of a fly-wheel in a machine.

Therefore, if speculation be the cause of these industrial depressions, it must be speculation in things not the production of labor, but yet necessary to the exertion of labor in the production of wealth—of things of fixed quantity; that is to say, it must be speculation in land.

That land speculation is the true cause of industrial depression is, in the United States, clearly evident. In each period of industrial activity land values have steadily risen, culminating in speculation which carried them up in great jumps. This has been invariably followed by a partial cessation of production, and its correlative, a cessation of effective demand (dull trade), generally accompanied by a commercial crash; and then has succeeded a period of comparative stagnation, during which the equilibrium has been again slowly established, and the same round been run again. This relation is observable throughout the civilized world. Periods of industrial activity always culminate in a speculative advance of land values, followed by symptoms of checked production, generally shown at first by cessation of demand from the newer countries, where the advance in land values has been greatest.

That this must be the main explanation of these periods of depression, will be seen by an analysis of the facts.

All trade, let it be remembered, is the exchange of commodities for commodities, and hence the cessation of demand for some commodities, which marks the depression of trade, is really a cessation in the supply of other commodities. That dealers find their sales declining and manufacturers find orders falling off, while the things which they have to sell, or stand ready to make, are things for which there is yet a widespread desire, simply shows that the supply of other things, which in the course of trade would be given for them, has declined. In common parlance we say that "buyers have no money," or that "money is becoming scarce," but in talking in this way we ignore the fact that money is but the medium of exchange. What the would-be buyers really lack is not money, but commodities which they can turn into money—what is really becoming scarcer, **is** produce of some sort. The diminution of the effective demand of consumers is therefore but a result of the diminution of production.

This is seen very clearly by storekeepers in a manufacturing town when the mills are shut down and operatives thrown out of work. It is the cessation of production which deprives the operatives of means to make the purchases they desire, and thus leaves the storekeeper with what, in view of the lessened demand, is a superabundant stock, and forces him to discharge some of his clerks and otherwise reduce his demands. And the cessation of demand (I am speaking, of course, of general cases and not of any alteration in relative demand from such causes as change of fashion), which has left the manufacturer with superabundant stock and compelled him to discharge his hands, must arise in the same way. Somewhere, it may be at the other end of the world, a check in production has produced a check in the demand for consumption. That demand is lessened without want being satisfied, shows that production is somewhere checked.

People want the things the manufacturer makes as much as ever, just as the operatives want the things the storekeeper has to sell. But they do not have as much to give for them. Production has somewhere been checked, and this reduction in the supply of some things has shown itself in cessation of demand for others, the check propagating itself through the whole framework of industry and exchange. Now, the industrial pyramid manifestly rests on the land. The primary and fundamental occupations, which create a demand for all others, are evidently those which extract wealth from nature, and, hence, if we trace from one exchange point to another, and from one occupation to another, this check to production, which shows itself in decreased purchasing power, we must ultimately find it in some

obstacle which checks labor in expending itself on land.
And that obstacle, it is clear, is the speculative advance
in rent, or the value of land, which produces the same
effects, as in fact, it is, a lock-out of labor and capital by
land owners.   This check to production, beginning at
the basis of interlaced industry, propagates itself from
exchange point to exchange point, cessation of supply
becoming failure of demand, until, so to speak, the
whole machine is thrown out of gear, and the spectacle
is everywhere presented of labor going to waste while
laborers suffer from want.

This strange and unnatural spectacle of large numbers
of willing men who cannot find employment is enough
to suggest the true cause to whomsoever can think con-
secutively.   For, though custom has dulled us to it, it *is*
a strange and unnatural thing that men who wish to labor,
in order to satisfy their wants, cannot find the opportunity—as, since labor is that which produces wealth, the
man who seeks to exchange labor for food, clothing, or
any other form of wealth, is like one who proposes to
give bullion for coin, or wheat for flour.   We talk about
the supply of labor and the demand for labor, but, evidently, these are only relative terms.   The supply of
labor is everywhere the same—two hands always come
into the world with one mouth, twenty-one boys to every
twenty girls; and the demand for labor must always
exist as long as men want things which labor alone can
procure.   We talk about the "want of work," but, evidently, it is not work that is short while want continues;
evidently, the supply of labor cannot be too great, nor
the demand for labor too small, when people suffer for
the lack of things that labor produces.   The real trouble
must be that supply is somehow prevented from satisfying demand, that somewhere there is an obstacle which
prevents labor from producing the things that laborers
want.

Take the case of any one of these vast masses of un-employed men, to whom, though he never heard of Mal-thus, it to-day seems that there are too many people in the world. In his own wants, in the needs of his anxious wife, in the demands of his half-cared-for, perhaps even hungry and shivering children, there is demand enough for labor, Heaven knows! In his own willing hands is the supply. Put him on a solitary island, and though cut off from all the enormous advantages which the co-operation, combination, and machinery of a civilized community give to the productive powers of man, yet his two hands can fill the mouths and keep warm the backs that depend upon them. Yet where productive power is as its highest development they cannot. Why? Is it not because in the one case he has access to the material and forces of nature, and in the other this access is denied?

Is it not the fact that labor is thus shut off from nature which can alone explain the state of things that compels men to stand idle who would willingly supply their wants by their labor? The proximate cause of en-forced idleness with one set of men may be the cessation of demand on the part of other men for the particular things they produce, but trace this cause from point to point, from occupation to occupation, and you will find that enforced idleness in one trade is caused by enforced idleness in another, and that the paralysis which pro-duces dullness in all trades cannot be said to spring from too great a supply of labor or too small a demand for labor, but must proceed from the fact that supply cannot meet demand by producing the things which satisfy want and are the object of labor.

Now, what is necessary to enable labor to produce these things, is land. When we speak of labor creating wealth, we speak metaphorically. Man creates nothing. The whole human race, were they to labor forever, could not create the tiniest mote that floats in a sunbeam—could not make this rolling sphere one atom heavier or one atom lighter. In producing wealth, labor, with the aid of natural forces, but works up, into the forms desired, pre-existing matter, and, to produce wealth, must, therefore, have access to this matter and to these forces —that is to say, to land. The land is the source of all wealth. It is the mine from which must be drawn the ore that labor fashions. It is the substance to which labor gives the form. And, hence, when labor cannot satisfy its wants, may we not with certainty infer that it can be from no other cause than that labor is denied access to land?

When in all trades there is what we call scarcity of employment; when, everywhere, labor wastes, while desire is unsatisfied, must not the obstacle which prevents labor from producing the wealth it needs, lie at the foundation of the industrial structure? That foundation is land. Milliners, optical instrument makers, gilders, and polishers, are not the pioneers of new settlements. Miners did not go to California or Australia because shoemakers, tailors, machinists, and printers were there. But those trades followed the miners, just as they are now following the gold diggers into the Black Hills and the diamond diggers into South Africa. It is not the storekeeper who is the cause of the farmer, but the farmer who brings the storekeeper. It is not the growth of the city that develops the country, but the development of the country that makes the city grow. And, hence, when, through all trades, men willing to work cannot find opportunity to do so, the difficulty must arise in the employment that creates a demand for all other employments—it must be because labor is shut out from land.

In Leeds or Lowell, in Philadelphia or Manchester, in London or New York, it may require a grasp of first principles to see this; but where industrial development has not become so elaborate, nor the extreme links of the chain so widely separated, one has but to look at obvious facts. Although not yet thirty years old, the city of San Francisco, both in population and in commercial impor-tance, ranks among the great cities of the world, and, next to New York, is the most metropolitan of American cities. Though not yet thirty years old, she has had for some years an increasing number of unemployed men. Clearly, here, it is because men cannot find employment in the country that there are so many unemployed in the city; for when the harvest opens they go trooping out, and when it is over they come trooping back to the city again. If these now unemployed men were producing wealth from the land, they would not only be employing themselves, but would be employing all the mechanics of the city, giving custom to the storekeepers, trade to the merchants, audiences to the theaters, and subscribers and advertisements to the newspapers—creating effective demand that would be felt in New England and Old England, and wherever throughout the world come the articles that, when they have the means to pay for them, such a population consumes.

Now, why is it that this unemployed labor cannot employ itself upon the land? Not that the land is all in use. Though all the symptoms that in older countries are taken as showing a redundancy of population are be-ginning to manifest themselves in San Francisco, it is idle to talk of redundancy of population in a State that with greater natural resources than France has not yet a million of people. Within a few miles of San Francisco is unused land enough to give employment to every man who wants it.. I do not mean to say that every unem-ployed man could turn farmer or build himself a house, if he had the land; but that enough could and would do so to give employment to the rest. What is it, then, that prevents labor from employing itself on this land? Simply, that it has been monopolized and is held at speculative prices, based not upon present value, but upon the added value that will come with the future growth of population.

What may thus be seen in San Francisco by whoever is willing to see, may, I doubt not, be seen as clearly in other places.

The present commercial and industrial depression, which first clearly manifested itself in the United States in 1872, and has spread with greater or less intensity over the civilized world, is largely attributed to the undue extension of the railroad system, with which there are many things that seem to show its relation. I am fully conscious that the construction of railroads before they are actually needed may divert capital and labor from more to less productive employments, and make a community poorer instead of richer; and when the railroad mania was at its highest, I pointed this out in a political tract addressed to the people of California;* but to assign to this wasting of capital such a widespread industrial dead-lock seems to me like attributing an unusually low tide to the drawing of a few extra bucketfuls of water. The waste of capital and labor during the civil war was enormously greater than it could possibly be by the construction of unnecessary railroads, but without producing any such result. And, certainly, there seems to be little sense in talking of the waste of capital and labor in railroads as causing this depression, when the prominent feature of the depression has been the superabundance of capital and labor seeking employment.

Yet, that there is a connection between the rapid con-

---

* The Subsidy Question and the Democratic Party, 1871.

struction of railroads and industrial depression, any one who understands what increased land values mean, and who has noticed the effect which the construction of railroads has upon land speculation, can easily see. Wherever a railroad was built or projected, lands sprang up in value under the influence of speculation, and thousands of millions of dollars were added to the nominal values which capital and labor were asked to pay outright, or to pay in installments, as the price of being allowed to go to work and produce wealth. The inevitable result was to check production, and this check to production propagated itself in a cessation of demand, which checked production to the furthest verge of the wide circle of exchanges, operating with accumulated force in the centers of the great industrial commonwealth into which commerce links the civilized world.

The primary operations of this cause can, perhaps, be nowhere more clearly traced than in California, which, from its comparative isolation, has constituted a peculiarly well-defined community.

Until almost its close, the last decade was marked in California by the same industrial activity which was shown in the Northern States, and, in fact, throughout the civilized world, when the interruption of exchanges and the disarrangement of industry caused by the war and the blockade of Southern ports is considered. This activity could not be attributed to inflation of the currency or to lavish expenditures of the General Government, to which in the Eastern States the comparative activity of the same period has since been attributed; for, in spite of legal tender laws, the Pacific Coast adhered to a coin currency, and the taxation of the Federal Government took away very much more than was returned in Federal expenditures. It was attributable solely to normal causes, for, though placer mining was declining, the Nevada silver mines were being opened, wheat and wool were beginning to take the place of gold in the table of exports, and an increasing population and the improvement in the methods of production and exchange were steadily adding to the efficiency of labor.

With this material progress went on a steady enhancement in land values—its consequence. This steady advance engendered a speculative advance, which, with the railroad era, ran up land values in every direction. If the population of California had steadily grown when the long, costly, fever-haunted Isthmus route was the principal mode of communication with the Atlantic States, it must, it was thought, increase enormously with the opening of a road which would bring New York harbor and San Francisco Bay within seven days' easy travel, and when in the State itself the locomotive took the place of stage coach and freight wagon. The expected increase of land values which would thus accrue was discounted in advance. Lots on the outskirts of San Francisco rose hundreds and thousands per cent., and farming land was taken up and held for high prices, in whichever direction an immigrant was likely to go.

But the anticipated rush of immigrants did not take place. Labor and capital could not pay so much for land and make fair returns. Production was checked, if not absolutely, at least relatively. As the transcontinental railroad approached completion, instead of increased activity symptoms of depression began to manifest themselves; and, when it was completed, to the season of activity had succeeded a period of depression which has not since been fully recovered from, during which wages and interest have steadily fallen. What I have called the actual rent line, or margin of cultivation, is thus (as well as by the steady march of improvement and increase of population, which, though slower than it otherwise would have been, still goes on) approaching the speculative rent line, but the tenacity with which a speculative advance in the price of land is maintained in a developing community is well known.*

Now, what thus went on in California went on in every progressive section of the Union. Everywhere that a railroad was built or projected, land was monopolized in anticipation, and the benefit of the improvement was discounted in increased land values. The speculative advance in rent thus outrunning the normal advance, production was checked, demand was decreased, and labor and capital were turned back from occupations more directly concerned with land, to glut those in which the value of land is a less perceptible element. It is thus that the rapid extension of railroads is related to the succeeding depression.

And what went on in the United States went on in a greater or less obvious degree all over the progressive world. Everywhere land values have been steadily increasing with material progress, and everywhere this increase begot a speculative advance. The impulse of the primary cause not only radiated from the newer sections of the Union to the older sections, and from the United States to Europe, but everywhere the primary cause was acting. And, hence, a world-wide depression of industry and commerce, begotten of a world-wide material progress.

There is one thing which, it may seem, I have overlooked, in attributing these industrial depressions to the speculative advance of rent or land values as a main and

---

*It is astonishing how in a new country of great expectations speculative prices of land will be kept up. It is common to hear the expression, "There is no market for real estate; you cannot sell it at any price," and yet, at the same time, if you go to buy it, unless you find somebody who is absolutely compelled to sell, you must pay the prices that prevailed when speculation ran high. For owners, believing that land values must ultimately advance, hold on as long as they can.

primary cause. The operation of such a cause, though it may be rapid, must be progressive—resembling a pressure, not a blow. But these industrial depressions seem to come suddenly—they have, at their beginning, the character of a paroxysm, followed by a comparative lethargy, as if of exhaustion. Everything seems to be going on as usual, commerce and industry vigorous and expanding, when suddenly there comes a shock, as of a thunderbolt out of a clear sky—a bank breaks, a great manufacturer or merchant fails, and, as if a blow had thrilled through the entire industrial organization, failure succeeds failure, and on every side workmen are discharged from employment, and capital shrinks into profitless security.

Let me explain what I think to be the reason of this: To do so, we must take into account the manner in which exchanges are made, for it is by exchanges that all the varied forms of industry are linked together into one mutually related and interdependent organization. To enable exchanges to be made between producers far removed by space and time, large stocks must be kept in store and in transit, and this, as I have already explained, I take to be the great function of capital, in addition to that of supplying tools and seed. These exchanges are, perhaps necessarily, largely made upon credit—that is to say, the advance upon one side is made before the return is received on the other.

Now, without stopping to inquire as to the causes, it is manifest that these advances are, as a rule, from the more highly organized and later developed industries to the more fundamental. The West Coast African, for instance, who exchanges palm oil and cocoanuts for gaudy calico and Birmingham idols, gets his return immediately; the English merchant, on the contrary, has to lay out of his goods a long while before he gets his returns. The farmer can sell his crop as soon as it is harvested, and for cash; the great manufacturer must keep a large stock, send his goods long distances to agents, and, generally, sell on time. Thus, as advances and credits are generally from what we may call the secondary, to what we may call the primary industries, it follows that any check to production which proceeds from the latter will not immediately manifest itself in the former. The system of advances and credits constitutes, as it were, an elastic connection, which will give considerably before breaking, but which, when it breaks, will break with a snap.

Or, to illustrate in another way what I mean: The great pyramid of Gizeh is composed of layers of masonry, the bottom layer, of course, supporting all the rest. Could we by some means gradually contract this bottom layer, the upper part of the pyramid would for some time retain its form, and then, when gravitation at length overcame the adhesiveness of the material, would not diminish gradually and regularly, but would break off suddenly, in large pieces. Now, the industrial organization may be likened to such a pyramid. What is the proportion which in a given stage of social development the various industries bear to each other, it is difficult, and perhaps impossible, to say; but it is obvious that there is such a proportion, just as in a printer's font of type there is a certain proportion between the various letters. Each form of industry, as it is developed by division of labor, springs from and rises out of the others, and all rest ultimately upon land; for, without land, labor is as impotent as would be a man in void space. To make the illustration closer to the condition of a progressive country, imagine a pyramid composed of superimposed layers—the whole constantly growing and expanding. Imagine the growth of the layer nearest the ground to be checked. The others will for a time keep on expanding—in fact, for the moment, the tendency will be to quicker expansion, for the vital force which is refused scope on the ground layer will strive to find vent in those above—until, at length, there is a decided over-balance and a sudden crumbling along all the faces of the pyramid.

That the main cause and general course of the recurring paroxysms of industrial depression, which are becoming so marked a feature of modern social life, are thus explained, is, I think, clear. And let the reader remember that it is only the main causes and general courses of such phenomena that we are seeking to trace or that, in fact, it is possible to trace with any exactness. Political economy can deal, and has need to deal, only with general tendencies. The derivative forces are so multiform, the actions and reactions are so various, that the exact character of the phenomena cannot be predicted. We know that if a tree is cut through it will fall, but precisely in what direction will be determined by the inclination of the trunk, the spread of the branches, the impact of the blows, the quarter and force of the wind; and even a bird lighting on a twig, or a frightened squirrel leaping from bough to bough, will not be without its influence. We know that an insult will arouse a feeling of resentment in the human breast, but to say how far and in what way it will manifest itself, would require a synthesis which would build up the entire man and all his surroundings, past and present.

The manner in which the sufficient cause to which I have traced them explains the main features of these industrial depressions is in striking contrast with the contradictory and self-contradictory attempts which have been made to explain them on the current theories of the distribution of wealth. That a speculative advance in rent or land values invariably precedes each of these seasons of industrial depression is everywhere clear. That they bear to each other the relations of cause and effect, is obvious to whomsoever considers the necessary rela. tions between land and labor.

And that the present depression is running its course, and that, in the manner previously indicated, a new equilibrium is being established, which will result in another season of comparative activity, may already be seen in the United States. The normal rent line and the speculative rent line are being brought together: (1) By the fall in speculative land values, which is very evident in the reduction of rents and shrinkage of real estate values in the principal cities. (2) By the increased effi. ciency of labor, arising from the growth of population and the utilization of new inventions and discoveries, some of which almost as important as that of the use of steam we seem to be on the verge of grasping. (3) By the lowering of the habitual standard of interest and wages, which, as to interest, is shown by the negotiation of a government loan at four per cent., and as to wages is too generally evident for any special citation. When the equilibrium is thus re-established, a season of renewed activity, culminating in a speculative advance of land values will set in.*   But wages and interest will not recover their lost ground. The net result of all these perturbations or wave-like movements is the gradual forcing of wages and interest toward their minimum. These temporary and recurring depressions exhibit, in fact, as was noticed in the opening chapter, but intensifications of the general movement which accompanies material progress.

---

* This was written a year ago. It is now (July, 1879) evident that a new period of activity has commenced, as above predicted, and in New York and Chicago real estate prices have already begun to recover.

CHAPTER II.

The great problem, of which these recurring seasons of industrial depression are but peculiar manifestations, is now, I think, fully solved, and the social phenomena which all over the civilized world appall the philanthropist and perplex the statesman, which hang with clouds the future of the most advanced races, and suggest doubts of the reality and ultimate goal of what we have fondly called progress, are now explained.

The reason why, in spite of the increase of productive power, wages constantly tend to a minimum which will give but a bare living, is that, with increase in productive power, rent tends to even greater increase, thus producing a constant tendency to the forcing down of wages.

In every direction, the direct tendency of advancing civilization is to increase the power of human labor to satisfy human desires—to extirpate poverty, and to banish want and the fear of want. All the things in which progress consists, all the conditions which progressive communities are striving for, have for their direct and natural result the improvement of the material (and consequently the intellectual and moral) condition of all within their influence. The growth of population, the increase and extension of exchanges, the discoveries of science, the march of invention, the spread of education, the improvement of government, and the amelioration of manners, considered as material forces, have all a direct tendency to increase the productive power of labor—not of some labor, but of all labor; not in some departments of industry, but in all departments of industry; for the law of the production of wealth in society is the law of "each for all, and all for each."

But labor cannot reap the benefits which advancing civilization thus brings, because they are intercepted. Land being necessary to labor, and being reduced to private ownership, every increase in the productive power of labor but increases rent—the price that labor must pay for the opportunity to utilize its powers; and thus all the advantages gained by the march of progress go to the owners of land, and wages do not increase. Wages cannot increase; for the greater the earnings of labor the greater the price that labor must pay out of its earnings for the opportunity to make any earnings at all. The mere laborer has thus no more interest in the general advance of productive power than the Cuban slave has in advance in the price of sugar. And just as an advance in the price of sugar may make the condition of the slave worse, by inducing the master to drive him harder, so may the condition of the free laborer be positively, as well as relatively, changed for the worse by the increase in the productive power of his labor. For, begotten of the continuous advance of rents, arises a speculative tendency which discounts the effect of future improvements by a still further advance of rent, and thus tends, where this has not occurred from the normal advance of rent, to drive wages down to the slave point—the point at which the laborer can just live.

And thus robbed of all the benefits of the increase in productive power, labor is exposed to certain effects of advancing civilization which, without the advantages that naturally accompany them, are positive evils, and of themselves tend to reduce the free laborer to the helpless and degraded condition of the slave.

For all improvements which add to productive power as

civilization advances consist in, or necessitate, a still further subdivision of labor, and the efficiency of the whole body of laborers is increased at the expense of the independence of the constituents. The individual laborer acquires knowledge of and skill in but an infinitesimal part of the varied processes which are required to supply even the commonest wants. The aggregate produce of the labor of a savage tribe is small, but each member is capable of an independent life. He can build his own habitation, hew out or stitch together his own canoe, make his own clothing, manufacture his own weapons, snares, tools and ornaments. He has all the knowledge of nature possessed by his tribe—knows what vegetable productions are fit for food, and where they may be found; knows the habits and resorts of beasts, birds, fishes, and insects; can pilot himself by the sun or the stars, by the turning of blossoms or the mosses on the trees; is, in short, capable of supplying all his wants. He may be cut off from his fellows and still live; and thus possesses an independent power which makes him a free contracting party in his relations to the community of which he is a member.

Compare with this savage the laborer in the lowest ranks of civilized society, whose life is spent in producing but one thing, or oftener but the infinitesimal part of one thing, out of the multiplicity of things that constitute the wealth of society and go to supply even the most primitive wants; who not only cannot make even the tools required for his work, but often works with tools that he does not own, and can never hope to own. Compelled to even closer and more continuous labor than the savage, and gaining by it no more than the savage gets—the mere necessaries of life—he loses the independence of the savage. He is not only unable to apply his own powers to the direct satisfaction of his own wants, but, without the concurrence of many others,

he is unable to apply them indirectly to the satisfaction
of his wants. He is a mere link in an enormous chain of
producers and consumers, helpless to separate himself,
and helpless to move, except as they move. The worse
his position in society, the more dependent is he on society; the more utterly unable does he become to do anything for himself. The very power of exerting his labor
for the satisfaction of his wants passes from his own control, and may be taken away or restored by the actions
of others, or by general causes over which he has no more
influence than he has over the motions of the solar system. The primeval curse comes to be looked upon as a
boon, and men think, and talk, and clamor, and legislate
as though monotonous manual labor in itself were a good
and not an evil, an end and not a means. Under such
circumstances, the man loses the essential quality of
manhood—the godlike power of modifying and control-
ling conditions. He becomes a slave, a machine, a commodity—a thing, in some respects, lower than the
animal.

I am no sentimental admirer of the savage state. I do
not get my ideas of the untutored children of nature
from Rousseau, or Chateaubriand, or Cooper. I am conscious of its material and mental poverty, and its low and
narrow range. I believe that civilization is not only the
natural destiny of man, but the enfranchisement, elevation, and refinement of all his powers, and think that it
is only in such moods as may lead him to envy the cud-
chewing cattle, that a man who is free to the advantages
of civilization could look with regret upon the savage
state. But, nevertheless, I think no one who will open
his eyes to the facts can resist the conclusion that there
are in the heart of our civilization large classes with
whom the veriest savage could not afford to exchange.
It is my deliberate opinion that if, standing on the
threshold of being, one were given the choice of entering

life as a Tierra del Fuegan, a black fellow of Australia, an Esquimaux in the Arctic Circle, or among the lowest classes in such a highly civilized country as Great Britain, he would make infinitely the better choice in selecting the lot of the savage. For those classes who in the midst of wealth are condemned to want suffer all the privations of the savage, without his sense of personal freedom; they are condemned to more than his narrowness and littleness, without opportunity for the growth of his rude virtues; if their horizon is wider, it is but to reveal blessings that they cannot enjoy.

There are some to whom this may seem like exaggeration, but it is only because they have never suffered themselves to realize the true condition of those classes upon whom the fron heel of modern civilization presses with full force. As De Tocqueville observes, in one of his letters to Mme. Swetchine, "we so soon become used to the thought of want that we do not feel that an evil which grows greater to the sufferer the longer it lasts becomes less to the observer by the very fact of its duration;" and perhaps the best proof of the justice of this observation is that in cities where there exists a pauper class and a criminal class, where young girls shiver as they sew for bread, and tattered and barefooted children make a home in the streets, money is regularly raised to send missionaries to the heathen! Send missionaries to the heathen! it would be laughable if it were not so sad. Baal no longer stretches forth his hideous, sloping arms; but in Christian lands mothers slay their infants for a burial fee! And I challenge the production from any authentic accounts of savage life of such descriptions of degradation as are to be found in official documents of highly civilized countries—in reports of Sanitary Commissioners and of inquiries into the condition of the laboring poor.

The simple theory which I have outlined (if indeed it

can be called a theory which is but the recognition of the most obvious relations) explains this conjunction of poverty with wealth, of low wages with high productive power, of degradation amid enlightenment, of virtual slavery in political liberty. It harmonizes, as results flowing from a general and inexorable law, facts otherwise most perplexing, and exhibits the sequence and relation between phenomena that without reference to it are diverse and contradictory. It explains why interest and wages are higher in new than in older communities, though the average, as well as the aggregate, production of wealth is less. It explains why improvements which increase the productive power of labor and capital increase the reward of neither. It explains what is commonly called the conflict between labor and capital, while proving the real harmony of interest between them. It cuts the last inch of ground from under the fallacies of protection, while showing why free trade fails to benefit permanently the working classes. It explains why want increases with abundance, and wealth tends to greater and greater aggregations. It explains the periodically recurring depressions of industry without recourse either to the absurdity of "over-production" or the absurdity of "over-consumption." It explains the enforced idleness of large numbers of would-be producers, which wastes the productive force of advanced communities, without the absurd assumption that there is too little work to do or that there are too many to do it. It explains the ill effects upon the laboring classes which often follow the introduction of machinery, without denying the natural advantages which the use of machinery gives. It explains the vice and misery which show themselves amid dense population, without attributing to the laws of the All-Wise and All-Beneficent defects which belong only to the short-sighted and selfish enactments of men.

This explanation is in accordance with all the facts.

Look over the world to-day. In countries the most widely differing—under conditions the most diverse as to government, as to industries, as to tariffs, as to currency —you will find distress among the working classes; but everywhere that you thus find distress and destitution in the midst of wealth you will find that the land is monopolized; that instead of being treated as the common property of the whole people, it is treated as the private property of individuals; that, for its use by labor, large revenues are extorted from the earnings of labor. Look over the world to-day, comparing different countries with each other, and you will see that it is not the abundance of capital or the productiveness of labor that makes wages high or low; but the extent to which the monopolizers of land can, in rent, levy tribute upon the earnings of labor. Is it not a notorious fact, known to the most ignorant, that new countries, where the aggregate wealth is small, but where land is cheap, are always better countries for the laboring classes than the rich countries, where land is dear? Wherever you find land relatively low, will you not find wages relatively high? And wherever land is high, will you not find wages low? As land increases in value, poverty deepens and pauperism appears. In the new settlements, where land is cheap, you will find no beggars, and the inequalities in condition are very slight. In the great cities, where land is so valuable that it is measured by the foot, you will find the extremes of poverty and of luxury. And this disparity in condition between the two extremes of the social scale may always be measured by the price of land. Land in New York is more valuable than in San Francisco; and in New York, the San Franciscan may see squalor and misery that will make him stand aghast. Land is more valuable in London than in New York;

and in London, there is squalor and destitution worse than that of New York.

Compare the same country in different times, and the same relation is obvious. As the result of much investigation, Hallam says he is convinced that the wages of manual labor were greater in amount in England during the middle ages than they are now. Whether this is so or not, it is evident that they could not have been much, if any, less. The enormous increase in the efficiency of labor, which even in agriculture is estimated at seven or eight hundred per cent., and in many branches of indus. try is almost incalculable, has only added to rent. The rent of agricultural land in England is now, according to Professor Rogers, 120 times as great, measured in money, as it was 500 years ago, and 14 times as great, measured in wheat; while in the rent of building land, and mineral land, the advance has been enormously greater. According to the estimate of Professor Fawcett, the capitalized rental value of the land of England now amounts to £4,500,000,000, or $21,870,000,000—that is to say, a few thousand of the people of England hold a lien upon the labor of the rest, the capitalized value of which is more than twice as great as, at the average price of Southern negroes in 1860. would be the value of her whole population were they slaves.

In Belgium and Flanders, in France and Germany, the rent and selling price of agricultural land have doubled within the last thirty years.* In short, increased power of production has everywhere added to the value of land; nowhere has it added to the value of labor; for though actual wages may in some places have somewhat risen, the rise is clearly attributable to other causes. In more places they have fallen—that is, where it has been possible for them to fall—for there is a minimum below

---

* Systems of Land Tenure, published by the Cobden Club.

which laborers cannot keep up their numbers. And, everywhere, wages, as a proportion of the produce, have decreased.

How the Black Death brought about the great rise of wages in England in the Fourteenth Century is clearly discernible, in the efforts of the land holders to regulate wages by statute. That that awful reduction in population, instead of increasing, really reduced the effective power of labor, there can be no doubt; but the lessening of competition for land still more greatly reduced rent, and wages advanced so largely that force and penal laws were called in to keep them down. The reverse effect followed the monopolization of land that went on in England during the reign of Henry VIII., in the inclosure of commons and the division of the church lands between the panders and parasites who were thus enabled to found noble families. The result was the same as that to which a speculative increase in land values tends. According to Malthus (who, in his "Principles of Political Economy," mentions the fact without connecting it with land tenures), in the reign of Henry VIL, half a bushel of wheat would purchase but little more than a day's common labor, but in the latter part of the reign of Elizabeth, half a bushel of wheat would purchase three days' common labor. I can hardly believe that the reduction in wages could have been so great as this comparison would indicate; but that there was a reduction in common wages, and great distress among the laboring classes, is evident from the complaints of "sturdy vagrants" and the statutes made to suppress them. The rapid monopolization of the land, the carrying of the speculative rent line beyond the normal rent line, produced tramps and paupers, just as like effects from like causes have lately been evident in the United States.

"Land which went heretofore for twenty or forty pounds a year," said Hugh Latimer, "now is let for fifty or a hundred. My father was a yeoman, and had no lands of his own; only he had a farm at a rent of three or four pounds by the year at the uttermost, and thereupon he tilled so much as kept half a dozen men. He had walk for a hundred sheep, and my mother milked thirty kine; he was able and did find the King a harness with himself and his horse when he came to the place that he should receive the King's wages. I can remember that I buckled his harness when he went to Blackheath Field. He kept me to school; he married my sisters with five pound apiece, so that he brought them up in godliness and fear of God. He kept hospitality for his neighbors and some alms he gave to the poor. And all this he did of the same farm, where he that now hath it payeth sixteen pounds rent or more by year, and is not able to do anything for his Prince, for himself, nor for his children, nor to give a cup of drink to the poor."

"In this way," said Sir Thomas More, referring to the ejectment of small farmers which characterized this advance of rent, "it comes to pass that these poor wretches, men, women, husbands, orphans, widows, parents with little children, householders greater in number than in wealth, all of these emigrate from their native fields, without knowing where to go."

And so from the stuff of the Latimers and Mores— from the sturdy spirit that amid the flames of the Oxford stake cried, "Play the man, Master Ridley!" and the mingled strength and sweetness that neither prosperity could taint nor the ax of the executioner abash—were evolved thieves and vagrants, the mass of criminality and pauperism that still blights the innermost petals and preys a gnawing worm at the root of England's rose.

But it were as well to cite historical illustrations of the attraction of gravitation. The principle is as universal and as obvious. That rent *must* reduce wages, is as clear as that the greater the subtractor the less the remainder. That rent *does* reduce wages, any one, wherever situated, can see by merely looking around him.

There is no mystery as to the cause which so suddenly and so largely raised wages in California in 1849, and in Australia in 1852. It was the discovery of the placer mines in unappropriated land to which labor was free that raised the wages of cooks in San Francisco restaurants to $500 a month, and left ships to rot in the harbor without officers or crew until their owners would consent to pay rates that in any other part of the globe seemed fabulous. Had these mines been on appropriated land, or had they been immediately monopolized so that rent could have arisen, it would have been land values that would have leaped upward, not wages. The Comstock lode has been richer than the placers, but the Comstock lode was readily monopolized, and it is only by virtue of the strong organization of the Miners' Association and the fears of the damage which it might do, that enables men to get four dollars a day for parboiling themselves two thousand feet underground, where the air that they breathe must be pumped down to them. The wealth of the Comstock lode has added to rent. The selling price of these mines runs up into hundreds of millions, and it has produced individual fortunes whose monthly returns can be estimated only in hundreds of thousands, if not in millions. Nor is there any mystery about the cause which has operated to reduce wages in California from the maximum of the early days to very nearly a level with wages in the Eastern States, and that is still operating to reduce them. The productiveness of labor has not decreased, on the contrary it has increased, as I have before shown; but, out of what it produces labor has now to pay rent. As the placer deposits were exhausted, labor had to resort to the deeper mines and to agricultural land, but monopolization of these being permitted,

men now walk the streets of San Francisco ready to go to
work for almost anything—for natural opportunities are
now no longer free to labor.

The truth is self-evident.   Put to any one capable of
consecutive thought this question:

"Suppose there should arise from the English Channel
or the German Ocean a No-man's land on which common
labor to an unlimited amount should be able to make ten
shillings a day and which should remain unappropriated
and of free access, like the commons which once com-
prised so large a part of English soil.   What would be
the effect upon wages in England?"

He would at once tell you that common wages
throughout England must soon increase to ten shillings
a day.

And in response to another question, "What would be
the effect on rents?" he would at a moment's reflection
say that rents must necessarily fall; and if he thought out
the next step he would tell you that all this would hap-
pen without any very large part of English labor being
diverted to the new natural opportunities, or the forms
and direction of industry being much changed; only that
kind of production being abandoned which now yields to
labor and to landlord together less than labor could secure on the new opportunities.   The great rise in wages
would be at the expense of rent.

Take now the same man or another—some hard-headed
business man, who has no theories, but knows how to
make money.   Say to him: "Here is a little village; in
ten years it will be a great city—in ten years the railroad
will have taken the place of the stage coach, the electric
light of the candle; it will abound with all the machinery and improvements that so enormously multiply
the effective power of labor.   Will, in ten years, interest
be any higher?"

He will tell you, "No!"

"Will the wages of common labor be any higher; will it be easier for a man who has nothing but his labor to make an independent living?"

He will tell you, "No; the wages of common labor will not be any higher; on the contrary, all the chances are that they will be lower; it will not be easier for the mere laborer to make an independent living; the chances are that it will be harder."

"What, then, will be higher?"

"Rent; the value of land. Go, get yourself a piece of ground, and hold possession."

And if, under such circumstances, you take his advice, you need do nothing more. You may sit down and smoke your pipe; you may lie around like the lazzaroni of Naples or the leperos of Mexico; you may go up in a balloon, or down a hole in the ground; and without doing one stroke of work, without adding one iota to the wealth of the community, in ten years you will be rich! In the new city you may have a luxurious mansion; but among its public buildings will be an almshouse.

In all our long investigation we have been advancing to this simple truth: That as land is necessary to the exertion of labor in the production of wealth, to command the land which is necessary to labor, is to command all the fruits of labor save enough to enable labor to exist. We have been advancing as through an enemy's country, in which every step must be secured, every position fortified, and every by-path explored; for this simple truth, in its application to social and political problems, is hid from the great masses of men partly by its very simplicity, and in greater part by widespread fallacies and erroneous habits of thought which lead them to look in every direction but the right one for an explanation of the evils which oppress and threaten the civilized world. And back of these elaborate fallacies and misleading theories is an active, energetic power, a power that in every country, be its political forms what they may, writes laws and molds thought—the power of a vast and dominant pecuniary interest.

But so simple and so clear is this truth, that to see it fully once is always to recognize it. There are pictures which, though looked at again and again, present only a confused labyrinth of lines or scroll work—a landscape, trees, or something of the kind—until once the attention is called to the fact that these things make up a face or a figure. This relation once recognized, is always afterward clear. It is so in this case. In the light of this truth all social facts group themselves in an orderly relation, and the most diverse phenomena are seen to spring from one great principle. It is not in the relations of capital and labor; it is not in the pressure of population against subsistence, that an explanation of the unequaled development of our civilization is to be found. The great cause of inequality in the distribution of wealth is inequality in the ownership of land. The ownership of land is the great fundamental fact which ultimately determines the social, the political, and consequently the intellectual and moral condition of a people. And it must be so. For land is the habitation of man, the storehouse upon which he must draw for all his needs, the material to which his labor must be applied for the supply of all his desires; for even the products of the sea cannot be taken, the light of the sun enjoyed, or any of the forces of nature utilized, without the use of land or its products. On the land we are born, from it we live, to it we return again—children of the soil as truly as is the blade of grass or the flower of the field. Take away from man all that belongs to land, and he is but a disembodied spirit. Material progress cannot rid us of our dependence upon land; it can but add to the power of producing wealth from land; and hence, when land is monopolized, it might go on to infinity without increasing wages or improving the condition of those who have but their labor. It can but add to the value of land and the power which its possession gives. Everywhere, in all times, among all peoples, the possession of land is the base of aristocracy, the foundation of great fortunes, the source of power. As said the Brahmins, ages ago—

"*To whomsoever the soil at any time belongs, to him belong the fruits of it. White parasols and elephants mad with pride are the flowers of a grant of land.*"

CPSIA information can be obtained
at www.ICGtesting.com
Printed in the USA
BVHW04*1412310818
526156BV00004B/18/P